DAVID FELLMAN
Vilas Professor of Political Science, University of Wisconsin
ADVISORY EDITOR TO DODD, MEAD & COMPANY

ELECTIONS IN AMERICA

CONTROL AND INFLUENCE IN DEMOCRATIC POLITICS

"For a long time before the appointed time has come, the election becomes the important and, so to speak, the all-engrossing topic of discussion. Factional ardor is redoubled, and all the artificial passions which the imagination can create in a happy and peaceful land are agitated and brought to light. . . . It is true that as soon as the choice is determined, this ardor is dispelled, calm returns, and the river, which had nearly broken its banks, sinks to its usual level; but who can refrain from astonishment that such a storm should have arisen?"

ALEXIS DE TOCQUEVILLE
Democracy in America

ELECTIONS IN AMERICA

CONTROL AND INFLUENCE IN DEMOCRATIC POLITICS

Gerald M. Pomper

Rutgers · The State University

DODD, MEAD & COMPANY
New York Toronto 1968

LIBRARY OF CONGRESS CATALOG CARD NUMBER: 68-56335

PRINTED IN THE UNITED STATES OF AMERICA

TO MARC, DAVID, AND MILES

in the hope that voters and politicians
will redeem their pledge
"to save succeeding generations
from the scourge of war"

EDITOR'S INTRODUCTION

THE AMERICAN commitment to democracy rests upon universal suffrage which expresses itself through periodical elections. Changes in the power to govern have been accomplished, since the very birth of the republic, through the instrumentality of voting. In view of the venerable age and centrality of these aspects of our political system it is really quite astonishing that there is such a dearth of political science scholarship on this vital subject. Addressing himself directly to students of American government, Professor Pomper's book is a truly original contribution to the literature available to those seeking to understand the meaning of voting in our elections.

Voting and elections would seem to be old and thoroughly familiar aspects of the American scene. Actually, as Professor Pomper demonstrates, the field is studded with folkloristic myths, many of which he explores and some of which he also explodes, such as the myth that state governors who raise taxes are bound to suffer significantly at the polls. This notion is widely held, but refined analysis demonstrates that it is not to be accepted uncritically as a sort of self-evident proposition which everyone is bound to accept as being true.

This book explores for the political science student the nature of the intellectual problems involved in seeking to understand the nature of American elections. Professor Pomper analyzes the concept of the ballot in political theory, the place of voting in the structure of American elections, and various theories concerning the nature of the voter. He then addresses himself to the seminal question: do elections in America matter? Do they matter very much? He finds materials for an answer to this question in studying the process of party change, the making and keeping of party election promises, and the contribution of voting to the Negro's struggle for a citizenship equal to that of the rest of the population.

One of the solid merits of this book is that it is not committed to any single method of political science analysis. In a day when professionals in this field contend with each other on the battlements of competing methodologies, it is refreshing to read a competent book which cheerfully makes use of various methodologies without being enslaved to any single one, and without making a fuss about it. Professor Pomper uses methodology properly, as a means, and not as an end. Where the historical approach best illuminates a topic, the author uses it. Similarly, he employs philosophical analysis where it seems appropriate. At the same time, the reader will find in this book effective use of very sophisticated quantification of the very latest styles where quantification best responds to the problem under study. Thus this book not only contributes to the student's understanding of voting and elections in America, but also demonstrates to him how the contemporary political scientist handles the diverse materials with which he is involved.

DAVID FELLMAN

PREFACE

I HAVE written this book because of three concerns, derived from my experiences as a citizen, political scientist, and college teacher. As a citizen, I have been disturbed by an apparent public cynicism about elections in the United States, and the consequent disdain for the political process. Many groups in America have become disillusioned with the efficacy of the ballot. Opponents of the Vietnam war, advocates of "black power," and ultraconservatives are alike in this respect. Some of the methods they employ in place of votes, such as non-violent demonstrations, are clearly legitimate within the democratic tradition. Nevertheless, their abandonment of politics is dismaying. By forsaking the use of elections, they imply that American democracy is weak and fraudulent. To respond to their diverse criticisms, fuller study of the true significance of elections is necessary. I believe the detailed examinations in this book will show that the vote remains an important means to achieve popular demands.

As a political scientist, I have been unhappy with the relative neglect of elections in the scholarly literature. The behavior of the voter has been carefully analyzed, and the actions of government have been investigated through a variety of methods. Elections provide the linkage between the behavior of the voter and the actions of government, but this vital linkage is rarely examined in its own light. By analyzing the effects of elections on public policy, I hope to provide a contribution to the scholarly literature.

Finally, as a teacher, I have been upset, and ultimately bored, by quarrels over methodology. Tenaciously but intolerantly, opposing dogmatists insist that meaningful research can only be conducted through their prized techniques. In this work, I have deliberately been eclectic in the use of methods. I hope that their use here will prove instructive in the use of various techniques, as well as contributing to substantive findings. Technical material on the various methods is presented separately in appendices to chapters 5–8. These can be omitted by the reader unconcerned with methodology.

I have employed both so-called "traditional" and "behavioral" methods. The former category commonly includes the study of political philosophy (Chapter 2), institutions (Chapter 3), legislation (Chapter 8), and history (Chapter 9). The latter group includes voting studies (Chapter 4), statistical and computer operations (Chapters 5 and 6), content analysis (Chapter 7), and legislative roll-call studies (Chapter 8). Throughout the work, I have attempted to remain conscious of the need for empirical generalization and theory in political science. The methodological conclusion to be derived from this book, hopefully, is that rigid categories are pointless, and that various methods can be usefully employed.

Elections are the unique institution of democracy, and a viable democracy requires meaningful elections. This book is a deliberate effort to show that elections do have significance. To be sure, the study of elections is of immense scope, and this work can only partially answer the many questions involved. By beginning to chart the subject now, it may become easier to conduct fuller mappings in the future. I hope to have promoted that exploration.

In writing this book, I have accumulated manifold debts, which I am happy to acknowledge here. As is customary, I accept responsibility for all errors, although I would be glad to distribute this burden, and would implore any true friend to assume his share.

Judson L. James and Gordon J. Schochet, two friends who also are colleagues, have been particularly helpful in hearing, reading, and criticizing my arguments. Their willingness to take time from their own research is deeply appreciated. Other scholars have been kind enough to criticize individual chapters. In particular, I would like to acknowledge the aid of Hugh Bone, Eugene Genovese, Richard McCormick, Alan Rosenthal, Stephen Salmore, Josef Silverstein, and Aaron Wildavsky.

Many of the ideas developed here benefited from the criticisms of students in my graduate seminar at Rutgers University in 1966. In addition to the help provided by all members of the group, Barbara Salmore and Barry Seldes performed the coding and card-punching for the computer's operations. I have also gained from discussions with Benjamin Baker, Donald Herzberg, Theodore Lowi, Neil McDonald, James Rosenau, and Frank Tachau.

This book was made possible through the generosity of the Rutgers University Research Council, which financed a year's research leave and other expenses. The cooperation of its director, Charles F. Main, is particularly appreciated. The computer operations of Chapters 5 and 6 were financed by liberal grants from, respectively, the Rutgers Center for Computer and Information Services and the University Research Council, and the Eagleton Institute of Politics.

Others have contributed to this work in a host of diverse but important ways. In particular, thanks are due to Elizabeth David, Leon Epstein, and David Fellman of the University of Wisconsin, Francois Grondin of the Rutgers library, William Keech of the University of North Carolina, Eve Lubalin and members of the staff of the Inter-University Consortium for Political Research of the University of Michigan, Doris Paul of the Rutgers Computer Center, and Jeanette Turniansky.

Earlier versions of the material presented in Chapters 2, 5, and 7 appeared, respectively, in the *Review of Politics,* the *Journal of Politics,* and the *Midwest Journal of Political Science.*

I am grateful to these publications for permission to incorporate these articles.

Ultimately, one derives the most help from his own family. Isidor H. Pomper has long been a brotherly support; for this book, he also provided mathematical instruction. Emanuel Michels contributed the common sense of a democratic citizen and a father-in-law. My sons—Marc, David, and Miles—to whom this work is dedicated, helped both directly and through humor and restraint. Marlene simply has been a wife, making her uniquely valuable contributions of criticism, diversion, and love.

G. M. P.

CONTENTS

TABLES

APPENDIX TABLES

FIGURES

CHAPTER 1

THE PROBLEM OF ELECTIONS

ELECTIONS are a mystery.

The mystery is pervasive. Although we consider elections crucial to the functioning of democracy, we have little knowledge of their true significance. Americans choose half a million public officials through the ballot, but the extent of popular control of government policy decisions is undetermined. Throughout the world as well, governments proclaim themselves democracies and hold mass elections, but the meaning of the ballot remains cloudy to the Soviet worker and the Mississippi Negro.

The mystery of elections is extended by the rites which characterize and sanctify the act of voting. The catechisms of civic education reputedly prepare the young for their future responsibilities. Exclusion of the unchurched, such as felons, transients, and aliens, underlines the importance of the franchise. Elaborate rituals and devices are employed to maintain the secrecy of the ballot—personal registration, bipartisan poll watching, and private voting booths.

The enigmas of elections remain after the polls close. The voice of the people is the voice of God, a scholar declared to Charlemagne, but the messages from both sources continue to be unclear. Computers and surveys now refine the insights of individual analysts. Information such as the partisan division of the vote among farmers or businessmen, for example, can now be known quickly and accurately. The causes of that vote and its policy implications are less apparent. In the 1964 presidential election, voters clearly preferred Lyndon Johnson to Barry Goldwater, but doubt remains about their other preferences. Thus, Goldwater professed to see a vindication of conservatism in the returns, whereas Johnson, perhaps with more reason, perceived a "mandate" for his "Great Society."[1]

The accumulation of empirical data can help to resolve conflicting interpretations and to provide a fuller understanding of the behavior of voters. It is now established, contrary to past beliefs, that campaigns change few minds, that independent voters are no wiser and usually less knowledgeable than committed Democrats and Republicans, and that the electorate is largely unconcerned with political philosophies, either liberal or conservative.[2] Some of the obscurity involved in the analysis of elections has been removed.

Mystery remains on the effect of elections. What difference do they make in American politics? The voters choose the men who will occupy the most prominent positions in government, but it is unclear how—or even whether—the electorate affects substantive policies. Popular majorities do not order troops to Vietnam, enact a civil rights law, or raise state taxes. What is the effect of voting, if any, on these actions of the President, Congress, and governors? The effect is certainly not obvious, but democracy would be inoperative if there were no relationship.

[1] *The New York Times*, November 4, 1964, p. 22 and November 5, 1964, p. 20.

[2] Bernard Berelson, Paul Lazarsfeld and William McPhee, in *Voting* (Chicago: University of Chicago Press, 1954), pp. 331–47, provide a useful comparison of findings through 1952. The most thorough analyses are Angus Campbell, Philip Converse, Warren Miller and Donald Stokes, *The American Voter* (New York: Wiley, 1960), and *Elections and the Political Order* (New York: Wiley, 1966). The subject is discussed more fully in chapter IV, below.

Perhaps their constituents influence, even if they do not actually decree, the actions of public officials. To Sidney Verba, "Influence, and consequently democracy, are defined in terms of the way in which governmental elites make decisions. . . . The government officials act in anticipation of certain consequences if they do not so act. They believe that if they do not act to benefit a group, that group will at some point in the future withdraw its support or its vote."[3] If this is the case, however, there are few attempts thoroughly to study these connections between the decisions of the electorate and the decisions of the government. The actions of voters and the actions of officials are investigated separately; scant attention is devoted to the relationships between the two groups. A true understanding of democracy demands insight into the vital democratic process of elections.

In the absence of knowledge, myths and unsubstantiated opinions are accepted by the people and the government as well. Thus, the ballot is widely considered a panacea for social ills. In its foreign policy, the United States government has often used the mere existence of elections as a touchstone by which to judge the quality of other governments. From the time of Woodrow Wilson, American recognition of foreign regimes has frequently depended on their acceptance of popular voting. In the belief of American statesmen, once elections were instituted, stability, progress, and decency would inevitably follow.[4]

The significance of elections, however, is more often assumed than investigated. This faith is long-standing. In ancient Athens, Pericles glorified popular participation: "We differ from other states in regarding the man who holds aloof from public life not as quiet, but as useless; we decide or debate, carefully and in person, all matters of policy, holding not that words and deeds

[3] Sidney Verba, "Political Participation and Strategies of Influence: A Comparative Study," *Acta Sociologica*, Vol. 6 (fasc. 1–2, 1962), pp. 23–24.

[4] See Theodore P. Wright, *American Support of Free Elections Abroad* (Washington: Public Affairs Press, 1964).

go ill together, but that acts are foredoomed to failure when undertaken undiscussed."[5] In seventeenth-century England, elections were regarded as a virtual guarantee of good government. "In all states where there is any face of common freedom," declared the Cromwellian army, "the people have a right to new and successive elections unto that great and supreme trust, at certain periods of time; which is so essential and fundamental to their freedom as it cannot or ought not to be denied them, or withheld from them, and without which the House of Commons is of very little concernment to the interest of the Commons of England."[6]

Trust in elections continues in our time. Many Americans have relied on elections as the means to end the long-standing evil of racial discrimination. In signing the Voting Rights Act of 1965, President Johnson said: "The right to vote is the most basic right without which all others are meaningless. It gives people—people as individuals—control over their own destinies. . . . The vote is the most powerful instrument ever devised by man for breaking down injustice and destroying the terrible walls which imprison men because they are different from other men."[7] In democratic ideology, then, the ballot holds an honored place—but its title is usually based on custom rather than on a careful search of its deed.

ELECTIONS UNDER ATTACK

Winning a share of political power has been a long and even violent struggle for most peoples. Thus, it is understandable that its importance has been emphasized and exaggerated. But the hopes placed on gaining the ballot have not been fully realized. Like the swing of a pendulum, the consequent disillusionment with the ballot has been as exaggerated as the most extreme

[5] Thucydides, *The Peloponnesian War*, trans. R. W. Livingstone (London: Oxford University Press), Book II, 40.

[6] "A Representation of the Army" (June 14, 1647), in A. S. P. Woodhouse, *Puritanism and Liberty* (London: J. M. Dent, 1938), pp. 406–7.

[7] *The New York Times*, August 7, 1965, p. 8.

hopes. Elections are under attack among both the general public and scholars. New myths may be superseding old ones; unsubstantiated despair may be replacing unsubstantiated optimism.

The evolution of the civil rights movement is one example of a disappointed faith leading to an attack on the worth of the ballot. For decades, the concentration of those seeking racial equality has been on securing access to the polls. In 1944, the Supreme Court nullified the "white primary," the most important legal barrier to Negro voting in the South.[8] Faith in elections was shown by the rapid increase of Negro registration. Presidential and congressional action later resulted in the passage of five civil rights statutes devoted to securing political freedom for black Americans.

The high hopes stirred by the development of law, however, have been often followed by frustration and disillusionment with the gains attainable through the electoral process. Though Negro registration increased by about 50 per cent in the Deep South in the year following the 1965 Voting Rights Act, this increase was far below the original predictions of a doubling of the nonwhite vote. In the North, where Negroes have voted freely for decades, conditions in the urban ghettos have deteriorated, not improved through political action. In both North and South Negro voting apparently has stimulated a "white backlash" and contributed to the election of overt or covert racists. Negroes' anger at the apparent apathy or opposition of the white voting majority has produced demands for "black power." Rejecting the concept of "coalition politics," two Negro militants wrote, "The two major political parties in this country have become non-viable entities for the legitimate representation of the real needs of masses—especially blacks—in this country."[9] With the abandonment of politics, many emphasize

[8] *Smith* v. *Allwright*, 321 U.S. 649 (1944). For a discussion of the impact of Negro voting, see chapter IX, below.

[9] Stokely Carmichael and Charles V. Hamilton, *Black Power: The Politics of Liberation in America* (New York: Vintage, 1967), p. 42.

instead methods of "direct action"—picketing, street marches, boycotts and, in a few extreme cases, violence.

Skepticism about the efficacy of elections extends to whites as well. This is most visible in the bitter debate over American intervention in Vietnam. Many persons opposed to the Johnson Administration's increased military action consider its policy not only immoral or improper, but also a betrayal of the popular will. They believe that Johnson's victory over Goldwater was a "mandate" against intervention and that the later escalation of the war by the United States was a direct violation of the 1964 "mandate." Senator Wayne Morse declared in 1966, "I have lost all confidence in the President's not expanding the war. In my judgment, he has been expanding it, expanding it, and expanding it, completely contrary to the promises he made in the 1964 campaign. . . . I see no difference in the result from what the result would have been had his opponent been elected in 1964."[10]

The propriety of American actions in Vietnam is not the issue here. What is relevant is that opposition to the policy has brought some critics to question the value of elections, to fear that "the American people have been losing their influence over events—events which determine whether their sons will go to war or go to school, whether their government will wipe out villages abroad or slums at home."[11]

A similar perception of popular impotence is evident among some conservatives. Reviewing the course of American domestic policy, they find a failure of electoral controls. "The system of restraints has fallen into disrepair," they complain. "The federal government has moved into every field in which it believes its services are needed. . . . The result is a Leviathan, a vast national authority out of touch with the people, and out of their control.

[10] *Congressional Record*, Vol. 112, 89th Cong., 2nd sess. (February 28, 1966), p. 4129.

[11] "Vote NOW on Vietnam!" an advertisement distributed nationally and published in *The New York Times*, March 13, 1966, Section IV, p. E5.

This monolith of power is bounded only by the will of those who sit in high places."[12] While the electorate at large may not share these views, 44 per cent of the voters do believe that "there doesn't seem to be much connection between what I want and what my representative does."[13]

These doubts about elections have been paralleled by institutional developments which restrict popular intervention in politics. The "short ballot" has resulted in a considerable decrease in the proportion of public officials chosen at the polls. Appointment and merit systems are appropriate for the selection of administrators and bureaucrats. They are even used, with less clear cause, for the choice of chief executives, such as city managers. The tenure of elected officials has become longer. Annual elections were once considered essential to liberty, but four-year terms are now most common for state governors and are increasingly common in legislatures. The initiative, the recall, and the referendum, once hailed as modern methods of direct democracy, are no longer widely trusted. To be sure, there are sound reasons for many of these reforms. The total pattern, however, indicates a widespread discontent with electoral processes.

A defensiveness is apparent in the arguments of many modern democratically minded scholars. They wish to preserve democracy, yet are hard-pressed to find logical support for their personal preferences. Modern experience and social-science findings have combined to raise problems about the "revolt of the masses," the "irrational man," and the "escape from freedom." Universal suffrage has not produced ideal societies, as evidenced by contemporary history from Nazi Germany to Vietnam. Racial prejudice, nationalistic frenzy, and cultural degeneration are apparently major characteristics of the contem-

[12] Barry Goldwater, *The Conscience of a Conservative* (New York: Hillman Books, 1960), pp. 19–20.

[13] Herbert McClosky, "Consensus and Ideology in American Politics," *American Political Science Review*, Vol. 58 (June, 1964), p. 371.

porary world. Even in democratic nations, large proportions of the voters have supported extremist parties.

In the United States, social scientists find large proportions of the citizenry ignorant of or opposed to presumably "fundamental principles of democracy." For example, a majority of voters would not allow a Communist to speak in their city.[14] The picture of democratic man drawn in the extensive studies of voting is one of an uninformed and only intermittently interested voter, responding to politics largely on the basis of vague symbols of party, issues, and candidates. Under these conditions an election cannot meet an ideal of a public debate on issues and a reasoned choice of candidates.

Given these findings, many commentators denigrate the role of elections. Their approaches differ but their conclusions are similar. One school offers recommendations, prescribing a limited influence for popular opinion as a desirable condition. The other school offers analysis, describing democratic politics as, in fact, giving voters little substantive power. Elections are found to be either dangerous or meaningless but, in either case, ridiculous.

To Walter Lippmann, of the first school, popular control is real and has been disastrous, particularly on questions of war and peace: "The unhappy truth is that the prevailing public opinion has been destructively wrong at the critical junctures. The people have imposed a veto upon the judgments of informed and responsible officials. They have compelled the governments, which usually knew what would have been wiser, or was necessary, or was more expedient, to be too late with too little, or too long with too much, too pacifist in peace and too bellicose in war, too neutralist or appeasing in negotiation or too intransigent. Mass opinion has acquired mounting power in this century. It

[14] James W. Prothro and Charles M. Grigg, "Fundamental Principles of Democracy: Bases of Agreement and Disagreement," *Journal of Politics*, Vol. 22 (May, 1960), p. 285.

has shown itself to be a dangerous master of decisions when the stakes are life and death."[15]

If public intervention inevitably brings ruin, decisions rightfully should be made by a talented elite or by a dictator. At most, the citizens may be allowed a small share of power in an autocratic system, in which "the people choose a leader in whom they have confidence. Subsequently, the chosen leader says, 'Be quiet and do as I say.' The people and the political parties can no longer interfere with what he does."[16] Elections eventually become unnecessary, for the will of the people is inferior to that of the oligarch and the despot, be it Stalin, Hitler or Sukarno.

Descriptive analysts present less severe but equally dismaying conclusions. Without necessarily endorsing the condition, such writers empirically find the ballot inconsequential. Elections are essentially charades by which the populace plays at controlling government; real decisions are made by a manipulating elite.

Disdain for elections is not unique to modern times. Plato presented similar arguments in his plan for an ideal state. In this utopia, the rulers' claim to power would be based on their superior wisdom. However, this claim would not be recognized by an uninformed multitude. To win acceptance of the philosophers' power, Plato suggested a myth, that men were made out of three metals of different quality. The choice of the elite would be carefully arranged in advance. Then, in order to win general consent, "We shall tell our people in this fable, that all of you in this land are brothers; but the god who fashioned you mixed gold in the composition of those among you who are fit to rule, so that they are of the most precious quality; and he put silver in the Auxiliaries, and iron and brass in the farmers and

[15] Walter Lippmann, *The Public Philosophy* (New York: New American Library, 1955), pp. 23–24.

[16] Max Weber, quoted by Herbert Tingsten, *The Problem of Democracy* (Totowa: Bedminster Press, 1965), p. 84.

craftsmen."[17] Once in power, the philosopher-kings would rule undeterred by mass opinion.

Elections are held to be the modern equivalent of Plato's myth, resulting in popular consent to the actual rule of an elite group. Murray Edelman's evocative analysis of American politics finds that the voters have little effect on public policy: the prime function of elections is a ritual of "symbolic reassurance" that serves to "quiet resentments and doubts about particular political acts, reaffirm belief in the fundamental rationality and democratic character of the system, and thus fix conforming habits of future behavior." Promoting social stability and political quiescence in this way is important, but the action of government, its allocation of benefits and deprivations, "what people get from government is what administrators do about their problems rather than the promises of statutes, constitutions, or oratory."[18] In the United States, Plato's myth and ruling oligarchy have become realities; elections are declared to be mere images of reality.

The critics attempt to destroy the mystery of elections. Analyzing the conventional myths of democracy, they find that the extravagant hopes occasionally placed on popular participation are supported by neither experience nor analysis. They suggest either fear or disdain in place of reverence for the ballot. They argue that elections result in disaster or deception rather than contributing to social well-being. The frustration and cynicism over the political process, evident among intellectuals as well as among less erudite Americans—from conservatives to radicals, from white "hippies" to black nationalists[19]—ultimately raises the issue of the viability of democracy itself.

[17] Plato, *The Republic,* trans. Francis W. Cornford (New York: Oxford University Press, 1945), Book II, 415.

[18] Murray Edelman, *The Symbolic Uses of Politics* (Urbana: University of Illinois Press, 1964), pp. 17, 193.

[19] See Murray B. Levin, *The Alienated Voter* (New York: Holt, Rinehart & Winston, 1960).

TOWARD ANALYSIS OF ELECTIONS

Faith in elections continues. It is evident even in the behavior of some of the detractors. Frustrated advocates of "black power" still attempt to build Negro political organizations in the Deep South. Senator Morse, in the same speech in which he criticized presidential action in Vietnam, appealed to the voters: "It is up to you, now, to exercise the check. It is up to you, now, to decide, through the ballot box, whether you want to send increasing numbers of American boys to their slaughter." Seeking to halt the growth of the welfare state, conservatives turned to political action and succeeded in winning control of the Republican party in 1964.

Is there any basis for this continuing faith in elections? To some extent, this faith must be accepted on its own terms, for confidence in the ballot rests on a fundamental moral judgment. The basic premise of a democratic system is "self-respect for everybody. Within this simple phrase is all that is or ought to be the democratic ideal . . . . If the ideal is to maintain self-respect for everybody permanently, everybody must help govern: The knowledge of self-direction is acquired in no other way than the having of it in the important affairs of life."[20] This fundamental premise cannot logically be proven or disproven, but it must be accepted as an axiom of democratic society. The ballot then becomes the necessary manifestation of "self-respect for everybody." Participation in meaningful elections is the political corollary of a moral presumption of individual worth.

To understand and defend elections, however, requires more than expressions of faith. Untested assumptions of the significance of the ballot must be clarified through probings in depth. The American political system provides ample material for examining the impact of elections. Concentrating on this system, the remaining chapters in this book are an attempt to begin

[20] William H. Riker, *Government in the United States,* 2nd ed. (New York: Macmillan, 1965), pp. 17–18.

those probings necessary for full comprehension of the processes of democracy.

In this examination, we will find a melding of two separate but related aspects of elections: the choice of government officials and the choice of government policy. In most cases, the voters can affect policy only through the election of politicians who will take actions desired by the majority of citizens.[21] The voters choose not an abstract program, but a party and its candidates, investing them with popular approval, the supreme legitimacy of a democratic system. In the process, the voters also legitimize the programs advanced and represented by that party and its leadership. If an election "mandate" exists, it is not conferred on the program itself, but on the public officials who advance the program.

The question remains, however, concerning the relationship between the voters' policy desires expressed through the choice of officials and the policy actions of those officials. After "the people have spoken," a winning politician could be reduced to a puppet of the popular majority or be independent, deaf to the inchoate speech of the voters. Aside from their policy effects, elections could conceivably fulfill other and manifold functions.[22]

We will concentrate on two broad alternative effects—direct and indirect results of popular elections. Direct voter control would be evidenced by elections in which the choice of men also clearly indicated popular preferences on policy issues. In such elections, the 1964 victory of Lyndon Johnson would indeed constitute a decision against large-scale inter-

[21] Voters make their own policy decisions when they pass on referenda or bond issues, but we will not deal with these cases. For an analysis of such elections, see James Q. Wilson and Edward C. Banfield, "Public-Regardingness as a Value Premise in Voting Behavior," *American Political Science Review,* Vol. LVIII (December, 1964), pp. 876–87.

[22] See the fine analysis of Richard Rose and Harve Mossawir, "Voting and Elections: A Functional Analysis," *Political Studies,* Vol. 15 (June, 1967), pp. 173–201.

vention in Vietnam. In the absence of such mandates, elections may have indirect significance. The actions of politicians might not be controlled in detail by ballots, but they might act in anticipation of voter reactions. Presidents could still wage war, but their actions would be taken after considering popular sentiments. A principal purpose here will be to assess the existence and relative importance of direct controls and indirect effects.

Before judging whether elections justify the continuing faith of democrats, we must know what to expect and which criteria to use. These expectations are found initially in the works of political philosophers and are discussed in the following chapter. Expectations are further affected by the character of American institutions, such as the two-party system, the Constitutional structure, and the diffusion of governmental power. The impact of institutions is analyzed in chapter III. The study of philosophy and of institutions leads to a common conclusion: elections in America can play a vital indirect role in protecting the interests of citizens, but they are unlikely to control governmental action directly.

To assess the actual impact of elections, we must uncover and examine the empirical evidence. If there is any direct influence of elections, it would come through popular voting. The import of voting surveys is studied in chapter IV. The portrait which emerges from these investigations is of a citizen of limited, but definite, competence, able to fulfill the expectations prescribed by political philosophy and provided by political institutions. But the portrait also shows that he is not likely to seek or obtain direct control over specific conduct.

The remaining chapters are original investigations of empirical material. The actions of the electorate are probed in two statistical studies. Voters' choices between parties in presidential elections between 1832 and 1964 are examined first. Second, the relationship between the outcome of state elections in the postwar period and the fiscal policies of state governors is investigated. Though dealing with different time periods and different political levels, chapters V and VI reinforce our earlier hypothesis: voters can and do intervene occasionally in the political system to express their vital interests, but they do not control the details of public policy.

If popular influence does not control policy actions in a direct manner, it may still be important in less obvious ways. Parties may seek to win mass support not only through platform promises but through subsequent actions. Elections have an indirect effect on policy by bringing the parties to consideration of popular needs, even though voters are not making explicit demands. The data presented in chapters VII and VIII indicate that platforms are far more meaningful than is commonly believed, and, despite the conventional folklore, that politicians usually keep promises to the voters.

Another indirect effect of elections may be the protection of the "natural rights" of voters—as hypothesized by democratic political philosophers. Politicians anxious to win or retain office would be expected to guard the interests of the electorate, even in the absence of explicit pressures. This expectation is tested by examining the protection of Negroes' rights to "life, liberty, and the pursuit of happiness" in the South from 1865 to the present. In chapter IX, we find that Negro rights were more secure at times and places that they exercised the suffrage and that their rights were jeopardized where and when they were disfranchised, indicating at least an indirect influence of the ballot. In the light of the previous findings, the concluding chapter is an attempt to generalize on the true significance of democratic elections.

Frankly underlying this book is the hope and belief that elections are important. To provide evidence in support of this proposition is more than a personal matter. The expectations of leaders and voters greatly affect political practice. If elections are widely considered dangerous or meaningless, actions may follow to restrict their importance and to minimize the power of ordinary citizens. Aware of this danger, V. O. Key, Jr., warned about interpretations of the voting studies which ridiculed the electorate. Such interpretations could become self-fulfilling prophecies: "Fed a steady diet of buncombe, the people may come to expect and to respond with highest predictability to buncombe. And those leaders most skilled in the propagation of buncombe may gain lasting advantage in the recurring struggles for popular favor."[23] Similarly, if elections are not respected, they could become unworthy of respect. The evidence presented in this book shows elections to be neither dangerous nor meaningless—the reports of the death of democracy have been exaggerated.

[23] V. O. Key, Jr., with the assistance of Milton C. Cummings, Jr., *The Responsible Electorate* (Cambridge: Harvard University Press, 1965), p. 7.

CHAPTER 2

THE BALLOT IN POLITICAL THEORY

THE SIGNIFICANCE of elections is our general problem. Before examining the impact of popular decisions in specific cases, we must establish our criteria. We must know what we expect before we know whether elections meet our expectations. In contemporary times, as we have seen, voting is both praised and damned. Much of the discussion today centers on the alleged "traditional theory of democracy," and our criteria for judging elections are derived implicitly from the works of political philosophy. From Plato to John Stuart Mill, philosophers have considered, approved, and condemned elections. To clarify our assumptions, therefore, we will examine in this chapter some major works of premodern European and American political thought.

The authors surveyed for this purpose are Plato, Aristotle, Machiavelli, Locke, Rousseau, Madison, Hamilton, Calhoun, and Mill, as well as disputants in the federal Constitutional Convention of 1787, the state conventions to ratify the Constitution, and the Congress on the Seventeenth Amendment, providing for the direct election of Senators.[1] This list includes both reputed friends and critics of democratic government. While other authors obviously could be added, this grouping seems a fair representation of premodern beliefs. An exhaustive examination of the specified writers, or of their entire theories, is not necessary here. We will also ignore the chronological evolution of ideas. Our emphasis is on the thoughts, of whatever historical period, relevant to an understanding and evaluation of the role of elections in government.

Political theorists of all eras have considered the functions of elections both in the choice of leadership and the determination of governmental action. They have differed, however, in their relative stress on the direct or indirect effects of the vote. Some writers have seen popular control as including both the choice of rulers and the precise delineation of policy. Others have seen the effects of elections as less obvious but still important. They have emphasized indirect impacts such as the stability and power of government, the development of personality and, especially, the protection of voter interests.

The theorists have also evaluated elections quite differently, expressing both enthusiastic support and fervent disdain for the ballot. Significantly, the criticism of elections usually has been expressed by writers who have expected direct popular control, whereas praise of elections has been more common among those who stressed indirect effects. The argument over elections, as we shall see, has been a dispute in which the opposing sides have not used the same criteria.

[1] The last debates are included because the Seventeenth Amendment appears to be the only important structural change in the original Constitution dealing with elections, and therefore the only occasion after 1789 for extended official debate on the issues involved. The only other amendment that might be considered is the two-term limit on the Presidency, but this change was not widely debated and its consideration centered on other issues. Amendments dealing with woman suffrage, the District of Columbia, and the poll tax have affected the size of the electorate, but not its functions.

DIRECT CONTROL: THE DANGERS OF ELECTIONS

Few philosophers have seen wise public action as the direct result of the electoral process. Machiavelli was an exception, believing the electorate competent to choose able leaders. Comparing popular and despotic governments, he held "that the people are more prudent and stable and have better judgment than a prince; and it is not without good reason that it is said, 'The voice of the people is the voice of God'. . . . We also see that in the election of their magistrates they make far better choices than princes; and no people will ever be persuaded to elect a man of inferior character and corrupt habits to any post of dignity, to which a prince is easily influenced in a thousand different ways."[2]

Rousseau was even more optimistic and emphasized policy decisions. Under suitable conditions, he wrote, "The general will is always right and tends to the public advantage."[3] While Rousseau's model community was a small, direct democracy, his beliefs were later extended to the American continental republic—first by the Jacksonians, and most extensively by the Progressives. Through elections, argued Oregon Senator Brown in 1911, "the accountability is always to the composite citizen—individual unknown—always permanent, never changing, the necessitated result being that the public servant must serve the composite citizen who represents general welfare."[4]

Most theorists who emphasize direct effects of elections are hostile to the ballot. They stress the need for skilled leaders in government and for wise policy decisions. Elections are judged on their ability to meet such goals and are found inadequate. Those who concentrate on these direct effects, therefore, become opponents of elections and fearful of their results.

[2] Niccolò Machiavelli, *Discourses on the First Ten Books of Titus Livius*, Modern Library ed. (New York: Random House, 1940), pp. 263–64.

[3] Jean Jacques Rousseau, *The Social Contract*, Everyman ed. (New York: Dutton, 1950), p. 27.

[4] *Congressional Record*, Vol. 46, 61st Cong., 3d sess. (1911), pp. 2595–96.

Criticism of the ballot is founded on an elitist premise. The theorists of this camp hold that certain discoverable abilities are needed to participate in government, that only a severely limited number of persons have these skills, and that all others should be excluded from politics. Specialists are necessary not only for the technical positions of a civil service; they are regarded as exclusively able to conduct all affairs of government. Hamilton argued this position gently, for he needed to court popular favor. "It is an unquestionable truth, that the body of the people, in every country, desire sincerely its prosperity; but it is equally unquestionable, that they do not possess the discernment and stability necessary for systematic government."[5]

Plato, unrestricted by political necessities, frankly expressed the elite theory and remains its most persuasive proponent. In perhaps his most celebrated paragraph, he wrote:

> Unless either philosophers become kings in their countries or those who are now called kings and rulers come to be sufficiently inspired with a genuine desire for wisdom; unless, that is to say, political power and philosophy meet together, while the many natures who now go their several ways in the one or the other direction are forcibly debarred from doing so, there can be no rest from troubles, my dear Glaucon, for states, nor yet, as I believe, for all mankind.[6]

The crucial problem in government is bringing the true elite to power. Governmental structure is of minor importance. "That can be the only true form of government in which the governors are really found to possess science, and are not mere pretenders, whether they rule according to law or without law, over willing or unwilling subjects, are rich or poor themselves—none of these things can with any propriety be included in the notion

[5] In the New York ratifying convention, in Jonathan Elliot, ed., *Debates on the Adoption of the Federal Constitution*, 2nd ed. (1888) (New York: Burt Franklin Research and Source Series 109), Vol. II, p. 132.

[6] *The Republic*, Book V, 473.

of the ruler."[7] Since specialists are required to run government, an elitist must have a way of discovering the experts.

Popular favorites are unlikely to have the required abilities. Indeed, elections have been held harmful because they actually promote the unqualified. The pursuit of office in elective systems is contrasted to the pursuit of wisdom characteristic of the most qualified rulers. "It is not in the natural course of things for the pilot to beg the crew to take his orders."[8] Elections deny society the benefit of its best leaders and advance the deficient. As Mill remarked, "The natural tendency of representative government, as of modern civilization, is toward collective mediocrity; and this tendency is increased by all reductions and extensions of the franchise, their effect being to place the principal power in the hands of classes more and more below the highest level of instruction in the community."[9] Deficient public policy will inevitably follow.

This concern was reiterated by Elihu Root, arguing against direct election of senators. "This change," he warned, "would prevent the Senate from having the benefit of . . . men who by lives of experience and effort have attained the respect of their fellow citizens and who are willing to undertake the burdens of public office, but are unwilling to seek it; men who will accept the burden as a patriotic duty . . . but who never would subject themselves to the disagreeable incidents, the labor, the strife, the personalities of a political campaign."[10]

Although elitists attack direct election of rulers, they find it more difficult to suggest alternative ways of selecting governors. In *The Republic*, for example, Plato provided only for the perpetuation of the philosophers' rule, through the control of public opinion and training of the guardians. He was unable

[7] Plato, *Statesman*, trans. B. Jowett, in *The Dialogues of Plato* (New York: Random House, 1937), 293.

[8] Plato, *The Republic*, Book VI, 489.

[9] John Stuart Mill, *Considerations on Representative Government* (New York: Liberal Arts Press, 1958), p. 114.

[10] *Congressional Record*, Vol. 46, 61st Cong., 3d sess. (1911), p. 2244.

to suggest a means of initiating the rule of the wise. Similar difficulties inhere in any plan for elite government.

To establish good government, and as an alternative to his ideal plan, Plato later suggested an elaborate system of laws and elections for a new commonwealth. Direct popular control was severely curbed. On the principle of specialization, the electorate was severely restricted. Only leisured citizens were admitted, "for he who is to secure and preserve the public order of the state has an art which requires much study and many kinds of knowledge, and does not admit of being a secondary occupation."[11] Even within this restricted group, some had greater influence than others. Most offices required special qualifications of age, property, or character, and long terms were common, with the principal rulers serving up to 20 years. Plato also divided the voters into classes on the basis of limited differences in wealth, with the richer classes having greater political influence.[12]

The elaborate system of elections was meant to serve as a second-best substitute for the ideal rule of the philosopher-king. The ideal still remained, however, and Plato returned to it. At the end of the *Laws*, he provided for a Nocturnal Council of the elderly wise men of the community, to whom is entrusted the education of new rulers and revision of the laws. Plato put his final trust in the creation of such a body. His ultimate proposal failed to guarantee wisdom, but it is the logical one for a firm believer in the need for specialized rulers. Elections may be carefully constructed and controlled, but they are a poor substitute for the rule of the wise. There is always the suspicion or conviction that the winners of elections need not necessarily be perceptive philosophers.

The voters are even less qualified to make policy decisions, according to the elitists. Since government is a specialized skill, it is madness to entrust it to the general public. Democratic

[11] Plato, *Laws*, trans. Benjamin Jowett, Book VIII, 846.
[12] *Ibid.*, Book VI, 753–68.

decision-making through elections is comparable to navigating a ship on which "the sailors are quarrelling over the control of the helm; each thinks he ought to be steering the vessel, though he has never learnt navigation and cannot point to any teacher under whom he has served his apprenticeship; what is more, they assert that navigation is a thing that cannot be taught at all, and are ready to tear to pieces anyone who says it can."[13] Elections are seen as involving policy decisions, and these decisions must inevitably be deficient.

Critical theorists have also attempted to specify the unwise policies they expect in elective governments. The recurrent fear is the asserted disregard of minority demands and the imposition of majority tyranny, the consequence of which is destruction of the state. "The instability, injustice, and confusion introduced into the public councils have, in truth been the mortal diseases under which popular governments have everywhere perished," wrote Madison in the most important exegesis on the Constitution. "Measures are too often decided not according to the rules of justice and the rights of the minor party, but by the superior force of an interested and overbearing majority." As a result, "democracies have ever been spectacles of turbulence and contention; have ever been found incompatible with personal security or the rights of property; and have in general been as short in their lives as they have been violent in their deaths."[14]

Those who have feared elections have seen them as the means by which selfish men advance their interests at the cost, even of the ruin, of others. To John Calhoun, every man "is ready to sacrifice the interests of others to his own. And hence, the tendency to a universal state of conflict, between individual and individual; accompanied by the connected passions of suspicion, jealousy, anger and revenge."[15] Elections provide no control

[13] Plato, *The Republic*, Book VI, 488.

[14] James Madison, *The Federalist*, No. 10.

[15] John C. Calhoun, *A Disquisition on Government*, in *Works*, Vol. I (New York: Appleton, 1854), p. 4.

over these tendencies. Rather, in a society of inevitable group conflict, elections contribute to the destruction of the rights of the minority. "There must, of necessity, be a governing and governed,—a ruling and a subject portion. The one implies the other; and in all, the two bear the same relation to each other; —and have, on the part of the governing portion, the same tendency to oppression and abuse of power. Where the majority is that portion, ... the minority, for the time, will be as much the governed or subject portion, as are the people in an aristocracy, or the subjects in a monarchy."[16]

Those fearful of elections tend to bolster their arguments by reference to a presumed "general welfare." "It does not follow that the public decisions are equitable," admitted Rousseau. On occasion, "the people is seduced by private interests, which the credit or eloquence of clever persons substitutes for those of the State; in which case the general will will be one thing, and the result of the public deliberation another."[17] Commonly, the general welfare is identified with interests and rights of particular minorities. To Madison, the protection of property interests from the attacks of "factions" is vital:

> By a faction, I understand a number of citizens, whether amounting to a majority or minority of the whole, who are united and actuated by some common impulse of passion, or of interest, adverse to the rights of other citizens, or to the permanent and aggregate interests of the community. . . . The most common and durable source of factions has been the various and unequal distribution of property. Those who hold and those who are without property have ever formed distinct interests in society. . . . The regulation of these various and interfering interests forms the principal task of modern legislation.[18]

[16] *Ibid.*, p. 23.
[17] Jean Jacques Rousseau, *A Discourse on Political Economy*, Everyman ed. (New York: Dutton, 1950), p. 291.
[18] *The Federalist*, No. 10.

Elections provide no protection against these dangers; indeed they only strengthen the position of the majority. Ideally, wrote Mill, the voter should consider the public interest, not his private welfare. "His vote is not a thing in which he has an option; it has no more to do with his personal wishes than the verdict of a juryman."[19]

Mill and others feared, however, that interests identified with the public welfare would be jeopardized by elections. To prevent this outcome, they created a variety of devices. Mill favored proportional representation, plural voting by educated citizens, disenfranchisement of paupers, and open ballots. Madison relied on social and institutional checks. He believed there would be a plurality of interests in a country as large as the United States. It was unlikely that any one interest would become a majority or would be sufficiently cohesive to be oppressive. Further insurance would be provided by the mechanisms of government: the filtration of popular views through representatives, separate means for the selection of each branch of government, and a variety of national checks and federal-state balances.

After the country's sixty years of experience under the Constitution, Calhoun was dissatisfied with Madison's solutions, but he carried his distrust of majority policy to an extreme. Calhoun recognized only two interests—free states and slave states. The Constitution had provided for the protection of slavery, he argued, by requiring a "concurrent majority" to pass legislation—not only a majority of population, but a majority of states as well. Unfortunately, the popular majority had become dominant. To provide for southern interests, new checks were needed, such as the equality of sectional representation in the Senate or the election of a second President with full veto power; otherwise, either the southern minority or the government must be destroyed.[20]

[19] *Considerations on Representative Government,* p. 155.

[20] *A Discourse on the Constitution and Government of the United States,* in *Works,* Vol. I, esp. pp. 381–96.

The policy decisions of the elective governments, then, are held to be unjust and destructive of vital interests. Ultimately, it is claimed, unchecked elections are dangerous to all, leading to instability and the destruction of the state. The principal cause of instability is the inability of the majority to restrain itself. Eventually, it infringes on some basic rights and intense beliefs of the minority, or one faction of the majority turns on another. "Cunning, falsehood, deception, slander, fraud and gross appeals to the appetites of the lowest portions of the community would take the place of sound reasoning and wise debate."[21]. The ultimate result is the end of all liberty, as repression by tyrannical rulers is substituted for popular rule. "That freedom which knew no bounds must now put on the livery of the most harsh and bitter servitude, where the slave has become the master."[22] The ultimate danger of direct control is the elimination of all control.

INDIRECT EFFECTS: THE BENEFITS OF ELECTIONS

Many philosophers have seen considerable benefit in the indirect influence of elections. The advantages of the ballot have been found largely apart from the personal abilities of the elected rulers or the content of public decisions. Rather, the favorable aspects have been found in the effects of popular intervention on the processes and functioning of government. Elections would improve the workings of government, even if they could not insure the wisdom of rulers or policies.

A principal procedural benefit has been the achievement of legitimate and stable government. The legitimacy of elective government has been grounded on a moral premise. "The liberty of man in society is to be under no other legislative power but that established by consent in the commonwealth," declared Locke, "nor under the dominion of any will, or restraint of any

[21] Calhoun, *Disquisition*, p. 42.
[22] Plato, *The Republic*, Book VIII, p. 569.

law, but what the legislature shall enact according to the trust put in it."[23] Madison later noted, but found it unnecessary to defend, "the fundamental principle that men cannot be justly bound by laws in making of which they have no part."[24]

While consent has been defended as morally necessary, political theorists have also tried to show that legitimacy is the empirical result of popular elections. In popular government, wrote Aristotle, the voters "have the power of electing the magistrates and calling them to account; their ambition, if they have any, is thus satisfied."[25] By contrast, argued eighteenth-century Americans, the denial of electoral power would stigmatize most persons as "suspicious characters, and unworthy to be trusted with the common rights of their fellow citizens" and "would create division among the people and make enemies of all those who would be excluded."[26]

To the framers of the Constitution, elections were unavoidable. Given the English tradition, no government could be considered legitimate unless popularly chosen. While many delegates to the Philadelphia convention were distrustful of popular wisdom, they also saw the practical necessity of popular elections. The franchise brought consent even if not ideal policies. As George Mason reminded the delegates, "Notwithstanding the oppressions and injustices experienced among us from democracy; the genius of the people is in favor of it, and the genius of the people must be consulted."[27]

Elections also have been held to increase the power of government, without determining the specific actions of that

[23] John Locke, *Of Civil Government*, Everyman ed. (New York: Dutton, 1943), Book II, p. 127.

[24] Max Farrand, ed., *The Records of the Federal Convention of 1787* (New Haven: Yale University Press, 1911), Vol. II, p. 204n. All unspecified references are to Madison's *Journal*. For a critique of the consent theory, see Hanna Pitkin, "Obligation and Consent—I," *American Political Science Review*, Vol. LIX (December, 1965), pp. 990–99.

[25] Aristotle, *Politics*, Modern Library ed. (New York: Random House, 1943), Book VI, 1318b.

[26] George Mason and John Rutledge in Farrand, ed., Vol. II, pp. 203–5.

[27] *Ibid.*, Vol. I, p. 101.

government. This empirical proposition was widely accepted at the Constitutional convention. Generally, those who wished a particular government body to be powerful favored popular election; those who wanted to restrict its power argued against popular election. James Wilson was "for raising the federal pyramid to a considerable altitude, and for that reason wished to give it as broad a base as possible," through direct election.[28] By contrast, Roger Sherman, a states-righter, opposed popular election of the Congress, while Mason, a believer in legislative supremacy, opposed the direct election of the President. Mason favored election of Congress but, when it came to the choice of an executive whose power he feared, "he conceived it would be as unnatural to refer the choice of a proper character for chief Magistrate to the people, as it would, to refer a trial of colors to a blind man."[29] The defense of elections was an expedient principle, supported on the basis of an empirical theory that elections conferred and increased government power.

Another general advantage claimed for elections is more intangible. Participation in government, of which voting is the most common means, is said to contribute to the personal development of the electors. Although often presented in value-free terms, this statement is a moral position based on certain tenets concerning the human personality. To Locke, self-determination is held essential to man generally, and consent is essential to political man. "He who would get me into his power without my consent would use me as he pleased when he had got me there, and destroy me too when he had a fancy to it." Furthermore, "this freedom from absolute, arbitrary power is so necessary to, and closely joined with, a man's preservation, that he cannot part with it but by what forfeits his preservation and life together."[30]

Mill shares the same moral premise, but his view of human character is more dynamic. A man's personality is not only

[28] *Ibid.*, Vol. I, p. 49.
[29] *Ibid.*, Vol. II, p. 31.
[30] *Of Civil Government*, pp. 125, 128.

recognized through participation in government; it is also developed. "The maximum of the invigorating effect of freedom upon character is only obtained when the person acted on either is, or is looking forward to becoming, a citizen as fully privileged as any other." Moreover, public responsibility stimulates him to widen his perspectives. "He is called upon, when so engaged, to weigh interests not his own; to be guided in cases of conflicting claims, by another rule than his private partialities. . . . He is made to feel himself one of the public, and whatever is for their benefit to be for his benefit."[31]

The most important virtue credited to elections is protection, or a check on power. Legitimate and strong government or moral development are important ends, but their benefit to individuals and groups is difficult to ascertain. To particular persons, the vote provides a vital means of defending their immediate interests and permits an indirect influence on government. The ballot is necessary not to guide the details of official action, but to make citizens secure. "Men, as well as women" summarized Mill, "*do not need political rights in order that they may govern, but in order that they not be misgoverned.*"[32]

While government is necessary, protection is also essential. Machiavelli and Madison share this basic premise. One "must start with assuming that all men are bad and ever ready to display their vicious nature, whenever they may find occasion for it."[33] Those who provide a role for elections do so because of a certain pessimism or realism about the possible misdeeds of men. Unlike Calhoun, however, who distrusted all men, advocates of elections are particularly suspicious of governors and more trustful of the governed. Madison wrote, "If angels were to govern men, neither external nor internal controls on government would be necessary," but in their absence, it becomes necessary to restrain government, and "a dependence on the people is, no doubt, the primary control."[34]

[31] *Considerations on Representative Government*, pp. 53–54. Cf. p. 130.
[32] *Ibid.*, p. 144. Italics added.
[33] Machiavelli, *Discourses*, p. 117.
[34] *The Federalist*, No. 51.

To be effective, Mill wrote, control must be exercised directly by those needing protection. Given the character of governors, their good intentions are an uncertain reliance. Possession of the vote, however, makes the expression of popular demands effective, because the government is obliged to attend to them.

> The rights and interests of every or any person are only secure from being disregarded when the person interested is himself able, and habitually disposed to stand up for them. . . . Rulers and ruling classes are under a necessity of considering the interests of those who have the suffrage; but of those who are excluded, it is in their option whether they will do so or not, and however honestly disposed, they are in general too fully occupied with things which they *must* attend to, to have much room in their thoughts for anything which they can with impunity disregard.[35]

Theorists who emphasize the protective aspects of elections reject the elitists' premises discussed earlier. The primary qualification of rulers is not considered their wisdom or talent, but their readiness to defend the rights of the voters. The electorate, in turn, is not judged by its ability to choose philosophers, but by its ability to choose politicians—men who seek power, not truth.[36] The virtue of elections is seen as bringing politicians to safeguard popular interests in order to promote their own quest for office. Protection, therefore, does not depend on the morality of rulers. As Patrick Henry scornfully declared, "Are we to go so far as to concede everything to the virtue of Congress? . . . I disdain to hold anything of any man. We ought to cherish that disdain."[37]

Popular protection is achieved in two distinctive but related ways. As summarized by Madison: "As it is essential that the

[35] Mill, *Considerations*, pp. 43, 131.

[36] The classic discussion of the character of the politician is Max Weber, "Politics as a Vocation," in H. H. Gerth and C. Wright Mills, *From Max Weber* (New York: Galaxy Books, 1958), IV.

[37] In the Virginia ratifying convention, in Elliot, ed., Vol. III, p. 167.

government in general should have a common interest with the people, so it is particularly essential that the [representatives] should have an immediate dependence on, and intimate sympathy with, the people. Frequent elections are unquestionably the only policy by which the dependence and sympathy can be effectually secured."[38]

"Dependence" means political restraint by the voters, who are aware of their interests, alert to their representatives' actions, and prepared to punish any misdeeds. "Do the members of Congress, says he, displease us, we call them home, and they obey. . . . Let these members know their dependence on the people and I say it will be a check on them, even if they were not good men."[39] Moreover, the representatives, knowing that they must face a new election shortly, will take care not to harm the voters. Whatever their personal character, officials will "have some hesitation before they abuse their powers."[40] Political necessity, not morality, provides protection.

Elections also serve as a check on power because of the "sympathy" between representatives and their constituents. This quality does not refer to the personal feelings of the legislator, but to the similarity between his social position and that of the voters. A representative would sympathize with his constituents because he would be of the same geographic area and status. The ideal legislature, in modern terms, would be a "random sample" of the voting population. For this reason, Aristotle characterized the choice of representatives by lot as the most democratic method.[41] The principle survives today in the ethnically "balanced ticket" or the militant Negro demand for "black power."

A properly constituted legislature was believed by Locke to be adequate for protection in almost all cases. Thus, while he

[38] *The Federalist,* No. 52.

[39] General Thompson, in the Massachusetts ratifying convention, in Elliot, ed., Vol II, p. 16.

[40] Machiavelli, *Discourses,* p. 224.

[41] *Politics,* Book IV, 1300a–b.

argues that "the supreme power cannot take from any man any part of his property without his own consent," this consent is equated with that "of the majority, giving it either by themselves or their representatives chosen by them."[42] No distinction is made between the voters and the representatives. With adequate elections, the actions of the legislature are equivalent to those of the voters themselves. The major political problem seen is the possible conflict between government and society, and the major function served by elections is to prevent oppression by government. Since the community is a united body, its common interest will be reflected in a properly constituted legislature.[43]

Protection is more complex when society is seen as comprising many different and divergent interests. The representative no longer can be the embodiment of a homogeneous community, but is likely to be more aware of some interests than others. Elections now provide a means of defending and advancing the specialized goals of groups. "In all elective offices each individual has a special interest, which it is presumed he has, under our general system of suffrage, a right to represent at the ballot box."[44] Government becomes not only a threat, but also a means of achieving specialized demands.

That representatives would promote particular interests has been widely accepted. Most of the controversies over suffrage in American history have been based on the tacit or explicit recognition that representatives would advance the relatively narrow goals of their constituency. The ballot has been sought by, and withheld from, the propertyless, Negroes, and women, because of the belief that their interests would be served—perhaps too well—if they could vote. Even if these groups did not make specific policy demands, it was expected that government

[42] *Of Civil Government*, pp. 187–89.

[43] The "right of revolution" is therefore severely restricted; see Locke, pp. 192–93.

[44] Senator Mitchell of Oregon, in *Congressional Record*, Vol. 21, 51st Cong., 1st sess. (1890), p. 3658.

would be responsive to their needs and thereby provide an indirect influence for the enfranchised.

While the empirical connection between interests and representation was widely accepted, the moral evaluation of this effect varied. According to one school, the advancement of particular interests will redound to the general advantage. "They who are already in place will be attentive to the rights of the people. . . . They who are out of office will watch them that are in, with a most critical eye, in order to discover and expose their malconduct if guilty of any, that so they may step into their places."[45]

The advancement of particular interests, however, could also be dangerous. Representatives are no longer a "random sample" of the population. They are likely to promote the goals of some groups while neglecting those of others. Some groups may be forgotten. Melancton Smith warned of an oligarchy: "A substantial yeoman, of sense and discernment, will hardly ever be chosen. From these remarks, it appears that the government will fall into the hands of the few and the great. This will be a government of oppression."[46] If the representative is no longer identified with the community, "sympathy" becomes less of a control, which now must come largely from his "dependence" on the voters. Unless the electorate is vigilant in defense of its interests, it may find these interests neglected. Protection is an important indirect effect of elections, but it demands attention on the part of the voters.

THE DEBATE OVER THE BALLOT

Theorists generally have evaluated elections unfavorably when they have focused on elections as direct choices of wise men or wise policies. In contrast, they have been well-disposed to the democratic process when they have considered the in-

[45] Samuel Stillman of Massachusetts, in Elliot, ed., Vol. II, p. 167.

[46] In the New York ratifying convention, in Elliot, ed., Vol. II, pp. 246–47. Cf. Hamilton in *The Federalist*, No. 35 and Patrick Henry in the Virginia convention, Elliot, Vol. III, p. 322.

direct effects of popular choice. The writers' different perspectives have led them to different conclusions. The debate over the ballot has therefore not been a true matching of ideas, for the two positions have employed different criteria.

The argument over elections, like that over democracy itself, begins with different premises of the nature of man. To the democrat, man is inherently good. He is of unique moral worth, and his individual personality is sacred and deserves protection. He has an inherent right to protect himself and the ability to make decisions for himself. Government is legitimate only when based on his consent. The right to vote follows from these premises. It is the means by which individuals protect themselves and express their consent. The individual's moral right to freedom becomes a political right of participation.

The opponent of elections and democracy is more pessimistic. Men are seen as basically selfish and ignorant. Not individuals, but the general welfare must be protected against such men. Participation in government is reserved for those who demonstrate knowledge and fitness of character. The inherent evil in all men justifies restriction of their political activities. Upon these different premises, political theorists have established contrasting criteria for the evaluation of elections.

The argument against elections has been focused on the ends of government, the achievement of wise decisions, and the content of policy. The fundamental premise is that there is a basic public good and that this good can be ascertained and achieved by wise rulers. Given this emphasis, broad popular participation is acceptable only if the voters have the competence to discern the public good. It is only the most optimistic theorists who have believed that the general electorate was wise enough to achieve the ideal. Rousseau is striking in his assertion: "When in the popular assembly a law is proposed, what the people is asked is not exactly whether it approves or rejects the proposal, but whether it is in conformity with the general will, which is their will. Each man, in giving his vote, states his opinion on that point; and the general will is found by counting votes."[47] The general will, however, is but an ideal which is often corrupted by special interests and by representation itself.

More commonly, an emphasis on the content of government policy leads to disparagement of elections. Wise policy cannot be achieved through popular control, for the voters lack capacity. The inevitable results are wrong decisions, disregard of public welfare, and depradations of the minority. "A government which is exposed to the hasty action of a people is the worst and not the best government on earth," according to a common argument.[48]

The argument favoring elections has been grounded on different premises. In this theory, liberal in tradition, the basic goal of political institutions is to prevent oppression and thereby to allow individual development. Elections are highly evaluated because they are effective means of providing protection for society and control over government. Decisions might be better or worse in content, but this consideration is not central. Elections, and democracy, are "no more than well-tried and, in the presence of a widespread traditional distrust of tyranny, reasonably effective institutional safeguards against tyranny."[49] Loyalty, stability, and governmental strength follow from the protection of citizens.

The argument over elections therefore has not been a true debate, for each side has begun on different premises and pursued different points. Opponents have seen the principal aim of politics to be the realization of wisdom, and have feared elections as giving power to the inexpert. Proponents have seen the primary purpose as protection and control of government and have praised elections for their contributions to these ends.

[47] *The Social Contract*, p. 106.

[48] Massachusetts Senator Hoar, in the classic defense of indirect Senate elections, *Congressional Record*, Vol. 25, 53rd Cong., special sess. (1893), p. 103.

[49] Karl R. Popper, "Plato as Enemy of the Open Society," in Thomas L. Thorsen, ed., *Plato: Totalitarian or Democrat?* (Englewood Cliffs: Prentice-Hall, 1963), p. 71.

To be sure, the debate has sometimes been directly joined. Democratic theorists have occasionally argued that competence is more likely to be achieved through the election of rulers, rather than through some ascriptive method such as hereditary succession. They have also argued that the promotion of each individual's self-interest would also result in greater development and substantively better policy, for only the individuals affected could truly know the consequences of public policy. Elitists have also claimed that the real interests of a society would be better guarded by a talented aristocracy than by mass intervention. Nevertheless, the thrust of each argument is in a different direction. Opponents do not necessarily favor the oppression of individuals, just as supporters do not endorse unwise government; the disagreement is over their relative order and importance. Those skeptical of elections place truth and capacity at the head of the priority list of values and hope protection will follow. The supporters of elections place more emphasis on self-protection and equality and expect better government to result.

Plato himself wryly recognized the difference, while indicating his elite preferences. In a democracy, he observed: "You are not obliged to be in authority however competent you may be, or to submit to authority, if you do not like it. . . . Democracy [is] an agreeable form of anarchy with plenty of variety and equality of a peculiar kind for equals and unequals alike."[50] In a more favorable manner, Winston Churchill said, "No one pretends that democracy is perfect or all-wise. Indeed, it has been said that democracy is the worst form of government except all those other forms that have been tried from time to time."[51]

Some theorists have tried to combine the values of competence and protection. Madison and Mill provide various means to permit the achievement of the public interest while not derogating the power of the electorate. Inevitably, the two

[50] *The Republic,* Book VIII, 557–58.

[51] 444 *House of Commons Debates,* 5th series (November 11, 1947), pp. 206–7.

values come into conflict. The promotion of equality threatens esteemed minority interests, while providing special protections for the minority violates the principle of equality.[52] Two different values are involved in the argument over elections. They must be distinguished logically and, in a practical situation, one must often be preferred over the other.

Many of the specific arguments about elections are derived from this primary conflict of values. The belief in the need for wisdom to achieve the overarching common interest leads to a demand for restrictions and qualifying tests for the electorate. The debate was conducted in the Constitutional convention, on the issue of direct election of the House. Sherman asserted that "the people want information and are constantly liable to be misled." Eldridge Gerry found direct election disadvantageous, for the people "are daily misled into the most baneful measures and opinions by the false reports circulated by designing men." In rebuttal, Mason rejected the necessity for wisdom in the electorate. Government "ought to know and sympathize with every part of the community. . . . We ought to attend to the rights of every class of the people."[53]

The threat of majority tyranny has been based on the same difference in premises and is indeed not a real issue in many ways. Majority tyranny can only be a threat if the majority in elections makes policy, the fearful assumption of those who regard elections as dangerous. De Tocqueville probably expressed this fear most graphically: "When an individual or a party is wronged in the United States, to whom can he apply for redress? If to public opinion, public opinion constitutes the majority; if to the legislature, it represents the majority and implicitly obeys it; if to the executive power, it is appointed by the majority and serves as a passive tool in its hands. . . . How-

[52] Robert Dahl brilliantly analyzes the logic and illogic of Madison's position in *A Preface to Democratic Theory* (Chicago: University of Chicago Press, Phoenix Books, 1963), chap. 1.

[53] Farrand, ed., Vol. I. pp. 48–49.

ever iniquitous or absurd the measure of which you complain, you must submit to it as well as you can."[54]

The support of elections, however, is rarely based on the policies which will result from the direct action of the majority. Rousseau and the American Progressives are distinctive in this regard. "Every law the people have not ratified in person is null and void—is, in fact, not a law," declared Rousseau. "The people of England regards itself as free; but it is grossly mistaken; it is free only during the election of members of Parliament. As soon as they are elected, slavery overtakes it, and it is nothing."[55] Putting this principle into practice, the Progressives favored the direct election of senators and judges, the direct primary, and the initiative and referendum.

Most supporters of elections have not spoken of majorities as having definable policy preferences. They have been concerned with the protection of the community as a whole, as was Locke, or with the protection of distinct interests within it, as Mill. Like any political device, popular elections will tend to protect some interests more than others. The effect of elections is to require government to pay greater attention to unorganized mass groups and comparatively less to elite groups of smaller numbers.

Protection is desired by both supporters and opponents of elections, but the more democratic position is concerned with the protection of broad social groups, and the opposition with smaller groups and their pursuit of "property, status, power or the opportunity to save mankind."[56] Each argument assumes some interests should be advanced, and some retarded by government; the dispute is over which interests deserve more attention—a value question answered differently by different persons.

[54] Alexis de Tocqueville, *Democracy in America,* ed. Phillips Bradley (New York: Vintage Books, 1954), Vol. I, p. 271.

[55] *The Social Contract,* pp. 94–95.

[56] Dahl, p. 31.

These value differences—the relative importance of competence and protection, and the preference for different interests, are the core of the argument over elections. In terms of empirical descriptions, there have not been great differences. Both sides agree that elections promote the interests of the voters, although this effect is evaluated differently. There is agreement as well that governments based on elections command mass loyalty and possess great strength, with opponents fearing this very strength as a prelude to tyranny.

The expectations of the theorists have provided material for our examinations of the significance of elections. To provide criteria for evaluating the ballot, we have focused on elements of the "traditional theory of democracy." Our analysis suggests that this theory has been misunderstood and, consequently, that many modern criticisms of elections are misplaced. Most of the critics, as cited in chapter I, implicitly assume that traditional theories of democracy provided for direct control by voters. Contemporary studies, however, have discovered a citizenry which is demonstrably inattentive to public affairs, uncertain of the principles of democracy, and unsophisticated in its attitudes toward parties, politicians, and policies. In the light of these findings, many commentators abandon or revise the "traditional" democratic theory.[57]

These writers may be missing the point. The advantages of elections have been seen in their indirect effects, particularly the protection of the voters, not in the wisdom of their decisions. To test the worth of elections, we should focus on these reputed benefits. A contrary emphasis on the failures of direct control would be based upon a false view of the theory of democracy, at least insofar as it relates to the theory of elections, described above. The assumption of these modern writers is that voters

[57] See Eugene Burdick, "Political Theory and the Voting Studies," in Burdick and Arthur Brodbeck, *American Voting Behavior* (New York: The Free Press, 1959), pp. 138–48. Bernard Berelson attempts to develop a new democratic theory in *Voting* (Chicago: University of Chicago Press, 1954), chap. 14.

are expected to make policy in elections. Since the evidence strongly indicates that voters do not make policy, the modern writers attack either the voters or the evidence. Yet, in accepting this assumption, they are also accepting the premises and criteria of the very persons who opposed elections. It was those who feared elections and democracy who considered wise policy and the competence of the citizenry the tests of good government. In judging modern voters by these standards, we accept the basis of their argument. It was Plato after all, not Mill, who measured the quality of a government by the wisdom of its rulers and the absolute truth of its decisions.

The agonizing reappraisal of democratic theory, then, is possibly unnecessary. We tend to apply the tests of the antidemocrats to democratic practice. After granting the premise that the proper test of an electoral system is the competence of the electors, it becomes difficult to remain a democrat. Admittedly, modern democracy has yielded neither philosopher-kings nor a utopian society. To this extent, the critics of elective government have been vindicated.

Those who supported elections, however, rarely expected these results. Even when the democratic voter was given a policy role, "these writers never claimed to be describing existing reality, for they were elaborating, at least in part, a set of ideals for a democratic society, which were also meant to be operative ideals for their own time."[58] In practice, elections would normally not meet these ideals, but would still serve important functions. To the democratic theorist, the voter need not know what is wise, but only what is personally satisfactory or obnoxious.

If we are to appraise the effects of elections in the light of modern experience it may be more appropriate to judge by the criteria of those who regarded elections as beneficial. These theorists have seen elections as a means of dealing with a

[58] Graeme Duncan and Steven Lukes, "The New Democracy," *Political Studies*, Vol. II (June, 1963), p. 161.

problem of high priority to them—controlling the government as the governed wish it to be controlled. Elections would give the voters a means of protection, a method of intervention in politics when their vital interests were being threatened. By their very existence, they would act as a restraint on government and tend to bring representatives to further the needs and wants of their constituents. Have elections provided protection for society and control over government? These seem the most appropriate questions to ask.

To provide protection and control, appropriate governmental institutions are necessary. We will examine the structure of American politics in the next chapter. Whatever the structure, however, the burden of his protection falls on the voter himself. What does he know and how does he act? Is there justification for universal suffrage? These questions will be considered in chapter IV. In the remainder of this study, we will attempt to determine the empirical character of elections.

CHAPTER 3

THE STRUCTURE OF AMERICAN ELECTIONS

OPTIMISTIC FAITH in the ballot has been particularly prevalent in the United States. Elections are the great public ceremonies of American life. We vote not only to choose public officials from President to coroner, but also to decide complex questions of fluoridation and constitutional revision, and to select college editors, All-Star teams, and beauty queens. Our pervasive faith is exemplified by the kindergarten student who brought a rabbit to school. One of his classmates asked if the animal were a boy or girl. How could one answer this vital question? Another youngster, familiar with American ways, quickly suggested: "Let's vote on it."

Adults, although presumably more aware of basic biology, also rely on the political process. Popular control through elections has been a dominant theme in American history. As early as the Jacksonian era, De Tocqueville found, "The people reign in the American political world as the Deity does in the universe. They are the cause and the aim of all things; everything comes from them, and everything is absorbed in them."[1] The practical manifestation of this belief was the rapid expan-

[1] Alexis de Tocqueville, *Democracy in America,* ed. Phillips Bradley (New York: Vintage, 1954), Vol. I, chap. 14, p. 260.

sion of the suffrage. By the time of the Civil War, and earlier in most states, voting was available to all white males.[2]

The widened suffrage was one of a series of developments which increased the importance of elections. Direct choice of public officials became prevalent; administrative responsibility was divided among several officers, each of whom was elected, but held power only for a short period; and representatives came to be "instructed" by the voters. "There was no appeal from the people, it was believed; the mass of the electorate was the highest law. The majority, using the tremendously lengthening lever of universal suffrage with the majority principle as a fulcrum, was the force which moved the whole nation."[3]

Elections have been seen as the means of resolving the most intense social conflicts. In 1858, as secession approached, Lincoln and Douglas engaged in their famous debates. At Freeport, Lincoln asked how it would be possible to exclude slavery from the territories in the light of the Supreme Court's decision[4] that any such action was unconstitutional. "It matters not what way the Supreme Court may hereafter decide as to the abstract question whether slavery may or may not go into a territory under the Constitution," Douglas answered, for "the people have the lawful means to introduce it or exclude it as they please, for the reason that slavery cannot exist a day or an hour anywhere unless it is supported by local police regulations. These police regulations can only be established by the local legislature, and if the people are opposed to slavery, they will elect representatives to that body who will by unfriendly legislation effectually prevent the introduction of it in their midst."[5] Douglas' doctrine was an artful attempt to satisfy

[2] See Chilton Williamson, *American Suffrage: From Property to Democracy, 1760–1860* (Princeton: Princeton University Press, 1960).

[3] Alfred de Grazia, *Public and Republic* (New York: Knopf, 1951), p. 114, and chap. 5.

[4] *Dred Scott* v. *Sanford,* 19 How. 393 (1857).

[5] Richard Hofstadter, ed., *Great Issues in American History* (New York: Vintage, 1958), Vol. 1, p. 372.

both the advocates and opponents of slavery. His principle of "popular sovereignty" also expressed an American belief in the overwhelming importance of elections.

Similar beliefs are evident in later years. After the Civil War came the enfranchisement of Negroes, the Progressive innovations of the initiative, referendum, recall, and nominating primary, the direct election of senators, and woman suffrage. In our own day, the belief in the importance of elections is evident in legislation to secure full voting rights for southern Negroes, proposals for direct popular election of the President, and demands for and resistance to equal apportionment of state legislatures and congressional districts.[6] Our faith in elections is evidenced by the contemporary existence of over half a million elected public officials in the United States, or an estimated average of one to every hundred families.[7] In California alone there are nearly 300 different kinds of public elections, conducted several times a year, in addition to numerous referenda.[8]

THE CHOICE OF RULERS

That Americans emphasize elections does not in itself make them meaningful. The institutions of the United States significantly affect their meaning and condition the influence of voters. As in football, the "rules of the game" greatly affect the actions of the individual players, the strategies employed by competing teams, the interest of the spectators, and even the final score.

In the American political game, the greatest influence of the voters, or spectators, comes in the selection of the players. The electorate does choose the people who are the government, or rather, the many governments, of the United States. The princi-

[6] Familiar arguments can be found in debates over reapportionment. See *Congressional Record*, Vol. 111, 89th Cong., 1st sess. (July 23 and 27, 1965), pp. 17395–404 and 17723–728.

[7] Daniel J. Elazar, *American Federalism: A View from the States* (New York: Crowell, 1966), p. 204.

[8] For the details of local elections, see Philip Schlessinger and Richard Wright, *Elements of California Government*, 2nd ed. (New York: Holt, Rinehart & Winston, 1966), p. 84.

pal executive officials—President, governors, and mayors—are designated by popular vote. Laws, made by directly chosen legislators, are administered by a bureaucracy under the supervision of one or more politically responsible executives, and are often interpreted by elected judges. These facts are obvious, but there is no inherent reason why any government official should be elected. Indeed, through most of history and in most of the world today, governments are not chosen in this way.

Even in nations holding free elections, officials are usually not designated by direct majority vote. In cabinet forms of government, the voters do not choose the nation's leaders. Instead, they choose legislative representatives, who bargain with each other to form a government. Unless one party has a majority in the legislature, the composition of this government is not determined by the popular vote, and it may change a number of times between elections, as the parties break old alliances and make new ones. In a presidential form of government, the voters do elect the nation's executive. If there are more than two contestants, however, it is unlikely that the winning candidate will have the support of a popular majority.

The two-party system is the most important fact about American elections. The existence of two, and only two, major parties makes the popular vote decisive in the choice of a government. The election then automatically provides one party with the majority in the legislature necessary to form a cabinet, or provides one party's candidate with a clear claim to executive power. The dominant characteristic and virtue of the two-party system is that it clearly indicates who will hold power and automatically produces majority control for one party.[9] Responsibility is placed on that party, and the stability of the government is promoted.

Although the two-party system determines who will hold power, there is no assurance that the majority party will be an

[9] E. E. Schattschneider, *Party Government* (New York: Holt, Rinehart & Winston, 1942), p. 84.

undistorted "mirror of opinion" held by the voters. Indeed, since opinions can rarely be reduced to two simple and coherent alternatives, the system inevitably distorts opinion, forcing the Harlem Negro and the Mississippi redneck into the same Democratic party, and Jacob Javits and Barry Goldwater into the same Republican party. As one critic complains, "It implies that representation . . . is at most of secondary importance, and that elections should be regarded as no more than a handy way of deciding which of two well-organized rival factions should be allowed to enjoy the sweets of office and to impose its particular doctrines on the community."[10] The emphasis is on securing a stable government with broad popular support, not on the faithful reflection of popular opinions.

The particular systems of voting employed in the American two-party system, to be discussed below, also distort the relative strength of the major parties. It is possible under the Electoral College for a President to be chosen with a minority of the total popular vote, as has happened 13 times since 1828, and even to be elected with fewer votes than an opposition candidate, as in the victories of Rutherford Hayes and Benjamin Harrison. It is theoretically possible as well for a party to win a majority of the seats in Congress, even though it receives only a minority of the popular vote, assuming its supporters are strategically situated.

The distortions of the electoral systems, however, usually are in the opposite direction, giving the majority party more electoral votes for President or more seats in Congress than would be proportionate to its share of the popular ballots. In the Electoral College, the candidate with the most popular votes in a state receives all of its electoral tallies, thereby exaggerating his strength. Thus, in 1964, Johnson received over 61 per cent of the popular vote, but over 90 per cent in the Electoral College. In congressional elections, a relatively small change in the

[10] J. F. S. Ross, *Elections and Electors* (London: Eyre & Spottiswoode, 1955), p. 50.

balloting brings a disproportionate change in the seats held by each party.[11] "The operation of the system is to exaggerate the victory of the strongest party and to discriminate radically against lesser parties. The system discriminates moderately against the second party but against the third, fourth and fifth parties the force of this tendency is multiplied to the point of extinguishing the chances of winning seats altogether."[12] A two-party system contributes to stability by giving one party the power of a majority. The electoral system strengthens that power by exaggerating the size of the majority.

The vital importance of the two-party system naturally leads to discussion of its sources. Frequently, methods of voting are considered the basic cause. In fullest use in America is the "single-member district, single-ballot, plurality" or "first past the post" method. Under this arrangement, each district elects only one representative, and each voter can make only one choice for a given office. The winner is the candidate who receives the most votes, even if it is a minority of the total ballots.[13]

A leading student of parties declares, as a "true sociological law," that this system itself produces a two-party system.[14] According to this hypothesis, since there is only one office in each district, small factions are unable to achieve a share of the spoils and are instead encouraged to attach themselves to one of the two major parties which have a reasonable hope of victory. Voters are considered reluctant to "waste" their ballots on a minor party and will support a major group in order to make their wishes "count."

[11] The precise mathematical relationship is presented in James G. March, "Party Legislative Representation as a Function of Election Results," *Public Opinion Quarterly*, Vol. 21 (Winter, 1957–58), pp. 521–42.

[12] Schattschneider, p. 75; italics in the original omitted.

[13] The theory and practice of electoral methods is discussed by W. J. M. MacKenzie, *Free Elections* (New York: Holt, Rinehart & Winston, 1958) and Duncan Black, *The Theory of Committees and Elections* (Cambridge: Cambridge University Press, 1958).

[14] Maurice Duverger, *Political Parties* (New York: Wiley, 1954), p. 217.

This explanation is plausible, but unconvincing. Historically, the single-member district did not become institutionalized in the election of the House of Representatives until 1842, after the two-party system had already been established.[15] Even in contemporary times, other methods are used, notably in the choice of a President, and a considerable proportion of state legislators are not chosen in single-member districts.[16] Moreover, in the Third French Republic and other nations, a two-party system did not follow from the "first past the post" method.[17]

The logic which derives the two-party system from electoral methods is also faulty. A single-member system may limit the number of parties in a given district to only two, but this factor does not explain why the same two parties dominate all states. A unifying national force is required. We must also be skeptical that voters deliberately refrain from "wasting" their ballots. Citizens do not usually make such intricate calculations—they simply choose the party they prefer.[18] Furthermore, if voters are reluctant to support a loser, they should vote only for the likely winner, not even for a large minority party. Despite the alleged fear of "wasting" ballots, however, millions fervently but futilely supported Stevenson in 1952 and Goldwater in 1964.[19]

[15] Joel F. Paschal, "The House of Representatives: 'Grand Depository of the Democratic Principle'?" *Law and Contemporary Problems*, Vol. 17 (Spring, 1952), pp. 280–87.

[16] Maurice Klain, "A New Look at the Constituencies: The Need for a Recount and a Reappraisal," *American Political Science Review*, Vol. 49 (December, 1955), pp. 1105–19.

[17] Philip Williams, *Politics in Post-War France* (London: Longmans, Green, 1954), pp. 309–13. However, the French system provided for two ballots. If no candidate won a majority in the first poll, a second election was held two weeks later, at which time a plurality was sufficient. Like the southern runoff primary, this system probably contributed to the viability of small factions and retarded party consolidation.

[18] Voters follow this course in both two-party and multiparty systems; see Anthony Downs, *An Economic Theory of Democracy* (New York: Harper & Row, 1957), chaps. 3, 9.

[19] A good analysis is found in Aaron B. Wildavsky, "A Methodological Critique of Duverger's *Political Parties*," *Journal of Politics*, Vol. 21 (May, 1959), pp. 303–18.

The Presidency, rather than the single-member district, probably has been the single most important institutional source of the American two-party system. A single office, it is indivisible among a coalition of parties. The President is chosen by direct popular vote in effect (although in fifty separate state elections), and his selection offers no opportunity for post-election bargaining among numerous factions. The power of the office has made it the supreme prize of American politics, bringing consolidation of differing factions in efforts to achieve a national majority.[20]

That the pursuit of Presidential power supports the two-party hegemony is illustrated by American history. There have been a multitude of minor parties, as well as continuous factionalism within the major groups. Despite their differences, the major parties have unified themselves and drawn support from the fringes because politicians have seen unity as essential to victory. Often the bonds have been only negative, with party cohesion the result of opposition to the policies of the incumbent administration, not of full agreement on alternative policies. New parties have been created and old parties reunited in efforts to wrest power from the incumbents. To win the Presidency, Jefferson, Madison, and Burr created the first Republican party, Jackson consolidated the enemies of John Quincy Adams, the Whigs brought together Jackson's and Van Buren's opponents, and the second Republican party united such disparate groups as Anti-Nebraskans, Know-Nothings, temperance advocates, and manufacturers. To win the Presidency, War Democrats and Confederates joined forces after the Civil War, Populists yielded their principles to support Bryan in 1896, and Theodore Roose-

[20] The effect of a single, directly elected executive is seen in contemporary France, where the advent of Charles de Gaulle stimulated movement toward unity among his diverse opponents—*The New York Times,* June 7, 1965, p. 1. After de Gaulle's narrow victory in the presidential election, these movements continued through the 1968 legislative elections.

velt abandoned the Progressive party in 1916 in an effort to defeat Wilson.[21]

The "rules of the game" in Presidential elections confine the competition to two teams. Each team recruits as much talent as it believes necessary for victory. If an important player becomes a holdout, the team will increase his rewards. The players on each team sometimes quarrel over the division of the gate receipts, but usually cooperate in attempts to take the winner's share. If a new club seems to be gaining some popularity, the two major clubs cooperate in limiting its exposure, bargain with its stars, or copy its style.

The attraction of the Presidency, however, does not fully explain the dominance of the major parties. In some ways, the Electoral College might be expected to reduce the pressures in this direction. Requiring the winner to receive an absolute majority of electoral votes makes it possible for a third party, if it wins a small bloc of states, to prevent the popular designation of a President. In such circumstances, the choice of the chief executive by the House of Representatives is an invitation to factional bargaining.[22] Even after the growth of the party system, major attempts to deny any candidate an electoral majority were made by the Whigs in 1836 and by southern Democrats in 1860. George Wallace of Alabama promised a similar strategy for 1964 and 1968.

Institutional factors alone, therefore, cannot explain why only two parties at any time have been able to mount and sustain nationwide appeals. Fundamentally, the two-party system is based on the total social conditions of the United States. American society has generally been united on the most funda-

[21] See Eugene Roseboom, *A History of Presidential Elections* (New York: Macmillan, 1959).

[22] In the Constitutional Convention, it was expected that the House would elect the President in almost all cases; see Max Farrand, *The Framing of the Constitution of the United States* (New Haven: Yale University Press, 1913), pp. 167–68.

mental social questions. Because policy issues have not been deeply divisive, nor factions irreconcilable, it has been possible to bring those of different viewpoints together in a common pursuit of electoral victory. While various issues were important, they have not been so numerous or mutually conflicting that the interests involved could not be satisfied within the minimum number of two parties.

Party schisms and disorganization are testament to the differences among factions. However, schisms have not been maintained for long periods of time, and the differences have been compromised because they did not involve profound moral claims or incompatible material interests. There has been general agreement on such fundamental matters as the Constitution, toleration of religious diversity, social equality, and a capitalist economic system. An expanding economy, geographical isolation and ethnic pluralism lessened the impact of debate on the distribution of wealth, on foreign policy, and on group status. "What differences exist do so in the area of secondary goals or over the means to agreed-upon goals. The stakes of politics are smaller, and the kinds of tolerance, compromise and concession necessary for a two-party system's majoritarian parties can prevail."[23] When, however, moral and inherently conflicting claims were made in the prelude to the Civil War, the parties could not hold together despite the institutional pressures toward unity.

The Presidency and the electoral system have tended to make unity desirable for American parties, and the social conditions of the United States have made it possible. The two-party system gives meaning to our elections. In biblical times, the Israelites asked God to give them a king. In modern America, the voters choose their own rulers. In one sense, it is therefore true that "the voice of the people is the voice of God." But men

[23] Frank J. Sorauf, *Political Parties in the American System* (Boston: Little, Brown, 1964), p. 30.

lack omniscience and the institutions of the United States guarantee that no man will be omnipotent.

LIMITS ON POPULAR POWER

To choose a government is not to choose governmental policies. Whereas the voters largely do determine the players in the game of American politics, they have far less control over the signals the players will call, the strategies they will employ, or the final score. The popular will, as represented by a majority of voters, does not determine public policy.

According to a well-established interpretation of American government, the limitations on the voters are principally institutional "separation of powers" and "checks and balances." J. Allen Smith, for one, vehemently denounced the Constitution as a reactionary attempt to restrict the popular will: "The efforts of the Constitutional Convention were directed to the task of devising a system of government which was just popular enough not to excite general opposition and which at the same time gave to the people as little as possible of the substance of political power."[24] In the same tradition, schoolboys and senators alike are prone to emphasize these limitations and to debate issues of national policy primarily in legal terms.

A literal reading of the Constitution often leads to an emphasis on the limitations of national power; it can also sustain Smith's description of the restricted role of popular majorities. In formal terms, the President is indirectly elected, the Senate is controlled by a minority of the nation's population, and judges are fully removed from popular influence.

A literal reading of this sort would also be a misreading of the contemporary Constitution. Regardless of formal structure, the President is chosen by popular vote, the Senate is usually more responsive to national majorities than the "democratic"

[24] J. Allen Smith, *The Spirit of American Government* (New York: Macmillan, 1907), p. 20.

House, and the Supreme Court "follows the election returns." Nor are the powers of the national government severely restricted today. The Constitution has evolved, through social necessity, political practice, and official interpretation, to an instrument which regulates the means by which national power is exercised but which imposes few substantial limitations on the ends toward which power is exercised.

It has now been over thirty years since a major act of Congress has been declared unconstitutional. On certain occasions, the Supreme Court does attempt to defend individual rights against the national government. For example, in a 1958 case dealing with the loss of citizenship by a military deserter, the Court ruled the penalty an unconstitutional punishment.[25] Otherwise, judicial review is no longer a significant limit on the power of Washington, although it remains effective against the states. The written Constitution supplies no explicit authority to desegregate restaurants, provide social security, or engage in undeclared wars, but the Court has incorporated these powers into the Constitution respectively, through interpretations of the power to regulate commerce, tax for the general welfare, and conduct foreign relations.[26]

The important limits on popular power no longer are found in the federal Constitution, but the limits do exist. One set of restrictions consists of environmental conditions beyond political control. In the constitutionally unrestrained British system, it is said that "Parliament can do everything but change a man into a woman or a woman into a man." Voters must accept these facts of life and others as well. The political discretion of a nation is restricted by its physical features and the limits of scientific invention. No farm subsidy program will make bananas grow in Alaska, and no Medicare law will produce a population of Methuselahs.

[25] *Trop* v. *Dulles*, 356 U.S. 86 (1958).

[26] *Katzenbach* v. *McClung*, 379 U.S. 294 (1964); *Steward Machine Co.* v. *Davis*, 301 U.S. 548 (1937); *U.S. v. Curtiss-Wright Export Corp.*, 299 U.S. 304 (1936).

The environment also includes social limitations. One nation, even one as powerful as the United States, cannot maintain the entire world order. A majority of Americans may favor the abolition of communism, but the Soviet Union is unlikely to agree. Established domestic institutions as well confine political choices. The American economy is largely controlled by corporate concentrations of capital, not by government or popular majorities. In 1960, the 500 largest business corporations conducted almost two-thirds of the nation's nonagricultural economic activity.[27] Although the actions of firms such as U.S. Steel and General Motors vitally affect employment, living conditions, population distribution, and even international relations, these decisions are barely affected by government, stockholders, or the imperfectly competitive marketplace.[28] Similarly, government must largely accept such social conditions as the birth rate, cultural values, and family structure. Politics can affect changes but, viewed in the context of the total environment, these changes must be marginal and incremental.

In the United States, political institutions further restrict the control of popular majorities. "Truly responsible government is only possible when elections are so conducted that a choice of men is a decision on policy," argues William Riker. To accomplish this goal, "the essential institutions of responsible government are, therefore, a system of two parties, each with strong leadership and one (as decided in elections) with the full power to govern. In the United States, we do have the two-party system though whether or not we have the other two essentials is far from certain."[29]

American parties are not cohesive units under strong leadership. Their organizational structure is best described as a

[27] Benjamin Baker and Stanley H. Friedelbaum, *Government in the United States* (Boston: Houghton Mifflin, 1966), p. 293.

[28] See Grant McConnell, *Private Power and American Democracy* (New York: Knopf, 1966), chap. 5.

[29] William H. Riker, *Democracy in the United States*, 2nd ed. (New York: Macmillan, 1965), pp. 84–5, 104.

"truncated pyramid." There is no supreme governing body at the apex of this pyramid. Whatever concentration of power exists is likely to be at intermediate heights, in the state or even county organizations. Even the truncated pyramid is not a solid piece of granite. There are faults in the stone, and there are many protected enclaves of power in which individual politicians and local groups reside.

The parties are not centralized because important rewards and crucial punishments of politics are also not centralized, but are shared among many governments and organizations. The nominating function, crucial in the internal government of parties, is widely dispersed. The massive numbers of state and local officers are obviously under the jurisdiction of the states, as are nominations to national office. Indeed, there is no such thing as a purely national election. Congressmen and senators are nominated in local primaries or conventions and are elected in their respective constituencies; the President is nominated by delegates chosen in similar primaries and conventions and is elected by the combined votes of separate states. Other important aspects of the electoral process are also predominantly in the states' domain, including party organization, voter qualifications, district boundaries, and election administration.[30]

The material rewards of politics are also concentrated at the state and local level. Patronage, contracts, and preferment are less plentiful in the federal government. The states and localities still spend more money, outside of defense, than the national government. They also have a very important role in the administration and outlay even of federal money, such as the extensive funds involved in grant-in-aid programs.[31] More-

[30] The leading work on the administration of elections remains Joseph P. Harris, *Election Administration in the United States* (Washington: The Brookings Institution, 1934). Important suggestions for reform—significantly, directed largely at the states—are in President's Commission on Registration and Voting Participation, *Report* (1963).

[31] Frederick C. Mosher and Orville F. Poland, *The Costs of American Government* (New York: Dodd, Mead, 1964), chap. 3.

over, national political leaders often have less discretion available than their state and local counterparts. Civil service regulations limit patronage more severely in Washington, and there are fewer choices possible in choosing among potential contractors for a supersonic airplane than in choosing among potential contractors for a state expressway.

Strong leadership is therefore unlikely in American parties, since the leaders do not have such disciplinary powers as the control of nominations, elections, or material rewards. The parties in Congress do nevertheless show considerable unity when issues come to a vote, and party membership is more closely associated with this voting than any factor such as constituency interest.[32] On important issues, about 80 per cent of the party will stand together. The parties are not monolithic but, given their decentralized structure, they are relatively cohesive.[33]

While some unity exists, defections can and do occur. "The parties are unable to hold their lines in a controversial public issue when the pressure is on."[34] Where a congressman perceives a conflict between the party program and the interest of his local district, he is likely to prefer the latter. Opposition to the party is therefore concentrated among such congressmen as Republicans from farm districts when the national party seeks to reduce price supports, or Democrats from the South when the party seeks to raise the minimum wage.[35] A congressman cannot be compelled to adhere to the party position, but loyalty to the constituency can be enforced directly, since its support is crucial for nomination and election.

[32] Important works on congressional voting include Julius Turner, *Party and Constituency* (Baltimore: Johns Hopkins University Press, 1951); David B. Truman, *The Congressional Party* (New York: Wiley, 1959); and Duncan MacRae, *Dimensions of Congressional Voting* (Berkeley: University of California Press, 1958).

[33] For further discussion, see chap. VIII, below.

[34] Schattschneider, p. 131.

[35] David R. Mayhew, *Party Loyalty among Congressmen* (Cambridge: Harvard University Press, 1966), chaps. 2, 4.

Further obstacles to popular control arise because the governments chosen by majorities in elections do not have the "full power to govern" in the United States. Their powers are insulated, reduced, and checked. Important elements of American government are deliberately insulated from the impact of elections. The largest number of public officials is included in the bureaucracy, which is protected, from clerks to important administrators, by civil service laws. While the bureaucracy is generally responsive, it has means of resistance when conflict arises between its ingrained practices and the programs of elected officials. Even a vigorous President like John Kennedy found his foreign policy initiatives frustrated by the traditions of the State Department. "Giving State an instruction, he remarked, snapping his fingers with impatience, is like dropping it in the dead-letter box. 'They never have any ideas over there,' he complained, 'never come up with anything new.'"[36]

Insulation from the direct impact of elections is found in many parts of the federal government. Judges are constitutionally protected during good behavior. The regulatory commissions are "independent" by statute. The autonomy of the commissions is not freedom from pressures by the regulated interests; indeed the commissions often become, not watchdogs of these industries, but their housepets. Their independence consists of freedom from the control of the President or other politically responsible officials. Other officials become insulated through a combination of achievement, public relations, power, and strategic alliances: the invulnerable position of J. Edgar Hoover is a leading example.

In state and local affairs, public authorities constitute another insulated center of power. These politically independent bodies are established to perform a governmental task which is beyond the abilities of existing agencies. The Port of New York Authority, the most impressive example, is responsible for all airports,

[36] Arthur M. Schlesinger, Jr., *A Thousand Days* (Boston: Houghton Mifflin, 1965), p. 406.

and a considerable proportion of the highways, commuter transit, and shipping in the nation's greatest metropolitan area. It imposes taxes in the form of tolls and fees, condemns property, borrows money on public credit, and regulates transportation for 16 million persons. Yet it is subject to no electoral control. The Authority's directors are appointed by the governors of New York and New Jersey for long, staggered, and fixed terms. Independent of Congress, its policies are theoretically subject to veto by the governors, but even this negative power is unexercised.[37]

Where government is not insulated from the influence of elections, its powers are often reduced. Popular desires as expressed in elections may be unfulfilled because the governments concerned lack the necessary power. The most severe restrictions apply to local governments. Legally regarded as merely corporate creations of the states, they can exercise very few independent powers. According to the long-established "Dillon's Rule," a municipality can exercise only those functions "granted in express words," "necessarily or fairly implied," or "essential . . . not simply convenient, but indispensable." Any doubt "is resolved by the courts against the corporation, and the power is denied."[38]

Nor do states exercise unlimited authority. The typical state constitution provides not only a framework of government, but a host of legislative details and limits on the power of the state. Details of public policy are encased in constitutional armor to protect them from any future attacks by legislative or popular majorities. The constitution of New York is not one of the longest or most detailed, yet it does specify the size and location of ski trails and roads in certain areas, while requiring other

[37] See U.S. Congress, House Judiciary Committee, *Port of New York Authority*, Hearings, 86th Cong., 2nd sess. (1961). For a critical appraisal, see Edward T. Chase, "How to Rescue New York from Its Port Authority," *Harper's*, Vol. 220 (June, 1960), pp. 67–74.

[38] John F. Dillon, *Commentaries on the Law of Municipal Corporations*, 5th ed. (Boston: Little, Brown, 1911), Vol. I, p. 448.

lands to be kept "forever wild."[39] Further restrictions are imposed on the states by the federal Constitution and courts. Whatever the wishes of a popular majority in a state, it may not secede, establish segregated schools, or regulate the length of interstate railroad trains.[40]

BARGAINING IN AMERICAN POLITICS

"The power to govern," in institutional terms, appears greatly restricted in American politics. In the political game, players are not always required to cooperate with one another and sometimes lack the necessary equipment to sustain a scoring drive. Further analysis indicates that political realities can be quite different from institutional appearances. Formally, the American system of government can seem to be a panoply of "clashing sovereignties," whose frustrated conflicts result in either domination or deadlock. In practice, however, legal positions are not pursued to ultimate conclusions, obstacles are overcome, and policies of mutual satisfaction are usually accomplished. The political players, though argumentative, want to score and to satisfy the fans. Despite their differences and the restrictions of the rules, they commonly can find the right plays.

Bargaining is the typical method of deciding issues in American government. Negotiation, compromise, and mutual concession are the dominant features of our politics, rather than insistence on separate legal powers and tests of strength. Through bargaining, the rigidities of institutions are relaxed. The process of negotiation can create new difficulties, further complicating popular control, but it provides the means by which political practice can mitigate legal constraints.

A politics of bargaining is not a means of direct voter control over policy. The electorate controls the choice of rulers, but the lack of discipline among officials and the limited powers of any

[39] New York State Constitution, Article XIX, Section 1.

[40] These limits are specified in the cases of *Texas* v. *White*, 7 Wall. 700 (1869); *Brown* v. *Board of Education*, 347 U.S. 483 (1954); *Southern Pacific* v. *Arizona*, 325 U.S. 761 (1945).

single government agency make the realization of popular mandates unlikely. Policy decisions result from the compromises and understandings within government. The electorate chooses the bargainers and can exercise an indirect influence on their negotiations, but it lacks the power to enforce detailed decisions.

Bargaining is possible because American politics is not ideological. The differences between President and Congress, or state and federal governments, or the two parties, are not matters of high principle. The typical disputes in America concern how to finance medical care, not whether to provide aid to the sick; where to locate a highway, not whether to build roads; how to increase the nation's military strength, not whether to assume international obligations. Since the participants in these disputes do wish to reach agreement, they are ready to bargain.

In an ideological politics, bargaining is inhibited. The gains of one group often mean vital losses to another. Communists and democrats in France cannot agree on the structure of government. Religionists and secularists in India or Israel cannot reach an accommodation. Demands for a fully independent Quebec cannot be reconciled with Canadian unity. In these situations, the disputants do not expect mutual gains from a settlement of their differences. Bargaining is not possible under these circumstances.[41]

In the United States, bargaining is feasible. It is initiated and usually successful because the formal powers available to any agency are commonly not sufficient to accomplish all of its purposes, both legal and political. Civil servants can ignore many Presidential requests, but they also need the support of

[41] A general statement of the nature of bargaining is found in Robert Dahl and Charles Lindblom, *Politics, Economics and Welfare* (New York: Harper & Row, 1953), chaps. 6–13. Nelson Polsby applied the model to national party conventions in "Decision-Making at the National Conventions," *Western Political Quarterly*, Vol. 13 (September, 1960), pp. 609–17. A recent important work is Lindbloom's *The Intelligence of Democracy* (New York: The Free Press, 1965).

the President and the Bureau of the Budget for legislation and appropriations. The Port of New York Authority can unilaterally condemn property and sell bonds for a World Trade Center, but it also needs building permits from New York City.[42] Municipalities have severely limited legal powers, but the votes of their residents are crucial in the election of state officials. The President cannot discipline his party in Congress, but his record will be a major issue in the individual districts. State parties are independent of national leaders, but the tides of national politics considerably affect local electoral fortunes.[43]

Bargaining is necessitated as much by political as institutional causes. The legal "checks and balances" are familiar. "The government of the United States was constructed upon the Whig theory of political dynamics, which was a sort of unconscious copy of the Newtonian theory of the universe. . . . The makers of our federal Constitution followed the scheme as they found it expounded in Montesquieu, followed it with genuine scientific enthusiasm. . . . Politics is turned into mechanics under his touch. The theory of gravitation is supreme."[44]

The institutional checks remain and can be significant. Federalism continues to be an important restraint, as illustrated in the case of civil rights. Although the federal government and the nation as a whole clearly favor equality for Negroes, action toward this end has been handicapped by the continuing power of the states over public safety, education, and voting qualifications.[45] Yet federalism is not primarily significant because of legal factors. The national government now has the constitutional power to protect civil rights, and recent legislation and

[42] To win the city's cooperation, the Port Authority eventually had to make a variety of concessions, including payments for various municipal programs—*The New York Times*, August 4, 1966, p. 1.

[43] See V. O. Key, Jr., *American State Politics* (New York: Knopf, 1956), chap. 2.

[44] Woodrow Wilson, *Constitutional Government in the United States* (New York: Columbia University Press, 1908), pp. 55–56.

[45] See Burke Marshall, *Federalism and Civil Rights* (New York: Columbia University Press, 1964).

court decisions have led to such action in regard to segregated schools and discrimination in voting and public facilities.

The actions of the national government, however, have been measured and severely limited to immediate problems, because of political checks. Decentralized parties, voter loyalty to state and local leaders, and the distribution of power within Congress are among the political factors which have bolstered, and even supplanted, the formal strengths of federalism. "The enumerated powers have been supplemented by the implied powers, the compact theory and state pretensions to sovereignty collapsed in the Civil War, and now the only real limits on the functions of the national government are the demands of the people and its own sense of self-restraint."[46]

Bargaining, rather than legal limitation, is also evident within the national government. The relationship of President and Congress, traditionally described as one of "separation of powers," is really one of "separated institutions sharing powers."[47] The separations are real. President and Congress (and each house of Congress) are chosen in different ways. Neither can fully dominate the other. The President cannot dissolve Congress and call for a new election, nor can he prevent obdurate congressmen from being elected, even under his own party label. Similarly, Congress cannot expect to use the rusty weapon of impeachment or even its well-sharpened legislative powers to bend the President to its will.

The constitutional separations between the branches, however, are no longer the primary reasons for their conflicts. Originally, each body was chosen in a distinct manner; today all are dependent, in reality if not formally, on direct popular vote. At one time, Congress and President were only related institutionally; today there are a plenitude of informal relations, including congressional oversight of administration, presidential leadership in budgeting and legislation, leadership

[46] Riker, p. 308.

[47] Richard Neustadt, *Presidential Power* (New York: Wiley, 1960), p. 33.

conferences, and most significant, the link of common party membership. In constitutional theory, the two branches are equal; today the center of American government is clearly in the White House.

Political, rather than institutional, factors are the basis of the contemporary separation. All branches are elected, but they are chosen by rather different constituencies. The President, selected by all voters, is most likely to be responsive to overt majority opinion and to national groups which are large but widely scattered. When a choice must be made between competing pressures, the mathematics of the Electoral College influence the President in a distinct direction. Because the entire electoral vote of a state is won by the candidate who receives a plurality of popular votes, particular presidential attention will be devoted to those states which have large blocs of electoral votes and which are competitive between the parties. These states contain large numbers of urban residents, industrial workers, and ethnic minorities, and aspirants for the White House will therefore be particularly responsive to their demands. Commonly, this results in a presidential emphasis on liberal social policies, including increased federal spending and welfare.[48]

The Senate's emphasis is most likely to be the unique interests of the states, as evidenced in its historical concern for silver miners or farmers. At present, the Senate shows much interest in urban problems because almost every state now includes a major metropolitan area, where a large proportion of the state's population votes. The House has been particularly devoted to narrow-gauge local interests. Rural and small-town voters, especially, have tended to have disproportionate power, because of the failure of state legislatures to reapportion con-

[48] See Allan P. Sindler, "Presidential Election Methods and Urban-Ethnic Interests," *Law and Contemporary Problems*, Vol. 27 (Spring, 1962), pp. 213–33, and Joseph E. Kallenbach, "Our Electoral College Gerrymander," *Midwest Journal of Political Science*, Vol. 4 (May, 1960), pp. 162–91.

gressional districts to reflect urban growth, and because of deliberate gerrymandering of these districts.

Even with fair apportionment and districting, stimulated by Supreme Court decisions,[49] the House will tend to emphasize relatively narrow interests. By the informal "locality rule," congressmen are virtually required to be long-term residents of their districts, whose attention is directed to the welfare of their local constituents, rather than to national questions.[50] Local control of nominations, including the direct primary, reinforces such parochialism. Moreover, the interests which predominate in a small constituency are different from those which are cumulated at the national level. Concentrated and geographically localized interests are preferred to those which are diffuse and continental. Conservative interests, those in support of the status quo, are likely to be favored. "It is in the small constituency that, other things being equal, power tends most to inequality of distribution. As a result representatives of small constituencies in a national forum will be more likely than representatives of large constituencies to take specific and extreme positions favoring the particular interests holding power in the constituent units . . . . The effect of a small constituency is to enhance the power of local elites, whatever their character or sources of power."[51]

The structure of power within Congress leads to further political conflicts with the President. American legislative power essentially depends on seniority, resulting from continued and unbroken re-election, and the greatest power accrues to representatives from districts in which party competition is no threat to tenure. Because of the seniority principle, southern Democrats and small-town Republicans gain disproportionate

[49] Equality of representation in Congress was mandated by *Wesberry* v. *Sanders*, 376 U.S. 1 (1964), equality in state legislatures by *Reynolds* v. *Sims*, 377 U.S. 533 (1964).

[50] Dennis Brogan, *Politics in America* (New York: Harper & Row, 1954), pp. 336–40.

[51] McConnell, pp. 108–9.

strength. The President, by contrast, has a relatively short tenure of four or eight years and wins election by appeals to the more competitive areas, particularly to non-southern and metropolitan areas. The leaders of Congress will represent the politically stagnant constituencies of the nation, the President the more dynamic areas. Conflict is likely to follow.

Each branch also responds to different pressures, aside from those of voters. The President is necessarily conscious of the demands of foreign nations, of the bureaucracy, and of the national party. Members of both houses of Congress must give greater weight to the demands of local business, of state and local officials, and of the decentralized party organizations. As much as their institutional divisions, these political differences between the branches create the necessity for bargaining between separated centers of power.

THE INFLUENCE OF ELECTIONS

Direct electoral control over policy is unlikely. The lack of centralization, limitations on power, and the complexities of government make simple majority rule infeasible, if not impossible. Even if voters have clear policy aims, they may not know where to direct their attention. "How does the citizen begin if he wishes to do something about his deteriorating neighborhood? Slum clearance involves three sets of law—local, state and federal—and perhaps half a dozen separate administrative agencies, each with its own body of regulations. Points of influence and centers of decision are diffuse and obscure. More often than not the citizen cannot name most of the officers he elects, or describe the responsibilities of the governments that serve him. How can he hope to make them responsive to his wishes?"[52]

Popular influence is real, but indirect. It exists because of the availability of bargaining. The very lack of centralized

[52] Morton Grodzins, *The American System*, ed. Daniel J. Elazar (Chicago: Rand McNally, 1966), p. 6.

power means that voters can attempt to influence decisions at many points and many times. Interested citizens need not restrict their attention to one election, after which there is no further means for popular intervention. The confusing multiplicity of governments also creates a comforting multiplicity of opportunities to influence policy. Grodzins appropriately terms the American system one characterized by "the multiple crack." . . . "The normal process of policy-making is one in which individuals and groups take their crack at influencing governmental policy at literally uncountable points in the legislative-administrative process. The process produces, among other things, the characteristic collaborative chaos of the American system."[53]

The dispersal of power limits the likelihood of totally unpopular policies. The various agencies involved in bargaining have a common aim of promoting public satisfaction. Their perceptions of the general welfare will differ, as will the influences which bear on them, and conflicting proposals can result. The shared interest in meeting popular needs, however, creates influences toward agreement in accord with the desires of the voters. The inability of any one agency to impose its will, moreover, increases the probability that agreed policies will be satisfactory to all.

The electors have their own powerful means of insuring that their interests are considered. Elected officials are important, even predominant, participants in the bargaining process, and the two-party system results in the direct choice of these officials by popular majorities. By controlling the tenure of these officials, voters also influence the policies they promote and negotiate. To win and retain power, elected officials will favor popular policies and will initiate programs which will arouse mass support.

The desire for electoral victory can facilitate bargaining. Politicians will agree more quickly when their agreement is

[53] *Ibid.*, pp. 14–15.

seen as necessary for individual success. The Presidency acts as a political magnet, unifying scattered filings into two parties. Congress and the President, despite their differences, join in improving the popular social security program. State and national party organizations cooperate in campaigns to win office on all levels. Rural legislators support urban programs considered necessary for statewide victory.

Electoral influence is also evident as a resource in the bargaining process. Because of the authority created by popular support, some agencies improve their negotiating position. Elections strengthen the Presidency against the courts, bureaucracy, and regulatory commissions; the states against the public authorities; the cities against the states; local areas against the federal government; and the national party against the decentralized organizations. In each of these pairs, the former agency can demonstrate greater popular support than the latter or can significantly influence its political future.

Elections do not determine the outcome of the bargaining process, but they can be a means by which bargainers gain resources. It is possible for an elected official to claim a "mandate" for his preferred policies, but the claim is unavailable to others. Thus, the British House of Lords agreed to its own loss of power after the voters supported the reformist Liberal party in 1910, and the U.S. Supreme Court ended its opposition to the New Deal after Franklin Roosevelt's landslide victory in 1936.

The voters, then, do have an influence on policy. The spectators at the political game select the players; only occasionally do they also call the signals. The men on the field, however, must satisfy the fans or be replaced or lose customers. The most important players can often dominate the game by asking the crowd to cheer in their support and to harass the opposition. The final score will result from the combined effect of the demands of the spectators, the restrictions of the rules, and the skills of the players.

Thus the voters play an indirect role in the determination of public policy. The actual decisions about the actions of government must be left to the initiatives of officials and their complex bargaining. Voters, however, can meaningfully intervene to support a leadership group which is seeking to enact a particular program. By their endorsement of particular contestants in the bargaining process, the voters can have the final word. The choice of governors can thereby become a choice of governmental policy.

Voters also can protest effectively when their interests are involved. Elections can therefore serve another indirect function, providing the benefits of protection emphasized by democratic theorists. The very complexity of institutions which makes it difficult to achieve a coherent program also provides numerous agencies to protect individuals and groups. Noncentralized parties and government allow voters repeatedly to seek a redress of grievances. Diverse institutions, each with limited power, may attempt to increase their bargaining advantages by winning popular support. The competition is untidy, even chaotic, but it can promote citizens' protection and interests.

Given American institutions and the politics of bargaining, elections cannot be definitive, but they can be decisive. Their empirical quality will depend greatly on the qualifications of the electorate. In the next chapter, we turn to an examination of American voters.

CHAPTER 4

VOTERS IN AMERICA

IF ELECTIONS have any significance, the character of the voters is obviously crucial. Direct control of public policy would require the citizens to be informed and interested in the broad range of governmental issues. Indirect influence of voters would require at least some awareness of their personal needs and interests. Voters must have some concern for the acts of politicians, else politicians will have little concern for the acts of the voters. In this chapter, we shall review the extensive findings of voting research in the United States. We will then proceed to analyze the actions of the electorate in presidential and gubernatorial contests.

Explanations of voters' attitudes have been advanced at least since the time of Socrates' trial for subversion in Athens. To win popular support, the philosopher was advised to rely on "pitiful appeals to the jury with floods of tears, and [to have] his infant children produced in court to excite the maximum of sympathy, and many of his relatives and friends as well."[1] Socrates rejected the advice but perhaps he erred, since the populace then voted the death penalty.

[1] Plato, *The Apology*, trans. Hugh Tredennick (London: Penguin Books, 1954), p. 34.

In recent decades, some reliable data on the electorate have become available. Opinion surveys, though sometimes faulty, do provide a means to learn the expressed beliefs of a representative sample of the population. The student of politics is no longer exclusively dependent on individual insight or on chance meetings with voters. From the initiation of the Gallup poll in 1936 through the continuing, elaborate studies of the Michigan Survey Research Center, a considerable amount of evidence has been accumulated. Using this material, we will deal with two sharply divergent descriptions, or "models," of the American voter.

One model is that of the philosophical citizen; the other, that of the manipulated subject. Whereas the first model is appropriate for direct popular control of policy, the second permits neither direct nor indirect influence. The philosophical citizen is an ideal voter, who individually seeks the common good by attention to policy issues. Upon fair consideration of all sides in an election, he supports the candidate most likely to advance the general welfare. As we shall see, this model does not fit empirical reality.

In reaction to some of the less gratifying findings of voting research, a pessimistic portrait of the voter has been drawn, a portrait of the manipulated subject. The individual is no longer seen as a participating citizen. He is regarded as subordinated by impersonal forces and forceful persons, a subject susceptible to manipulation by socioeconomic influences, propaganda, and glamorous candidates. Democratic sensibilities are enraged at this portrait. Fortunately for these sensibilities, this model also can be shown to be empirically invalid.

Voters are neither philosphical citizens nor manipulated subjects. They may be best described by a third model, that of the meddling partisan. The real character of the voter does not make direct policy control likely, but it does permit indirect influences of elections.

THE PHILOSOPHICAL CITIZEN: INDIVIDUALITY

In the first model, the voter is politically autonomous. Citizens ideally make their decisions privately and on the basis of their independent judgment. They seek the common good, not personal or group advantage. As Mill defined the ideal, "The voter is under an absolute moral obligation to consider the interest of the public, not his private advantage, and give his vote to the best of his judgment, exactly as he would be bound to do if he were the sole voter and the election depended on him alone."[2] We still hold to this belief, as seen in individualistic voting rituals—the restriction of electioneering near the polls, the locked ballot box, and appeals to "vote for the best man."

Despite theory and ritual, voting is not a private action, except in the most literal sense. A ballot is cast by each individual—at least where honesty prevails—but the voter's decision is not the result of isolated contemplation. Rather, the individual is influenced by the groups to which he belongs and with which he identifies. "A person thinks, politically, as he is, socially,"[3] wrote the authors of the first academic election survey. This statement is an exaggeration, but it correctly points to the social influences upon the voter.

If electoral judgments were simply individual decisions, there would be only random differences in the voting patterns of social groups. White-collar and manual workers, college and high school graduates, Protestants and Catholics, northern and southern European immigrant stocks, small-town and big-city residents, Caucasians and Negroes—each group would divide its vote between the parties in similar proportions. In fact, these groups differ in their political behavior. In each of the pairs listed, the first group shows relatively more support for the

[2] John Stuart Mill, *Considerations on Representative Government* (New York: Liberal Arts Press, 1958), p. 156.

[3] Paul Lazarsfeld *et al.*, *The People's Choice*, 2nd ed. (New York: Columbia University Press, 1948), p. 27.

Republicans, and the second group is more favorable to the Democrats. The division of the vote in three recent elections is presented in Table 4.1.[4]

Of the various groups which affect political man, the most important is the political party itself. Voters do not view public events with unaided vision, but through the lens of partisanship. Table 4.1 indicates the strong loyalty of Democrats and Republicans to their party's candidates. Repeated investigations also have shown a deep sense of "party identification" by most of the population. At least three-fourths of American adults feel a meaningful and continuing loyalty to either the Democrats or Republicans, and only about a tenth are confirmed Independents. This loyalty affects not only their vote but their perceptions of the entire political world.[5]

Party identification is quite firm. It develops early in life, before there is any detailed understanding of public issues and governmental institutions. By the fourth grade, a majority of schoolchildren identify with a political party.[6] For the most part, children assume and later retain the same party loyalty as their fathers and mothers. Even among adults, nearly 80 per cent hold

[4] The data for Table 4.1 are from the voting studies of the Survey Research Center of the University of Michigan. The results for 1952 were published in Angus Campbell, Gerald Gurin, and Warren E. Miller, *The Voter Decides* (Evanston: Row, Peterson, 1954), pp. 70–77. The data for 1960 and 1964 were derived from the surveys of those years and provided through the courtesy of Mrs. Eve Lubalin of the Inter-University Consortium for Political Research. Similar figures from the Gallup poll are reported in *Congressional Quarterly Weekly Report*, Vol. 22 (December 25, 1964), p. 2846. I have used *The Harris Survey* of January 11, 1965 for the figures on residence and ethnic group in 1960 and 1964, since the questions asked by the Survey Research Center on these topics changed somewhat in the later years.

The percentages for each category indicate both votes and preferences of nonvoters among persons in that category. Where the two-party figures do not add to 100 per cent, the remaining persons either voted for a minor party or did not answer the question.

[5] On the distribution and stability of partisanship, see Angus Campbell *et al.*, *The American Voter* (New York: Wiley, 1960), chaps. 6, 7.

[6] Fred I. Greenstein, "The Benevolent Leader: Children's Images of Political Authority," *American Political Science Review*, Vol. LIV (December, 1960), pp. 934–43.

Table 4.1 Demographic Division of Presidential Preferences
(In Percentages of National Opinion)

	1964		*1960*		*1952*	
	Goldwater	*Johnson*	*Nixon*	*Kennedy*	*Eisenhower*	*Stevenson*
Occupation						
Prof., Business	44	56	55	45	66	32
White Collar	31	69	54	46	61	37
Skilled Workers	19	81	39	61	45	52
Unskilled Workers	12	88	45	55	31	63
Farmers	39	58	66	34	59	35
Age						
21–34	26	74	48	52	50	48
35–44	31	69	48	51	52	45
45–54	30	70	46	53	55	42
55 and over	35	64	57	43	57	38
Sex						
Men	33	67	48	51	53	44
Women	29	71	52	48	54	43
Education						
College	45	55	64	35	71	28
High School	29	71	46	53	55	44
Grade School	18	81	48	52	46	48
Residence						
Metropolitan	27	73	38	62	52	46
Towns-Cities	40	60	54	46	53	44
Rural Areas	45	55	56	44	58	35
Religion						
Protestant	42	58	61	39	57	39
Catholic	21	79	20	80	46	53
Jewish	30	70	10	90	23	77
Ethnic Group						
Scotch-English	44	56	59	41	69	31
Irish	34	66	40	60	41	59
Italian	26	74	33	67	44	56
Polish	23	77	22	78	51	49
German	40	60	53	47	74	26
Negro	4	96	25	75	19	81
Region						
Northeast	25	75	50	50	57	40
Midwest	29	71	54	46	59	39
South	32	68	50	49	44	50
West	33	66	45	55	54	44
Party						
Democrats	13	87	23	76	27	73
Independents	44	56	50	49	67	33
Republicans	80	20	93	7	96	4

to the same faction as their parents. Once established, this loyalty is highly resistant to change: less than a fifth of Americans have ever fully reversed their party fidelity, although many have occasionally voted for an opposition candidate.

The effects of party identification are pervasive. It is not surprising to find that Democrats tend to select Democratic candidates and that Republicans also follow the path of electoral regularity. The consequences of partisanship, however, are much broader. The strength of party loyalty is directly related as well to apparently nonpartisan characteristics. Individuals who identify strongly with parties also show more civic interest and knowledge, devote more attention to political reports in the mass media, vote more frequently, are better able to deal with complex ballots, and are more committed to democratic goals of individual participation.

Political attitudes also are related to party identification, often in surprising ways. Although General Eisenhower was a national hero in 1952, evaluations of his personal characteristics, apart from his policies or party, were strongly affected by political loyalty. In comparison to Stevenson, 60 per cent of the strong Republicans favored the Eisenhower personality, while only 17 per cent of the strong Democrats made the same evaluation.[7]

Although identification and attitudes are often related, they are not identical. Partisanship exists independently. Most white southerners, for example, are both Democrats and segregationists, and southern Democrats are actually more favorable to segregation than Dixie Republicans. This loyalty is surely not a reflection of recent political events, for the Democrats have become recognized supporters of Negro civil rights while, at least in 1964, the Republican position was more appealing to

[7] *The Voter Decides*, p. 145. For detailed comments, see *The American Voter*, pp. 54–59. The widespread effects of partisanship are documented throughout the latter source, esp. chap. 6.

segregationists.[8] Democratic identification is a reflection of the historical events of the Civil War and Reconstruction which, although irrelevant to present politics, continue Democratic dominance in most southern elections.

The strong partisans are not individual philosophical citizens. They do not regard politics dispassionately, but rather with a definite bias in favor of Democrats or Republicans. Yet these are the same voters whose other political characteristics are relatively closer to the civic ideals of interest, knowledge, and participation. By contrast, the uncommitted Independents are more individualistic. Not committed to either party, they are more receptive to the conflict of ideas and candidates. Unfortunately, the uncommitted also tend to be the uninterested. "Independents tend as a group to be somewhat less involved in politics. They have somewhat poorer knowledge of the issues, their image of the candidates is fainter, their interest in the campaign is less, their concern over the outcome is relatively slight, and their choice between competing candidates, although it is indeed made later in the campaign, seems much less to spring from discoverable evaluations of the elements of national politics."[9] Social and party influences strengthen the individual's interest and participation in public life, even while they condition his perceptions.

THE PHILOSOPHICAL CITIZEN: ISSUES

Our first model further assumes that individuals will make electoral decisions primarily on the basis of policy questions. Direct electoral control is possible because of the voters' concern for issues. "This classic view implies that the policy of the government, the political issues, the parties' attitude toward

[8] Donald Matthews and James Prothro, *Negroes and the New Southern Politics* (New York: Harcourt, Brace & World, 1966), pp. 374–75. Nationally, by 20–1, the voters recognize the Democrats as more favorable to integration: Inter-University Consortium for Political Research, *1964 Election Study Codebook*, Question 68, Deck 13, col. 49.

[9] *The American Voter*, p. 143.

these, the activities of the parties, their programmes and their actions, will influence the voting choice and that this choice is neither the outcome of group influences nor predictable with the aid of a few attributes."[10] Arguing for an extended suffrage, Mill wrote, "It is by political discussion that the manual laborer, whose employment is a routine, and whose way of life brings him in contact with no variety of impressions, circumstances, or ideas, is taught that remote causes and events which take place far off have a most sensible effect even on his personal interests; and . . . learns to feel for and with his fellow citizens and becomes consciously a member of a great community."[11]

It is assumed here that the voters will be concerned with the most general and vital issues. Like the belief in individual decision, the assumption that general policy is central to the electorate is contrary in major respects to empirical evidence. Voters conforming to this part of the model would be knowledgeable about political events; they would have some coherent conceptual scheme with which to interpret these events; and they would relate their party loyalty to this interpretation. For large proportions of the electorate, each of these conditions is not realized.

Unhappily, the degree of popular ignorance about political events is easily illustrated. On a televised "current events test" in 1967, the average viewer (who was probably better informed than the general population) was only able to score 48 per cent on a series of simple factual questions. (A score of 60 was considered equivalent to a tenth-grade education.) At a time when Communist China had been in the headlines for months, only 58 per cent, given three choices, correctly identified that nation's leader as Mao Tse-tung, rather than Chiang Kai-shek (selected by 25 per cent) or Ho Chi-minh (17 per cent).[12]

[10] H. Daudt, *Floating Voters and the Floating Vote* (Leiden: Stenfert Kroese, 1961), p. 161.

[11] Mill, p. 130.

[12] Columbia Broadcasting Company, "National Current Events Test," January 3, 1967.

Another example is provided by public awareness of the Taft-Hartley Act, regulating the relations of unions and management. In 1953, six years after its passage, the act had been vigorously attacked and defended in three national campaigns and had been intensely argued by business, labor, and government. Nevertheless, two-thirds of the nation was ignorant of the law, and only one of six respondents had any specific idea of the changes they believed desirable in the statute.[13]

The mass electorate is also unlikely to have any coherent philosophy by which to judge events and to make decisions on specific policy questions. Asked to describe the parties and their policies, only a small minority of the voters spontaneously describe them in terms of general principles, or a political ideology. In 1956, only 2.5 per cent of the population, or 3.5 per cent of the actual voters, were "ideologues," who "clearly perceived a fundamental liberal-conservative continuum on which various of the political objects might be located." If less elaborate conceptual schemes of politics are included, this group still constitutes only 12 per cent of the population, or 15 per cent of the voters.[14]

In a further analysis in 1960, the voters were asked directly to classify the parties as "conservative" or "liberal" and to explain the meaning of these terms. Even with this stimulus, only 15 per cent could correctly identify the parties and provide an extended explanation of their "ideologies." In nearly a majority of these cases, moreover, the explanation of "liberal" and "conservative" did not refer to any fundamental philosophical differences, but to presumed Democratic inclinations to increase public spending, and Republican desires to economize.[15] Even the apparently ideological campaign of 1964 brought no change

[13] V. O. Key, Jr., *Public Opinion and American Democracy* (New York: Knopf, 1961), pp. 83–84.

[14] *The American Voter*, pp. 227–34. Almost no ideologies other than liberal or conservative were advanced by the voters.

[15] Philip E. Converse, "The Nature of Belief Systems in Mass Publics," in David E. Apter, ed., *Ideology and Discontent* (London: The Free Press of Glencoe, 1964), pp. 219–23.

in these perceptions.[16] There is a further lack of coherence when the electorate is asked about specific policy questions. There is no meaningful relationship, for example, between opinions on federal aid to education and federal aid to housing, nor between attitudes on foreign economic aid and military assistance abroad.[17]

Party loyalty does not provide a substitute for individual ideology. Conservatives and liberals, as defined by a personality index, are found to some degree in both parties.[18] Moreover, on none of 24 specific policies do Democratic and Republican voters show any statistically significant differences. Overwhelming proportions of both parties favor increased federal aid to education, for example, while similarly large proportions are unenthusiastic about more public ownership of natural resources.[19]

Policy questions, then, are not central considerations for many voters. There are, of course, many persons who are aware of political issues—if even 15 per cent of the electorate are ideologues, we are dealing with the formidable number of 11 million voters. However, those who show this concern are also more likely to be strong partisans and to be least likely to change their votes in the course of a campaign. On the other hand, those who vacillate are also those who are "the less concerned and the less attentive."[20] Policy considerations, therefore, cannot be said generally to determine campaign outcomes.

[16] Philip E. Converse *et al.*, "Electoral Myth and Reality: The 1964 Election," *American Political Science Review*, Vol. LIX (June, 1965), pp. 334–35.

[17] "The Nature of Belief Systems in Mass Publics," p. 228. The Goodman-Kruskal gamma for education and housing is .12; that for foreign policy attitudes is .16. For explanation and use of this statistic, see the Appendix in chap. VI, below.

[18] Herbert McClosky, "Conservatism and Personality," *American Political Science Review*, Vol. LII (March, 1958), pp. 27–45; *The American Voter*, pp. 209–15.

[19] Herbert McClosky *et al.*, "Issue Conflict and Consensus among Party Leaders and Followers," *American Political Science Review*, Vol. LIV (June, 1960), pp. 406–27.

[20] See Angus Campbell, "Surge and Decline: A Study of Electoral Change," in *Elections and the Political Order* (New York: Wiley, 1966), chap. 3, p. 48.

Voters who change their vote between elections rather than during the campaign itself are somewhat different. They are more akin to other policy-oriented citizens, even if they are not fully "philosophical." Such voters are not clearly distinct from consistent partisans in terms of education or political knowledge. However, if we focus only on those who swim with the tide, those who are recruits to the winning party do appear to be less interested in politics and therefore further from the ideal of the philosophical citizen. For example, of those who voted Republican in both 1948 and 1952, 36 per cent claimed a "great deal of interest" in politics. Of those who switched from Truman to Eisenhower, following the trend, only 25 per cent placed themselves in this category, and only 16 per cent of those who did not vote in 1948, but supported the Republicans in 1952, were greatly interested.

In 1960, the tide was running toward the Democrats, and the same pattern appeared in mirror image. Of the Kennedy voters who were also Stevenson supporters in 1956, 32 per cent claimed great interest. Those who changed from Eisenhower to Kennedy were less concerned, 19 per cent placing themselves in the high-interest group, along with only 16 per cent of the 1956 nonvoters who backed the Democrats four years later.[21] Reversals of party fortunes apparently do not depend on the changed opinions of those most involved.

The policy-oriented philosophical citizen does not appear often in voting studies. Direct electoral control of policy, therefore, seems unlikely. A summary demonstration of the point is provided by the Wisconsin gubernatorial election of 1962. This contest centered on a clear issue of tax policy, with Republican Philip Kuehn favoring an extension of the state sales tax, and Democrat John Reynolds seeking an increase in the income tax. Although the policy difference was clear and important, the election was not clearly decided on this basis.

[21] V. O. Key, Jr., with the assistance of Milton C. Cummings, Jr., *The Responsible Electorate* (Cambridge: Harvard University Press, 1966), pp. 99, 141.

Of the less than 60 per cent who came to the polls, almost half could not correctly identify both parties' positions. In the balloting, a third made the "wrong" choice—that is, favored the sales tax, but voted for the Democrats, or favored the income tax, but voted for the Republicans. Only about a fourth of the support won by each party was due solely to the tax issue. Even among these self-styled "tax voters," as Table 4.2 indicates, the bulk of the support for each party came from traditional Democrats or Republicans. Of all voters, as many voted their party loyalty as voted for a candidate supporting their tax position. In the end, the Democrats won the governorship by a handful of votes, but lost the legislature. Clearly, this election

Table 4.2 Sources of the 1962 Gubernatorial Vote in Wisconsin
(In Percentages of Votes Received)

	Democratic	*Republican*	*Total*
Tax Voters			
Party Loyalists	17	14	16
Independents, Others	10	5	7
Party Switchers	3	3	3
Nontax Voters			
Party Loyalists			
Favor Candidate's Tax Position	28	20	24
Do Not Favor Position	16	31	24
Independents			
Favor Candidate's Tax Position	12	9	10
Do Not Favor Party's Position	10	12	11
Party Switchers			
Favor Candidate's Tax Position	2	2	2
Do Not Favor Position	2	4	3
Total Vote from Party Loyalists	61	65	63
Total Vote Congruent with Tax Position	72	52	62
Totals	100%	100%	100%
Number of Voters	208	210	418

constituted no mandate for a specific tax policy.[22] Other elections are even less likely to evidence direct popular control.

THE MANIPULATED SUBJECT: INDIVIDUALITY

The empirical rarity of philosophical citizens in America has led some observers to an opposite model of the voter, that of the manipulated subject. Neither direct nor indirect electoral influence would be possible in this conception. Because individuals are affected by their group memberships, it is argued that their views are determined by these affiliations. Because party identification is a crucial influence, it is held to be unchanging and a sufficient explanation of the vote. Policy questions are presumed to have no influence on electoral judgments because voters do not have a developed philosophy of government. Since policy judgments are often based on partial or incorrect information, the voters are presumed incompetent or subject to manipulation by artful strategists. The import of the opinion surveys has been so exaggerated that Key found it "perverse and unorthodox" to argue "that voters are not fools . . . strait-jacketed by social determinants or moved by subconscious urges triggered by devilishly skillful propagandists."[23]

The evidence of the voting studies does not justify such extreme conclusions. It is simply untrue that "social characteristics determine political preferences."[24] Sociological influences are not controlling or fixed. Never complete, they also vary with individual involvement in the group and with

[22] Leon D. Epstein, "Electoral Decision and Policy Mandate: An Empirical Example," *Public Opinion Quarterly*, Vol. XXVIII (Winter, 1964), pp. 564–72. Table 4.2 is based on Tables 3–5 in this article and on recalculations of the original data supplied through the courtesy of Professor Epstein and Mrs. Elizabeth David of the University of Wisconsin. I have assumed that all "tax voters" made choices for governor congruent with their policy views. However, even in this group, only 70 per cent could correctly identify both parties' tax position.

[23] *The Responsible Electorate*, p. 7.

[24] Lazarsfeld, p. 27.

political circumstances. A glance at Table 4.1 indicates the limitations of sociological explanations. Groups are usually divided between the two major parties. There are tendencies toward the Democrats or Republicans, but a sizable minority almost always acts in opposition to the trend.

Individuals, moreover, fall into more than one category—a social class, a religion, a residential group, and so on. In a considerable proportion of the cases, belonging to different categories causes "cross-pressures" on the individual. As a Catholic an individual may be prone to support the Democrats, but as a businessman he may tend to vote Republican. It is difficult to learn the votes of such individuals on the basis of sociological collectives alone. Attempts to predict votes on the combined basis of class, religion, and residence succeed in only 60 per cent of the cases (even excluding nonvoters). Since absurd guessing would succeed in at least half and as much as 61 per cent of the cases, this is not an impressive performance. If we were to add more categories, such as age or ethnic groups, we would find still more "cross-pressures" and be even less accurate in predicting the vote.[25]

Sociological groups do not determine the vote, because they are often no more than artificial categories created by researchers for their own purposes of analysis. An individual may be classified as a worker, but unless he subjectively identifies with the working class, this classification will have little meaning. We find that partisanship varies considerably within a group. An illustration is provided by a study of the United Automobile Workers in Detroit. Two-thirds of the UAW members voted for Stevenson in 1952. Of those strongly attached to the union,

[25] If, as a guess, we predicted that every vote would be for the winning party, the correct guesses would be equal to the national percentage of the winner—varying from Kennedy's 50 per cent to Johnson's 61 per cent. Of course, this is not a serious method, but it does provide a baseline from which to judge other techniques. See also Daudt, pp. 110–13 and Morris Janowitz and Warren E. Miller, "The Index of Political Predisposition in the 1948 Election," *Journal of Politics*, Vol. 14 (November, 1952), pp. 710–27.

however, nearly three-fourths voted Democratic, while little more than half of those with weak attachments to the union voted for Stevenson.[26]

The effect of group memberships can also vary by elections. The nature of a given contest can increase the relevance of some groups and decrease that of others. Comparison of the elections of 1952 and 1960 is pertinent here. In 1952, economic or class issues were of greater importance; in the latter election, Kennedy's Catholicism made a great impact on the voters. Table 4.3 shows the differing results. In 1952, class differences are larger than religious schisms. In 1960, the class division within the same religion is small, but the religious difference within the same class is large.[27]

Table 4.3 Democratic Vote in 1952 and 1960, by Religion and Class
(In Percentages)

	1952			*1960*		
	Catholic	*Protestant*	*Total*	*Catholic*	*Protestant*	*Total*
Manual	64	52	56	85	47	60
Nonmanual	38	28	34	75	29	45
Total	55	42		81	38	
Total Class Difference			22%			15%
Total Religious Difference			13%			43%

The results of an election are not foreordained by the pattern of group preferences. Depending on political events, different group memberships will be politically salient, with different par-

[26] Arthur Kornhauser *et al.*, *When Labor Votes* (New York: University Books, 1956), p. 150. For similar findings in regard to religious groups, see Gerhard Lenski, *The Religious Factor* (Garden City: Doubleday Anchor, 1963), pp. 174–202.

[27] Robert R. Alford, *Party and Society* (Chicago: Rand McNally, 1963), pp. 242–43. The figures differ slightly from those in Table 4.1 because of the use of different sources.

tisan effects.[28] In 1960, religious memberships were most significant. It is possible, through computer simulation, to estimate the results if other factors had been dominant. An emphasis on foreign policy, for example, would probably have resulted in an overwhelming Nixon victory, a demonstration of the flexibility of the electorate.[29]

Political factors make some sociological groups more relevant than others at a given time. These same factors are also responsible in large part for the loyalty of a group to a particular party. Why should Negroes or workers be Democrats? This party loyalty is clearly not inevitable, since the Republican party enjoyed majority support by both groups in the early twentieth century. The origins of present fidelity must be sought in such political factors as the history of the New Deal, party programs, and the activities of local organizations. Sociological influence "indeed explains a certain uniformity of choice but not the political direction of the choice. An explanation will always have to be sought in outside factors, and it is probable that, in the last resort, these factors will be the activities of the parties and the government in the present and past."[30]

Party identification, unlike sociological groupings, is clearly related to individual perceptions and to political events. Its relationship to the vote itself is therefore more obvious and more consistent. Thus, in the strongly Republican year of 1952, only 57 per cent of trade-union members supported Stevenson, but 84 per cent of the "strong" Democrats stayed with their party's candidate. In 1964, as seen in Table 4.1, Goldwater was deserted by a majority of the professionals and businessmen, who are

[28] For a further discussion, see V. O. Key, Jr., and Frank Munger, "Social Determinism and Electoral Decision: The Case of Indiana," in Eugene Burdick and Arthur Brodbeck, eds., *American Voting Behavior* (New York: The Free Press, 1959), pp. 281–99.

[29] Ithiel de Sola Pool, *Candidates, Issues and Strategies* (Cambridge: M.I.T. Press, 1964), p. 89.

[30] Daudt, p. 94.

"sociological Republicans," but kept the support of four out of five party-identifiers, even though most Republicans would have preferred another candidate for the G.O.P.[31]

Because party identification is an important influence on the vote, it is often misunderstood as controlling most votes. A common misinterpretation is to regard the two parties as assured of support by a large core of steadfast loyalists, while the decisive votes are cast by a small minority of manipulated subjects. Indeed, Berelson seems to find this situation desirable: "Those who change political preferences most readily are those who are least interested, who are subject to conflicting social pressures, who have inconsistent beliefs and erratic voting histories. Without them—if the decision were left only to the deeply concerned, well-integrated, consistently-principled ideal citizens—the political system might easily prove too rigid to adapt to changing domestic and international conditions."[32]

Actually, the electorate is more flexible than is generally thought. Not only the disinterested change votes, but even many of the strong partisans, although in lesser proportions, as demonstrated in the behavior of Democrats in 1952 and Republicans in 1964. About half of the voters have supported the opposition party at least once in a presidential election.[33] In any given year, three of every ten voters will either be switching from one party to the other, or will be previous nonvoters. For example, John Kennedy's 1960 victory was not accomplished simply by Democratic loyalists. Of his 34 million votes, 10 million came from those who switched from Republican support in 1956, and another 5 million from those who did not vote in the previous contest.[34]

[31] On 1952, see *The Voter Decides,* pp. 73, 109. On 1964, see "Electoral Myth and Reality," pp. 323–27. "Strong" Democrats are those who identify themselves in this manner.

[32] Bernard Berelson, *Voting* (Chicago: University of Chicago Press, 1954), p. 316. See also Eugene Burdick, "Political Theory and the Voting Studies," in Burdick and Brodbeck, pp. 136–49.

[33] *The American Voter,* p. 148.

[34] *The Responsible Electorate,* pp. 20, 27.

Party loyalty is a basic element in the vote, but loyalty does not necessarily mean unchanging homage. Voting can be strongly affected by short-term forces such as issues and candidates.[35] "The popular majority does not hold together like a ball of sticky popcorn. Rather, no sooner has a popular majority been constructed than it begins to crumble . . . . Old friends are sustained, old enemies are converted into new friends, old friends become even bitter opponents, and new voters are attracted to the cause."[36]

Even party identification itself shows less stability than is commonly assumed. The evidence for stability is largely based on aggregate figures, not on analysis of individual behavior. Stability in over-all figures, however, does not prove stability in individual loyalty. In fact, many individuals have changed parties in their lifetime—about 22 per cent of the nation, according to 1964 data. Change is also evident between generations. While most voters retain the party identification of their parents, about a fifth have left the political faith of their fathers. (This fifth is not necessarily the same as those who have changed parties during their adult lives.) Party loyalty has often been compared to religious fidelity, but it is obviously less tenacious. There are few religious converts; there apparently are a large number of political apostates.

Considerable proportions of the electorate are sufficiently individualistic to change their party or to abandon their traditions. The fact that four-fifths always retain the same loyalty, or hold to that of their parents, indicates the solidity of partisanship. However, a change by 20 per cent can completely overturn the political system. In fact, a change by a small proportion of voters in the New Deal period had that very result, converting the Democrats from a persistent minority to a dominant majority

[35] See Philip E. Converse, "The Concept of a Normal Vote," in *Elections and the Political Order*, chap. 2, and Donald E. Stokes, "Some Dynamic Elements of Contests for the Presidency," *American Political Science Review*, Vol. LX (March, 1966), pp. 19–28.

[36] *The Responsible Electorate*, p. 30.

party for the next thirty years. Neither sociological nor partisan groupings completely determine the outcome of elections.

THE MANIPULATED SUBJECT: ISSUES

In the model of the manipulated subject, policy questions have little relationship to the vote. Any noticeable degree of electoral influence on government is absent. The bulk of the voters are unthinking partisans. Almost all of the remaining persons are Indifferents, "those who respond to a carefully thought-out strategy, who act more from emotion than reason, who are the least passionate in their political conviction, who couldn't care less." From this premise, it follows that the means to win elections can include the exploitation of admittedly false statements, an emphasis on the "image" of candidates, and the development of "cell groups" for covert campaigns. Another method is the use of "foot-soldiers" to exploit the voters' "hunger for identification." "The foot-soldiers are not commissioned to try to convince by logic. Their single assignment is to say: 'Mr. Jones is a good man. Please vote for Mr. Jones.' . . . If the person called upon is not strongly committed to one candidate, this personal plea for his vote from a neighbor may be the only truly compelling reason he will have to make a choice between the candidates on election day."[37]

These suggestions are advanced in *How to Win an Election*, an ironic title for a book whose author lost his own race for senator from Arizona and who was a principal adviser to Barry Goldwater. This view of the electorate could be disregarded if confined to a few pretentious propagandists, but it is held more widely. The television debates of 1960, for example, were

[37] Stephen C. Shadegg, *How to Win an Election* (New York: Taplinger, 1964), pp. 24, 127–29.

condemned by many liberals who believed that the electorate would be unable to understand the policy issues argued.[38] Furthermore, Kelley has suggested that the Republican campaign of 1964 may have been designed to appeal principally to ideological canvassers, disregarding an electorate to whom policy questions were deemed unimportant. "An explicit conservative appeal need not hurt the party at the polls," it was believed, "since the votes that decide presidential elections come mainly from persons who know or care little about issues of public policy."[39]

The possibilities for manipulation are far more apparent in the plans of propagandists than in the voting studies. The mass media offer fewer opportunities for "brain-washing" than is often supposed. Repeatedly, it has been shown that those who are most committed in their votes also devote the greatest attention to a campaign: the propagandists are largely dealing with an immovable audience. Moreover, party loyalty provides a protective screen for the voter. He is apt to perceive propaganda in ways consonant with his political preferences. A majority of Democrats, for example, believed that Kennedy "won" the 1960 debates, while Republicans were convinced that Nixon triumphed.[40] Not all of the campaign messages, however, are distorted in this way. The media do have some impact, but there is no proof that their effect is an increase in irrationality. A detailed analysis of the television debates, for example, reveals that they were less vague and provided more information than ordinary campaign speeches. Interviews with viewers show they did

[38] See Sidney Kraus, ed., *The Great Debates* (Bloomington: Indiana University Press, 1962), pp. 127–50. Other writings tending to this view are Murray B. Levin, *The Alienated Voter* (New York: Holt, Rinehart & Winston, 1960), and the satire by John G. Schneider, *The Golden Kazoo* (New York: Dell, 1956).

[39] Stanley Kelley, "The Presidential Campaign," in Milton C. Cummings, Jr., ed., *The National Election of 1964* (Washington: The Brookings Institution, 1966), p. 57.

[40] Kraus, p. 199. Compare Berelson, chap. 11.

learn more about issues from the programs and became aware of the candidates' policies.[41]

It would also be unwise for any party to concentrate only on Indifferents. There is probably an irreducible tenth to a fifth of the population which cannot be brought to the polls even by the most clever tricks.[42] Furthermore, a party cannot assume that it is assured of the votes of its partisans. Attention only to Indifferent voters can lose it established support. As we have seen, large numbers will temporarily abandon their preferred party, while some will even change loyalty. The Goldwater experience demonstrated that a party must protect its established preserves even while it goes hunting "where the ducks are."

To win an electoral majority, a party must devote itself to policies as well as images, to the heavy artillery of issues as well as to the neighborliness of foot-soldiers. Although it is true that the voters do not see the parties in broad philosophical terms, they do have a policy-tinted vision. Only a relatively small one-sixth of the voters see no issue content to the parties. The largest group, 42 per cent of the population and 45 per cent of actual voters, conceive of the parties in terms of group benefits. Democrats and Republicans are liked or disliked because of their perceived attitudes toward union interests or because of their farm policies. This is a relatively narrow, but certainly meaningful, standard by which to judge politics—particularly if one is a union member or a farmer.

Another quarter of the electorate judges the parties according to the "nature of the times." A party in power during periods of peace and prosperity is praised; a party associated with depression, war, or broken promises is condemned. The voters judge government retrospectively, by its performance. This

[41] John W. Ellsworth, "Rationality and Campaigning: A Content Analysis of the 1960 Presidential Campaign Debates," *Western Political Quarterly*, Vol. 18 (December, 1965), pp. 794–802; Kraus, pp. 200–203.

[42] See William A. Glaser, "Fluctuations in Turnout," in William McPhee and William Glaser, *Public Opinion and Congressional Elections* (New York: The Free Press of Glencoe, 1962), chap. 2.

seems a clearly reasonable criterion.[43] A similar awareness of policy questions is indicated by popular reactions to the terms "liberal" and "conservative." Most voters do not have an elaborate understanding of these ideologies, as we have seen. When questioned at length, however, a majority can correctly label the parties and give at least a narrow but correct definition of the terms. Conceptual clarity is even greater among the mass electorate when issues involve group interests.[44]

For a great many voters, policy does have some relation to their party preferences, although issues are not viewed philosophically. However, it is not clear that it would be more appropriate for voters to deal with policy questions in broad ideological terms. The parties do not lend themselves to such analysis. The difference between Democrats and Republicans is not really a philosophical conflict. Both parties contain ideologues of all brands, but are preponderantly composed of neither doctrinaire liberals nor dogmatic conservatives. So far as these terms have meaning in American politics, they commonly center on the "spending versus saving" debate which is perceived by the voters.

Most often, the appeals of the parties are cast in terms of group benefits and the nature of the times. "A New Deal for the American people," or "Time for a Change," after all, are not capsule statements of ideologies, but attempts to win votes on the basis of tangible promises and in reaction to popular discontents. As chapter VII will show, the parties offer group benefits and better times, not philosophies. The voters' perceptions of the parties are reasonably in accord with their true character.

In these terms, there is a clear relationship between the public's policy preferences and its votes, and this relationship is stronger than the association of sociological groupings and the vote. Two examples may be useful. In 1952, voters were placed

[43] *The American Voter*, pp. 234–49.
[44] "The Nature of Belief Systems in Mass Publics," pp. 219–27, 234–38.

into five groups on the basis of their positions on four vital issues, from those who took the Democratic position on all questions to those completely supporting the Republicans. Stevenson did best among those in full agreement with the Democrats, winning 81 per cent of this vote. He did successively worse as Republican policy preferences increased, finally receiving only 14 per cent of the vote among those taking the G.O.P. position on all of the four issues. These four subjects alone did not delineate the vote. Other issues (particularly Korea), party identification, and candidate preference were also important. However, even without these factors considered, opinion on policies and the vote did coincide strongly.[45]

Issues in 1960 provide another example. In one survey, respondents were first asked to designate "the most important problem facing the country" and were then asked which party would handle the problem better. By asking the individual to select a problem, we come closer to reaching the basis for his vote. In the entire nation, only 3 per cent failed to vote for the party they considered better qualified to deal with the issues accorded priority. The actions of vote switchers are particularly relevant. Of Stevenson voters of 1956 who thought the Republicans more adept in 1960, 89 per cent changed to Nixon. In the opposite case, some Eisenhower supporters now looked with favor on the Democrats, and 96 per cent of this group changed to Kennedy. The same pattern prevailed among those who did not participate in the previous election.[46]

These findings are not unique—policy and partisan preferences are congruent in elections generally. In the Wisconsin gubernatorial election of 1962, it may be recalled, nearly two-thirds of the voters chose the party with whose tax position they agreed, whether knowingly or not. The consonance seems obvious—until it is compared to the model of the manipulated subject. Group pressures, traditions, and propaganda do not explain elections. They are usually reinforced by opinion on

[45] *The Voter Decides,* p. 131; see also p. 169.
[46] *The Responsible Electorate,* pp. 133–34.

issues. When party identification or group membership is not consistent with policy preferences or other short-term forces, a significant proportion will desert their "natural" party. New voters, who are less committed, will follow their opinions as much as their sociological or partisan instincts. As Key wrote, "the electorate behaves about as rationally and responsibly as we should expect, given the clarity of the alternatives presented to it and the character of the information available to it."[47]

On occasion, the policy alternatives offered by the parties are clear, and this difference is also perceived by the voters. In such circumstances, the policy meaning of an election is apparent. Such was the case in 1964 in regard to civil rights. Goldwater's strength was clearly related to the "white backlash." As seen in Table 4.4, voters opposing civil rights were

Table 4.4 Opinion on Civil Rights and Presidential Preference, 1964
(In Percentage of National Opinion)

	"High Backlash"	*"Low Backlash"*
Goldwater Preference	26	11
Johnson Preference	15	48

predominant among Republican supporters. Those in the "low backlash" category were largely Johnson voters.[48] The decisive Democratic victory was a definite indication that American voters were willing to continue action toward racial equality. These results help to explain the swift passage of the 1965 Voting Rights Act. Votes clearly influenced public policy.

[47] *Ibid.*, p. 7.

[48] Derived from *The Harris Survey*, September 29, 1964. At this point, Harris was forecasting a 63 per cent vote for Johnson, slightly more than his actual percentage. The coefficient of correlation is a very high .77. "High backlash" respondents were those who took at least two of the following positions: believed the pace of civil rights was "too fast"; opposed the 1964 civil rights act; were more worried than a year ago about safety in the streets. "Low backlash" were those voters who took one or none of these positions.

THE MEDDLING PARTISAN

The evidence of the voting studies confirms neither the theory of the philosophical citizen nor that of the manipulated subject. Voting is not an isolated act, but neither is it fully determined by sociological memberships or party identification. Voters do not have broad factual knowledge or an integrated ideology, but they do react to the parties in terms of the group benefits they provide and their records in office.

A model of the American electorate which finds support in empirical studies is that of the meddling partisan. In this model, we recognize the great effect of party identification. Loyalty to the Democrats and Republicans will affect the perceptions and actions of the voter to a considerable degree. We also see the voter as something more than an obedient soldier in the party ranks. The voter's involvement is sporadic—in the nature of meddling rather than continuing participation. Meddling is not a constant process. The electorate intervenes periodically, and only when the occasion is of considerable importance. The voter becomes involved in direct relation to his personal concerns. His party loyalty is dependent on the satisfaction of his particular needs. He is ready to bolt the party when he perceives his immediate and vital interests at stake.

In this model, partisanship is pervasive. Because of party loyalty, most voters do not wait for a campaign to begin before deciding for whom to vote. Party provides a lens with which to focus the confusing and divergent stimuli of politics, a mechanism to relieve the individual of the impossible demands made of the philosophical citizen. Events, issues, and candidates take on meaning for the individual and enable him to make an electoral decision long before he enters the polls.

Parties also organize the stimuli for the voter. Not only his perceptions, but the objects which he perceives are selected by party activists. A popular fondness for war heroes or for Catholics only becomes relevant when an Eisenhower or a

Kennedy is a presidential candidate. Foreign involvement or a concern for civil rights become salient only when these issues are presented to the electorate.

Party loyalty makes it difficult for the voter to be a philosophical citizen. He cannot deal with the full range of politics, but only with the stimuli presented by the parties. His perception of candidates and issues is not clear. He cannot easily be convinced by the opposition, for he ignores many of the messages of politicians and distorts other communications because of his partisan bias. The very loyalty which makes the voter difficult to reach, however, also makes him more difficult to control. He is not easily made into a manipulated subject. Political hucksters can try to manufacture issues and attractively to package candidates of little worth. These attempts can succeed at times. Nevertheless, the voter is protected from these efforts by his own indifference and by his predispositions. Political messages must be consonant with his partisanship and his perceived interests to be heard. A strong Democrat can hardly be convinced of the virtues of Barry Goldwater, and a Negro can scarcely be persuaded of the virtues of white supremacy.

Partisan attachments alone are insufficient to win an election. Even the most committed voters must be persuaded to come to the polls and to continue to support their traditional party. The undecided, apathetic, and even the opposition must be courted. Party loyalty is held strongly, but also shed easily when appropriate, like a favorite hat. Because politics is not vital to the lives of most voters, and because most have no ideological stake in the outcome of elections, they are willing to vote for either party when the occasion is suitable.

Electoral victory, it should be emphasized, is always a matter of marginal support. Because of party loyalty, each major faction knows it will survive even electoral disaster, but each wants more than bare survival. In the search for victory, it appeals to all groups in attempts to win crucial increments of votes. Winning a majority of Negro votes is not enough for Democrats—they seek an overwhelming majority. Obtaining half of the Independent vote is not as good as winning three-fifths. Most Republicans will back the G.O.P. nominee, but Democrats would rather reap a 25 per cent minority than a 10 per cent share of this vote.

To win these crucial increments of votes, the parties must satisfy the demands of a meddling populace. Meddling is a selective process. Voters are not concerned or knowledgeable about the entire political world. They are apt to cast their ballots largely on matters of direct and personal significance. Most voters, it will be recalled, see the parties in terms of the group benefits they provide and of the nature of the times. They will support that party which better provides benefits, or can bring better times. When a party fails to accomplish these ends, these voters are particularly ready to subordinate their party identification. In 1956, for example, change was particularly notable among those viewing the parties in these terms. Two-thirds of the Democrats who voted for Eisenhower perceived politics in terms of group benefits and the nature of the times. While ideological voters tended to stay with the party, from 20 to 46 per cent of those on the less philosophical levels bolted to the Republicans.[49] Their meddling was decisive in the contest.[50]

Selective meddling by the voters is also evident in the reaction to policy issues. Sophisticated understanding of issues is not widespread, but there are different "issue publics" scattered throughout the electorate. Whereas few voters have an interest in and understanding of the entire range of issues, many

[49] *The American Voter,* p. 284. The Democrats with no policy perceptions also had a high rate of defection, 36 per cent. However, because few persons in this group actually vote, only a fifth of the total defections (the rate of defections multiplied by the proportion of the actual voters) came from this group.

[50] The benefits provided by parties are subject to considerable selective perception by the voters. Those who believe their economic position to be improving —whatever the objective reality—are more likely to support the incumbent party than those personally unhappy with their position. See Warren E. Miller, "The Socio-Economic Analysis of Political Behavior," *Midwest Journal of Political Science,* Vol. II (August, 1958), pp. 239–55.

do have an interest and understanding of a small number of issues. If we examine these separate "issue publics," rather than concentrating on the total electorate, we find considerable sophistication, and a direct relationship between policy views and the vote.[51]

The relationship found between opinions on "the most important problem" and party reference is indicative. Most voters may not care about civil rights—but Negroes and Mississippi rednecks do. Similarly, oil-drillers understand oil depletion allowances, and some union leaders and employers are concerned about the Taft-Hartley Act, though most voters remain uninterested in these subjects. The combination of a considerable number of "issue publics" introduces a plethora of policy considerations to the election. All of the promises or actions of a party are not important to all voters, but almost all will be concerned about some particular policy of personal significance. They are prepared to meddle selectively in the political system by granting their vote to the party which seems best able to deal with their personal concerns. Parties are likely to appeal to these "issue publics" through their platforms, as we will see in chapters VII and VIII. Elections thereby exert an indirect influence over policy.

The voter, then, is a meddling partisan. Normally, politics does not touch his personal concerns. His attachment to a particular party is in keeping with family tradition, habit, and his social environment. Supporting this party saves him the impossible task of fully understanding all issues and following all candidates. So long as the party he supports continues to be identified with those programs, leaders, and groups to which he is attached, he will retain his loyalty.

On occasion, however, the party no longer serves these purposes. The group benefits he expects, whether material or psychological, are no longer provided. Times are not good even under his party's leadership. Its candidates no longer conform

[51] "The Nature of Belief Systems in Mass Publics," pp. 245–46.

to his preferences. This is the occasion for abstaining, voting for the opposition, or even for permanently transferring his loyalty. When the Democratic party is no longer segregationist, or when Harry Truman leads the nation into a frustrating war in Korea, or when a Republican candidate threatens the welfare state, partisanship is subordinated to self-interest. Party performance can overcome party loyalty.

The quality of the American voter makes his direct control over policy unlikely. The American citizen largely reacts to the political world. His meddling is stimulated by external events; rarely is it an attempt to impose a coherent scheme on that world. Since voters are not ideological, and coherent majorities do not support specific and integrated programs, public officials are not severely restricted in their actions. Extensive "mandates" are improbable.

The electorate does not determine the full governmental program in advance, but it can judge its effects later, at the next election. If group interests have been protected, and times are perceived as good, the party in power will be returned to office. If the voters feel disquieted with the course of public events, or feel some vital interest is being damaged, they will turn to the opposition party. "A majority party, once it is in office, will not continue to accrue electoral strength; it may preserve for a time its electoral majority, but the next marked change in the party vote will issue from a negative response of the electorate to some aspect of the party's conduct in office, a response that tends to return the minority party to power."[52] The judgment of the voters, therefore, is primarily a retrospective one, a statement of satisfaction and dissatisfaction with the past performance of government.

The behavior of the American electorate does permit indirect popular influence over public policy. The electorate does not decide policy; it accepts or rejects politicians associated with policies. In making its favorable or unfavorable judgments about

[52] *The American Voter,* p. 554.

their past conduct, however, it can also affect future policies. Politicians will continue those policies which result in popular approval and revise those which lead to popular condemnation. Approval of Roosevelt's New Deal in 1936 therefore led the parties to support greater welfare measures in later years, while disapproval of the Democrats' leadership during the Korean War led to the conclusion of a truce agreement.

In practice, voting is most likely to affect policy by providing a protection for the vital interests of the citizens. An electorate of "meddling partisans" is well-suited to enforce protection. The populace is not rigidly fixed in its positions, nor fully controlled. Party loyalty, the foundation of voting, is itself grounded in self-interest. Voters are able and willing to desert their party, particularly when their private concerns are threatened. The institutions of American government, such as the two-party system and the Presidency, provide an efficient means for an electorate bent on rebuking its rulers. The government is not obligated to follow any prescribed program, but it must respect the vital interests of its citizens and promote the general goals of "good times." Governors, knowing they must soon face the voters' retrospective judgment, have every motive to safeguard the citizens' vital interests.

The evidence of the voting studies, then, is that voters, by their meddling in elections, can protect themselves. Action of this sort is not irrational, unless rationality is bounded by the absolute truths of the idealist philosopher. Indeed, the voters seem to use elections for the most suitable purpose, the advancement of those particular interests which they are best able to judge. This is the practical qualification which Aristotle found in the general electorate: "There are some arts whose products are not judged of solely, or best, by the artists themselves, namely those arts whose products are recognized even by those who do not possess the art."[53]

[53] Aristotle, *Politics*, Modern Library ed. (New York: Random House, 1943), Book III, 1282a.

The portrait of the American voter sketched above is consistent with the expectations of democratic political theorists and with the place provided for the electorate in American institutions, as discussed in the last two chapters. The voter is not likely to exercise the direct control feared by the opponents of elections. He is able to fulfill the realistic expectations of democratic theorists, who saw elections as a means of individual and group advancement. The political structure of the United States allows the voters to make vital decisions on the choice of rulers, while restricting the electorate's influence over specific government decisions. From the evidence of the voting studies, this is precisely the role the electorate is best able to perform.

We have now dealt with the expectations held of elections, their institutional character, and the quality of the voters. In the remaining chapters, we will seek to uncover new empirical evidence to assess the impact of American elections. We first turn to the actions of the voters in elections for chief executives—Presidents and state governors. The voters at least control the tenure of these politicians. We must seek to determine if, in voting for individuals, the electorate is also making decisions relevant to the parties and policies which American chief executives represent.

CHAPTER 5

PARTY CHANGE IN PRESIDENTIAL ELECTIONS

THE VOTERS' most striking intervention in American politics comes in presidential elections. Popular influence is of obvious importance at such times, for the choice of a chief executive may determine the fate of the entire world. The voters' influence goes beyond the one-day choice of a four-year government. A party as well as a candidate is invested with power, and the composition and commitments of the winning party will greatly shape the course of future events.

Through the choice of party, the electorate is also choosing policy. Victory for Democrats or Republicans is also an endorsement of Democratic or Republican policies. The voters thus indirectly affect governmental action by supporting or rejecting the men associated with these actions. In this chapter we seek to locate the historical occasions of party change in presidential elections and to assess the policy effects of these changes.

Partisanship is basic to the electoral decision, as we have seen in the previous chapter. When involved in a particular campaign, such as 1968, we are apt to consider only the candidates' personalities and such immediate matters as Vietnam or racial policy. Contemporary factors, however, will have an effect only within the larger framework of the voters' underlying party loyalties.

Usually, these loyalties favor one party over the other. The dominant party holds the support of a distinct coalition of geographic areas and social groups. By supporting the party, the voters also support its policies. Party actions, in turn, are directed toward meeting the needs and demands of this electoral coalition. The arguments of the dominant party establish the agenda of public debate, and its deeds set the course of public policy. Historically, "our political solar system, in short, has been characterized not by two equally competing suns, but by a sun and a moon. It is within the majority party that the issues of any particular period are fought out; while the minority party shines in reflected radiance of the heat thus generated."[1] In a particular election, the "sun" may be eclipsed, but it is still the center of the system.

The long-term significance of an election is its effect on the majority party coalition, rather than the victory of particular men or the resolution of unique issues. The voters promote stability or innovation. When basic cleavages are fundamentally unaffected, the long-term effect of an election is likely to be limited. If the incumbents retain office, they will continue their policies, considering victory an endorsement of their record. If the incumbents are defeated, some changes are likely in those particular policies which aroused public dissatisfaction. In the absence of a basic change in party support, however, striking departures from previous party principles or governmental action are unlikely. Each party will continue to appeal to its known constituency, public debate will still center on persistent issues, and official actions will be in accord with established practices.

Where loyalties change, however, whether incumbents win or lose, vital effects on the political system are more likely. The majority party is now supported by a new coalition of voters. It must recognize different demands from the past. New issues are likely to come to the fore, and initiatives in public policy are

[1] Samuel Lubell, *The Future of American Politics*, rev. ed. (Garden City: Doubleday Anchor, 1956), p. 212.

more likely. As outdated issues and group alignments are replaced by a more relevant party system, government is more likely to respond to contemporary needs.

VARIETIES OF ELECTORAL CHANGE

A presidential election always evidences both stability and change. Figure 1 is a visual representation of the different influences. The lines on the graphs trace the percentage of the vote obtained by one party in a hypothetical series of elections. If party loyalty were a constant and complete influence on voting, the party percentage would be a straight horizontal line, as in the first diagram. The composition of the party's coalition would remain the same, and change would come only from variations in turnout.

In fact, partisanship is never this unshakable. Short-term forces result in small increments and losses. Although the coalition supporting the party remains the same, the degree of support from its members shifts temporarily, resulting in turnover in control of the White House. In 1952, for example, the personal appeal of Dwight Eisenhower and dissatisfaction with the Korean War led to a general swing to the Republicans. However, voting surveys indicate that the composition of the parties and the underlying Democratic majority in the nation were not drastically changed.[2] The combined effect of party loyalty and short-term forces is pictured in Figure 1 (b).

An election can also revise the basic cleavages in the electorate. On these occasions, parties not only win or lose, they are transformed as major social groups take on altered and persistent loyalties. Thus, the victories of Franklin Roosevelt were not only personal triumphs. His Democratic majorities reflected the strength of a new voting coalition of urban workers and ethnic minorities and the massive electoral changes brought by economic distress. Even as "Depression babies" suffer "middle-

[2] See Angus Campbell *et al.*, *The American Voter* (New York: Wiley, 1960), chaps. 3, 4.

aged spread," these events continue to strongly condition our politics. Party change led to policy change.

Basic alterations of the political system may come through cumulative social trends and gradual changes in group attachments. The electorate is always changing, as in an unending motion picture. Voters come to maturity, die, move, leave or gain jobs, hear new arguments, and benefit or lose from governmental policy. As the film of life advances, political loyalties are reinforced, activated, weakened, or changed. A presidential election is only one frame of the unending film, but the frame which may reveal the end of this slow process of "secular realignment," which has overturned the party system.[3]

The combined effect of party loyalty, short-term forces, and secular realignment is seen in Figure 1 (c). The crucial change is in the composition of the party's support. For the sake of simplicity, we may assume that the new cleavage also is to the net benefit of our imaginary party. In reality, there usually are countervailing movements of voting groups, so that gains in some areas are partially balanced by losses elsewhere.[4]

Change can also come in a short period or be precipitated by the nature of a particular election. Large numbers of voters may be shaken permanently from their traditional partisanship by events such as depression or war or by the unusual character of the candidates. V. O. Key first pointed to such "critical elections," in which "the decisive results of the voting reveal a sharp alteration of pre-existing cleavages within the electorate. Moreover, and perhaps this is the truly differentiating characteristic of this sort of election, the realignment made manifest in the voting in such elections seems to persist for several succeeding

[3] See V. O. Key, Jr., "Secular Realignment and the Party System," *Journal of Politics*, Vol. 21 (May, 1959), pp. 198–210.

[4] See Donald E. Stokes and Gudmund Iversen, "On the Existence of Forces Restoring Party Competition," in Angus Campbell *et al.*, *Elections and the Political Order* (New York: Wiley, 1966), pp. 180–93.

elections."[5] Party loyalty and short-term forces continue to affect the vote, but the composition of the party has changed from the past. See Figure 1 (d).

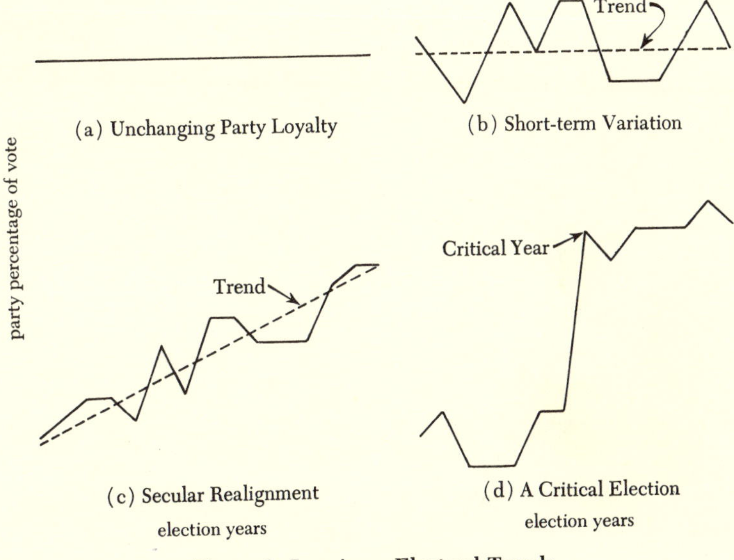

Figure 1. Imaginary Electoral Trends

Presidential elections have different effects when the underlying cleavages are retained or altered. To learn the significance of popular intervention in an election, we must examine both its immediate outcome and the degree of change in the basic attachments of the voters.

American presidential elections have been decided by popular vote since 1828. This long historical period provides abundant data for analysis. We can go beyond the results of particular con-

[5] V. O. Key, Jr., "A Theory of Critical Elections," *Journal of Politics*, Vol. 17 (February, 1955), pp. 3–18. Further work on the subject includes Duncan MacRae, Jr. and James A. Meldrum, "Critical Elections in Illinois: 1888–1958," *American Political Science Review*, Vol. LIV (September, 1960), pp. 669–83; and Charles Sellers, "The Equilibrium Cycle in Two-Party Politics," *Public Opinion Quarterly*, Vol. XXIX (Spring, 1965), pp. 16–38.

tests and focus on the similarities of different elections and abstract patterns of party change from the historical realities. Classification of national elections represents the first step in this examination.

Classification is based on two criteria, or dimensions. The first dimension is the outcome of the election, the victory or defeat of the normal majority party. This characteristic is immediate and obvious. The second dimension is the degree of continuity or change in electoral cleavage. Continuity exists where only short-term forces affect basic partisanship. Change occurs through secular realignment or in a critical election.

Combining these two criteria, as in Figure 2, provides a fourfold classification. When basic loyalties are stable, a victory for the majority party is considered a Maintaining election, and its defeat, because of short-term forces, is termed a Deviating result. Where basic change in party support does take place, the normal majority party may retain its dominant position or be displaced. The former case is considered a Converting election, and the latter a Realigning contest.[6] With appropriate methods, it may be possible to locate all presidential races since 1828 in one of these four categories.

ELECTORAL CLEAVAGE	MAJORITY PARTY: *Victory*	MAJORITY PARTY: *Defeat*
Continuity	"Maintaining"	"Deviating"
Change	"Converting"	"Realigning"

Figure 2. A Classification of Presidential Elections

[6] All of these terms except Converting were originally defined in *The American Voter*, pp. 531–38. The same authors discuss the subject further in *Elections and the Political Order*, chaps. 4, 7, and 10. For a fuller discussion and greater elaboration of the methods used here, see Gerald Pomper, "Classification of Presidential Elections," *Journal of Politics*, Vol. 29 (August, 1967), pp. 535–66.

CLASSIFICATION OF ELECTIONS

Proper categorization of elections involves many problems. The horizontal dimension of Figure 2 presents no difficulties, since victories or defeats of the majority party are historical facts. Complexities arise in regard to the vertical dimension, in knowing whether a particular result signifies electoral continuity or change. Since both are partially present in every contest, there can be no simple solution. Some reasonable means is needed to distinguish a Maintaining from a Converting victory of the majority party and a Deviating from a Realigning triumph of the minority.

For our survey of all elections since 1828, the most feasible course is to concentrate on the geographical distribution of the vote. A change in a party's support may be defined as a change in the party's relative strength in each of the states. When basic loyalties change, the state-by-state distribution of the party's vote would be different from the past: traditional strongholds would fall, while new areas of strength would become evident. In 1964, for example, the massive voting shifts in individual states lead to a suspicion that the parties were transformed. Maine, once the most Republican state, gave nearly two-thirds of its vote to Johnson, while Mississippi, where Republicans previously were considered virtually criminals, voted 87 per cent for Goldwater.

If we wish to learn how closely the results in any given election are related to the results in the past, statistical procedures and computers must be employed. In technical language, the results in the given election constitute one variable, and the results in the past are a second variable. The relationship between the two variables is found by a correlation coefficient. The first variable is measured by the Democratic party's percentage of the total vote in each state in the given election (e.g., 1964).[7]

[7] The percentages are from Svend Petersen, *A Statistical History of the American Presidential Elections* (New York: Ungar, 1963); *Congressional Quarterly Weekly Report*, Vol. 21 (March 26, 1965), p. 466.

The second variable is measured by the Democratic party's average percentage in each state in the four preceding elections (e.g., 1948 to 1960).[8] Through the common statistical procedure of linear correlation, the results in each state are matched against each other, and the total relationship is then calculated.[9]

Linear correlation will indicate the relative degree of electoral continuity or change. If there is high continuity from past results in a given election, regardless of partisan victory or defeat, the correlation coefficient should be high. The highest possible figure is 1.0. This result would be obtained if the Democratic party percentage in each state in a particular year were exactly the same as the four-election average Democratic vote in that state. If there is change, even if the same party wins all the elections considered, we will find a relatively low coefficient. A figure of zero would indicate no relationship between past and present voting patterns. A negative correlation, down to a limit of −1.0, would indicate a reversal of the party's geographical base.[10]

[8] Third-party votes are considered separately. For each election in which there were significant splinter groups, the third-party percentage was added to the Democratic share, and new calculations were made. In the analysis of the results, however, only the Democratic percentage of the total vote is used, except in 1860 where the Douglas and Breckinridge percentages are combined, and in 1948, where the Truman and Thurmond percentages are combined. The previous four elections were chosen as a measurement of past results in order to eliminate influences due solely to particular candidates or similar factors, while avoiding the inclusion of too many elections to detect significant changes.

[9] Linear correlation is described in any statistics textbook. The formula for calculation where X and Y are the two variables, N the number of cases, Σ the sum of individual cases, and r the correlation coefficient, is:

$$r = \frac{\Sigma XY - \frac{(\Sigma X)(\Sigma Y)}{N}}{\sqrt{\left[\Sigma X^2 - \frac{(\Sigma X)^2}{N}\right]\left[\Sigma Y^2 - \frac{(\Sigma Y)^2}{N}\right]}}$$

[10] For uses of this method using county data, see V. O. Key, Jr. and Frank Munger, "Social Determinism and Electoral Decision: The Case of Indiana," in Eugene Burdick and Arthur Brodbeck, *American Voting Behavior* (Glencoe: The Free Press, 1959), pp. 281–99, and Thomas A. Flinn, "Continuity and Change in Ohio Politics," *Journal of Politics*, Vol. 24 (August, 1964), pp. 521–44.

Figure 3 pictures the correlation of the vote in each election year with the past results. The peaks of the diagram indicate that the states' support of the Democrats in the designated year was highly related to that in the preceding four contests. The valleys indicate a change in source of support. Significant changes in electoral cleavages appear to have occurred five times in American history: (1) Van Buren's victory in 1836; (2) the Civil War period, particularly Lincoln's re-election in 1864; (3) the Populist-McKinley-Bryan period of 1892–96; (4) the period before and during the New Deal, with the election of 1928 outstanding; and (5) the current era, particularly the victories of Kennedy and Johnson in the last two elections. These results are somewhat surprising, for the elections involving Van Buren, Lincoln,

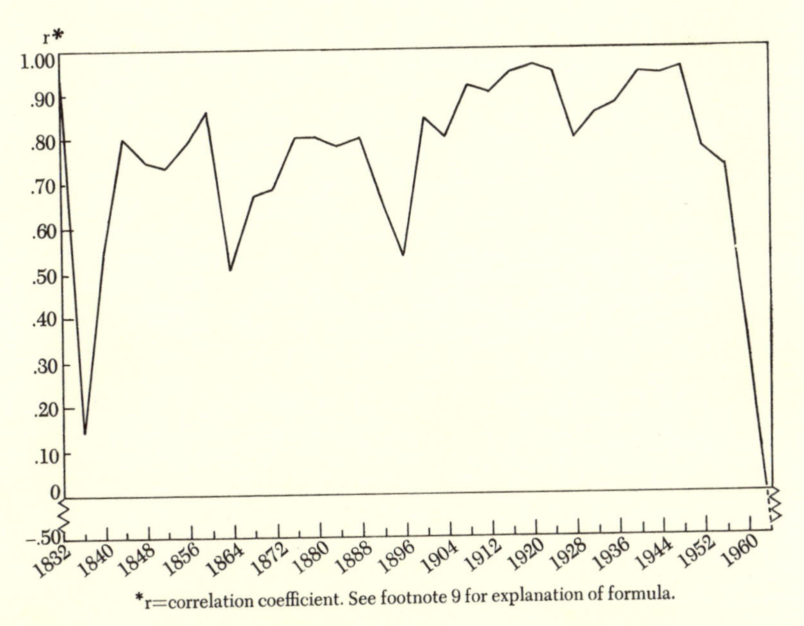

Figure 3. Correlation of Presidential Vote in Given Years with Average of Previous Elections, 1832–1964

Kennedy, and Johnson have not been commonly described in the same way as the triumphs of McKinley or Franklin Roosevelt. To provide further evidence it would be helpful to attempt another analysis.

In a critical election, we may recall, the party's vote in individual states would be notably different from the past. However, these changes would not be uniform across the nation. The factors making for change would operate strongly in some states, but have little net effect on traditional partisanship elsewhere. Concern over civil rights in 1964 thus brought a great shift in the vote in Mississippi but had little apparent impact in Idaho.

The standard deviation provides a statistical gauge of such variations. It measures the spread, or dispersal, of state differences from the average change in the nation. In an election in which there is no fundamental change, the shifts of the individual states from their past votes will be similar to one another. A low standard deviation will result. If every state followed the national trend, the figure would be zero. When cleavages are fundamentally altered, the shifts of individual states will vary considerably, and the standard deviation will be relatively high.[11]

Figure 4 shows the standard deviation of state results in each presidential election. Contrary to the previous graph, change in party cleavages is indicated here by the peaks of the curve, and stability by the low points. The pattern corroborates our earlier conclusions, although there are some differences. We also see that change does not come only in isolated elections. The regular slopes of the curve indicate periods of developing cleavages before a crucial contest, and periods of assimilation of these changes after a decisive vote. The 1964 peak, for example, was

[11] The standard deviation is simply calculated. Where σ is the standard deviation, and x is the individual deviation from the mean,

$$\sigma = \sqrt{\frac{\Sigma x^2}{N}}$$

preceded by generally increased deviations in the four earlier elections.

Thus far, we have concentrated on locating the elections in which there is change from past voting patterns. The period between crucial contests also needs to be analyzed. By focusing on these intervening elections, we can identify periods of stability, in which the coalition of voters included in each party remains substantially the same, even as particular candidates gain victory or suffer defeat.

When a stable and persistent voter coalition is established, the party's relative support from any particular state will remain

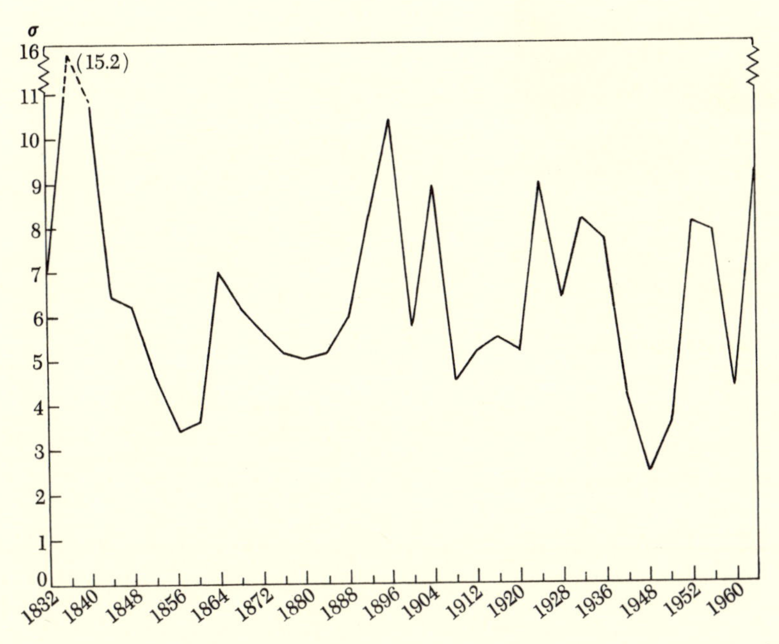

Figure 4. Standard Deviation of Differences from Average State Votes in Presidential Elections, 1832–1964

fairly constant over a number of elections. While there will be fluctuations due to short-term forces, the individual states can be clearly identified throughout the period as to their partisan leanings. In the New Deal era, for example, some voters temporarily shifted in Mississippi or Maine, but these states remained among the most loyal Democratic and Republican areas, respectively.

Stable periods can be statistically isolated, through methods described in the Appendix.[12] The correlations obtained indicate the following four periods to be eras of electoral stability: (1) 1844–60, the span from Van Buren to the Civil War; (2) 1876–88, the time between Reconstruction and the upheavals of the Populists; (3) 1900–20, an era of Republican party supremacy; and (4) 1932–48, the heyday of the New Deal coalition. More recent elections show marked changes. Of the total of 34 presidential contests since the initiation of broad popular participation, twenty can be clearly classified within these four eras of electoral stability.

Our measure now enables us tentatively to categorize presidential elections. To summarize, a Converting or Realigning election would be likely to show a low linear correlation to the average vote in the four preceding elections, a high standard deviation of state differences from past votes, and state-by-state results different from the individual elections which preceded and followed it. In a Converting election, the majority party would retain its status; in a Realigning contest, the former minority would become dominant. On the other hand, in a Maintaining or Deviating election, the opposite statistical results would be evident. The majority party would win the White House in the Maintaining case, but would be temporarily displaced in a Deviating outcome.

[12] The method employed here, correlation of nonsuccessive elections, was suggested by MacRae and Meldrum, p. 670. The use of matrices, presented in the Appendix, is adopted from David B. Truman, *The Congressional Party* (New York: Wiley, 1959).

Since some change is evident in every election, disagreement is likely over particular cases. However, using the categories drawn in Figure 2, we may reach some conclusions. The data point to the presidential elections of 1836, 1896, 1960, and 1964 as Converting, and those of 1864, 1928, and 1932 as Realigning. The victories of the first Harrison, Taylor, Lincoln in 1860, Cleveland, Wilson, and Eisenhower are deemed Deviating elections, and the remaining results can be classified as Maintaining outcomes. It now remains to assess the historical impact of these results.

A SURVEY OF PRESIDENTIAL ELECTIONS

The first critical contest in the history of the Presidency did not come until 1836, the thirteenth national election. A party system had been established shortly after the initiation of the Constitution, and a stable political coalition had been forged by Thomas Jefferson in 1800, but popular participation in these events was limited. Although there were democratic developments even at that time, the choice of the chief executive was still confined to a relatively small elite.[13]

The history of the elective Presidency began in 1828. Westward expansion, the development of democracy, and the first stirrings of industry were producing a new nation. When Andrew Jackson entered the White House, his Democratic-Republican party was also a new organization, not simply a reincarnation of the Jeffersonian faction. An odd amalgam of western frontiersmen, southern planters, Pennsylvania manufacturers, and New York's Tammany Hall, the coalition was inherently unstable.

The party system gained definition through the course of Jackson's eight years in office. His poorly organized opponents of 1828 were more fully prepared in 1832, when a convention of "National Republicans," the first held by a major party, unanimously nominated Henry Clay for President. At the same time,

[13] See William N. Chambers, *Political Parties in a New Nation* (New York: Oxford University Press, 1963).

unity increased among the Democrats. In 1832, Jackson sponsored the first convention of his party to legitimize the selection of Martin Van Buren as the vice-presidential candidate and the exclusion of John Calhoun from national power.

The Democratic coalition became more coherent, with Jackson "the unchallenged chieftain of a compact militant party combination consisting of the residuum of faithful followers remaining after the successive defections of the lukewarm. Thousands who had at first supported him as the supposed champion of internal improvements were no doubt impelled by the Maysville veto to turn to Clay . . . . The state-rights Virginia planters under John Tyler now turned away from the nationalist President who had prepared to crush the nullificationists with military force and went over to the opposition . . . . Prosperous Jacksonians had difficulty stomaching the bank veto, however much it elated the common man."[14]

In 1836, these changes culminated in Van Buren's victory. The leadership of both parties shifted strongly, with the center of gravity of the Democrats moving away from the South toward the Middle Atlantic states. Opposition groups formed in all states. In the South, "the vague kind of one-party politics that had prevailed came to an abrupt end, and by 1836 there were competitive parties in every state. Although the new alignment did not become firm in some states until after 1837, the basic outlines of what were to be the Democratic and Whig parties had been delineated."[15] The basis of party support shifted strongly in the balloting. The Democrats gained 10 or more percentage points in the six New England states; they lost a similar proportion of the vote in ten states, seven of them slave areas.

Van Buren's victory constituted a Converting election, in which the Democrats were returned to power on the basis of a

[14] Wilfred E. Binkley, *American Political Parties*, 4th ed. (New York: Knopf, 1962), p. 140. For a theoretical analysis, see William H. Riker, *The Theory of Political Coalitions* (New Haven: Yale University Press, 1962), pp. 58–59.

[15] Richard P. McCormick, *The Second American Party System* (Chapel Hill: University of North Carolina Press, 1966), pp. 338–39.

new voter coalition. By 1844, the voter cleavage was established. The majority party did not win all following contests. Unusual events such as the depression of 1837 or the Mexican War, and attractive opposition candidates such as William Harrison or Zachary Taylor brought Deviating outcomes in 1840 and 1848. Nevertheless, the Democrats constituted the "sun" of the political solar system, the Whigs being the less luminous "moon." Democrats led the debate on the issues of national policy, such as territorial expansion, tariffs, banking, and the most vital question, the extension of slavery. Their actions reflected the demands of their voting coalition, just as their inability to solve the slavery question reflected the uneasy alliance of northern and southern groups. When the party could not reach a united policy on slavery, the nation itself could no longer remain united.[16]

Social trends were preparing a new political order. Territorial expansion was followed by railroads, population dispersal, new patterns of trade, and new constituencies in the West. The first waves of immigration and the development of manufacturing brought urban growth and demands for land. All questions were ultimately and intimately involved as well with the slavery issue. Instability in the political system was evident from the division of the Whig party, the consequent rise of the Republicans in 1856, and the deadlocked Democratic convention of 1860. But past voting patterns persisted even as civil war neared. The combined Douglas and Breckinridge vote of 1860 closely parallels earlier Democratic support. The party did not change its geographical base, but its constituents divided into two factions, resulting in a Republican victory and southern secession.[17]

Changes in party loyalty came with the Civil War and the Reconstruction. The conflict was a traumatic experience for the

[16] See Roy Nichols, *The Disruption of American Democracy* (New York: Macmillan, 1948).

[17] The persistence of past voting patterns in the South in 1860 is shown by Seymour Lipset, *Political Man* (Garden City: Doubleday, 1959), chap. 11.

United States. Deaths in the conflict numbered 600,000, a larger number than in any American war and, on a proportionate basis, the contemporary equivalent of seven million killed. Virtually every family in the nation was affected by the battles, the economic transformations, the hardships of Reconstruction, and the emancipation of the slaves.

The political result was a definite break in the traditional sources of party support. The new Republican party became dominant in the nation, with 1864 marking a Realigning election. The degree of change to the Republicans in this year is exaggerated by the absence of the Confederate states, but the signs of transformation are evident in the northern states alone, as the Republicans assimilated former Whigs, Know-Nothings, Constitutional Unionists, and even Democrats. The party bore the new name of Union in 1864, and "it is a much debated question," writes Denis Brogan, whether it had much "in common with the agglomeration of 'Anti-Nebraska' men of 1854, or even with the Republican party of 1856 or 1860. At any rate, it was no longer a party of a moral idea; for some it was not a party that needed moral ideas. It had something better; it had possession of power in the federal government."[18]

The Republican party continued its dominance after Appomattox. Although its victories were often tainted or perilously narrow, the party was defeated for the Presidency only by Grover Cleveland for the rest of the century. There was some return to antebellum loyalties, but not to the Democrats' previous position as the majority party. As the upheavals of Reconstruction ended with the 1876 election, a new era of electoral stability began.

The vital decisions of public policy were now made predominantly by Republicans. The initial stress on Union and Reconstruction, which first brought the party to the White House, was replaced by new concerns. The majority coalition now consisted of farmers, manufacturers, and veterans of the Grand

[18] Denis Brogan, *Politics in America* (New York: Harper & Row, 1954), p. 55.

Army of the Republic, with occasional support from southern Negroes and former Whigs. With this backing, the party promoted farm homesteads, agricultural extension services, expansion of a national railroad system, high tariffs, hard money, veterans' pensions, and limited efforts toward the protection of Negroes.[19]

As the century waned, a new transformation of American politics developed. The industrialization of the nation, the closing of the frontier, the growth of urban complexes through internal and foreign immigration, and the blurring of Civil War memories prepared the foundation for a new party system. These social changes began to find political expression in 1892. Spurred by agricultural distress, the Populists won a million votes. In an appeal addressed to the economically underprivileged of all regions, they sought free coinage of silver to inflate the currency, government regulation of railroads, an income tax, and the eight-hour day for industrial workers.[20] The severe depression of 1893 provided further stimulus to the realignment of party loyalties.

In 1896, the competition between McKinley and Bryan provided the occasion for conversion of the Republican majority. Dislocations from past practice were evident in both parties. The Democrats appropriated the main principle in the Populist program, free coinage of silver; repudiated their incumbent President, Grover Cleveland; nominated the thirty-six-year-old Bryan; and willingly accepted the loss of their substantial conservative faction. The Republicans moved to consolidate a new coalition. While silverite votes were neglected, a major effort was made to recruit other groups. "The strategy looked to the

[19] The shifting Republican policy toward the South can be traced in David Donald, *The Politics of Reconstruction* (Baton Rouge: Louisiana State University Press, 1965), C. Vann Woodward, *Reunion and Reaction*, rev. ed. (Garden City: Doubleday Anchor, 1956); Stanley P. Hirshson, *Farewell to the Bloody Shirt* (Bloomington: Indiana University Press, 1962).

[20] See John D. Hicks, *The Populist Revolt* (Minneapolis: University of Minnesota Press, 1931).

retention of the support of manufacturing interests, the solidification of the loyalties of financial groups, and the recruitment of a substantial vote from industrial labor. . . . The cumulative effect of the planks shaped for specific sectors of the population was a broad appeal to all those of conservative instinct. The crusading Bryan was pictured as a leader of a ragtag band of radicals that would upset the foundations of the Republic."[21]

The election was the first thoroughly convincing victory in the history of the Republican party. Transformations in party support were geographically widespread. Nineteen states changed more than 10 percentage points from their average vote in the four previous elections. Ten states showing Democratic losses were all located in the Northeast. Nine states with large Democratic gains were all in the South and West. A new electoral majority was formed of the East and Midwest.[22]

The electoral cleavage initiated in 1896 was sealed still more firmly in the twentieth century. Until 1932, Woodrow Wilson alone was able to win Deviating elections for the Democratic party. Aside from some years of his administration, national policies were based on the G.O.P.'s principles of high tariffs, restricted immigration, limited governmental regulation of the economy, territorial expansion, and unilateral action in international affairs.

The Republican majority coalition began to splinter in the 1920's. Underlying social forces again were making for change. The decline in the rural population, the growth of the cities, and what Samuel Lubell wryly called "a little matter of birth rates" brought increasing numbers of Catholics, urban residents, and recent immigrants into the electorate.[23] Negro migration began the slow erosion of the solid South. World war, radio, and the automobile hastened the transformation of the

[21] V. O. Key, Jr., *Politics, Parties and Pressure Groups*, 5th ed. (New York: Crowell, 1964), p. 171.

[22] See Stanley L. Jones, *The Presidential Election of 1896* (Madison: University of Wisconsin Press, 1964).

[23] Lubell, pp. 29–35.

United States toward a cohesive technological society. In 1924, the third-party candidacy of Robert La Follette indicated the weakening of past loyalties. Voters dissatisfied with the conservative character of both parties, particularly former Republicans, supported the new Progressives.

Four years later, transformation of the party coalitions quickened. The turnout of voters increased more than 25 per cent, and the Democratic vote almost doubled in comparison to 1924. The urban vote became Democratic, a premonition of its future decisive impact in national elections.[24] For the first time since Reconstruction, a Republican candidate sought and won southern electoral votes, while the Democrats' nomination of Al Smith marked their turn toward the urban, Catholic, and working-class constituencies of the North. In response to these new alternatives, the Democratic vote declined 10 percentage points or more in seven southern or border states. It increased as much in seven other states, four of them urban and heavily Catholic, the rest largely rural and Progressive.[25]

The Democrats did not achieve majority status until later elections. The transformations wrought in 1928 were solidified and extended by new events. The coming of the Depression reinforced loyalties first expressed in 1928 and brought additional converts to the party, particularly among first-time voters. The actions of the Roosevelt administration and the benefits of the New Deal further unified the majority Democratic coalition. "The long-entrenched Republican sympathies of the electorate may not have given way easily in the early years of the Depression. Had not Roosevelt and his New Deal won the confidence of many of these people during his first term—or even during his second—there might well have been a return to

[24] See Samuel J. Eldersveld, "The Influence of Metropolitan Party Pluralities in Presidential Elections since 1920," *American Political Science Review*, Vol. XLIII (December, 1949), pp. 1189–1205.

[25] On the 1928 election, see Ruth C. Silva, *Rum, Religion and Votes* (University Park: Pennsylvania State University Press, 1962), and Key, "A Theory of Critical Elections."

earlier party lines similar to that which occurred in 1920. From this point of view we might speak not of a realigning election but of a realigning electoral era."[26]

The new voting coalition continued to be evident through 1948, providing the voting support for major innovations in national policy. The federal government became a major influence in American life, while supporting new activities on the part of state and local agencies as well. Government began to assume responsibility for maintaining economic prosperity, providing minimum levels of social welfare, equalizing power between labor and management, and easing racial discrimination. At the same time, the historic policy of international isolation was replaced by intervention in world conflict and diplomacy. These initiatives of the Democrats were soon accepted by the minority Republican party as well.

Social trends in the postwar period have prepared the way for new political transformations. Population growth now comes in the suburbs, not in the cities. Farming has been converted to a large-scale industry conducted by a small minority. Employment is increasingly in service and professional occupations, not in blue-collar jobs. Mass migration has brought a majority of Negroes outside of the South, making race the most vital issue in all regions of the country. The peacetime draft and an uncertain "cold war" have made foreign policy a domestic concern.

Political change is also evident in the past four presidential contests, and our measures suggest that the Democratic majority underwent Converting elections in 1960 and 1964. Strains in the New Deal coalition were already evident in 1948, when the Dixiecrats temporarily split the party. There were no fundamental alterations in that year, but some change in voter alignment is evident in 1952. Shifts toward the Republicans occurred in all social groups and in all parts of the nation. Geographical

[26] *The American Voter*, p. 535, italics omitted. See also pp. 152–60.

variations were evident within the general trend. Differences from the average vote in the past were greatest in sixteen states, all in the South or mountain regions.[27] By 1960, southern dissidents were organizing an "independent electors" movement. The Democrats lost important support in the South and West, while making important gains in New England and the Middle Atlantic states.

The 1964 election bears many of the hallmarks of a critical election. The party nominations were a break from tradition. The Democrats named their first southern candidate since James Polk, and the Republicans were led by an extreme conservative who took uncompromising right-wing positions. The post-New Deal consensus was broken, and policy differences between the parties were sharply drawn. The candidates openly concentrated on areas of erstwhile opposition. President Johnson sought and won support from the industrial community, newspaper publishers, and suburbanites, while Senator Goldwater solicited traditional Democratics in the Deep South and among white ethnic minorities. In financing their campaigns, contrary to past practice, Democrats relied on relatively few contributions by the rich, while the Republicans collected less money through small contributions by a large number of donors.[28]

The results showed great geographical change in the parties' support. Of course, the total Democratic vote increased substantially as Johnson gained the largest percentage of the total vote ever achieved by a Democrat. The important point, however, is that the gains were not relatively equal in all states, as would tend to be the case if the voters were reacting only to the temporary oddities of 1964. Instead, there was considerable variation. The Democratic vote decreased from its four-election

[27] See Angus Campbell *et al., The Voter Decides* (Evanston: Row, Peterson, 1954), and Donald S. Strong, "The Presidential Election in the South, 1952," *Journal of Politics,* Vol. 17 (August, 1955), pp. 343–89.

[28] See Herbert Alexander, *Financing the 1964 Election* (Princeton: Citizens' Research Foundation, 1966), chaps. 4, 5.

average in the five Black Belt states of the South carried by Goldwater, while it increased over 18 percentage points in eleven states of the Northeast and five of the Midwest.

Voting surveys also provide some evidence of a recent and meaningful shift in the political system. The general emphasis in these studies has been on the persistence and stability of party identification. Table 5.1 supports this conclusion, revealing that close to four of five persons in each of the elections from 1952 to 1964 retained the same underlying partisan loyalty. On the other hand, the table also shows that over a fifth of the voters in each election had changed their loyalty at some time before the election.

Table 5.1 Continuity and Change in Party Identification, 1952–64
(Percentage of All Respondents in Election Year)

	1952		*1956*		*1960*		*1964*	
No Change in Identification		*79.2%*		*79.6%*		*77.9%*		*78.0%*
Democrats	39.4		38.3		36.6		43.7	
Republicans	19.0		23.1		23.3		18.2	
Independents	11.9		14.1		13.3		14.0	
None, Other	8.9		4.1		4.7		2.1	
Change in Previous Four Years		*3.3°*		*6.2*		*3.9*		*6.0*
From One Party to the Other			3.2		3.1		3.7	
Fron One Party to Independent			3.0		.8		2.3	
Change Before Last Four Years		*4.5°*		*10.3*		*12.2*		*8.6*
From One Party to the Other			6.0		6.4		5.8	
Fron One Party to Independent			4.3		5.8		2.8	
Change of Indefinite Date		*11.0*		*1.7*		*4.4*		*3.0*
Other Probable Changes		*2.0*		*2.2*		*1.6*		*4.4*
Total		*100.0%*		*100.0%*		*100.0%*		*100.0%*
N		1,899		1,742		1,925		1,556

° Data do not permit further analysis.

If we examine these figures closely, we find five bits of evidence that 1964 was particularly notable in the transformation of party loyalties: (1) There was a slight decrease in the total proportion which maintained an unchanging identification. (2) Very few 1964 respondents were completely apolitical; only

2 per cent had neither a past nor present identification. (3) The disparity between the proportions of loyal Democrats and loyal Republicans widened considerably in the 1960–64 period. (4) Complete conversion from one party to another was particularly high in 1964. In earlier years, change either was less, or the switchers were likely to escape into the compromise status of "independent." (5) Of those who definitely or probably had changed at some time before the election, a greater proportion in 1964 made the switch in the preceding four years, rather than in the more distant past. All of these factors indicate a heightened political involvement among the voters in 1964.[29]

The changes in voter identification are not as clear and dramatic as the shifts in the parties' geographical support.[30] Final analysis must await the elections of 1968 and 1972, for the ultimate sign of a critical election is persistence of new cleavages. It is possible that the great movement of voters between the parties was only a temporary reaction to the admittedly unusual circumstances of 1964. It would, however, be quite remarkable if such were the case.

The outcome of the past election has left its mark in Democratic control of state legislatures and redistricting, organizational changes and conflicts in both parties, and the memories of the voters. The new Democratic coalition, begun with Kennedy and expanded with Johnson, provided the political energy

[29] Table 5.1 is based on data from the election studies of the Survey Research Center, recoded and computed by courtesy of the Inter-University Consortium for Political Research. The last two rows include respondents for which the data was inadequate to provide further classification. The basic data for 1964 are found in variables 611–614 of the *1964 Election Study Codebook*, and data for earlier elections are found in the corresponding codebooks and variables.

[30] Donald Stokes finds "almost no perceptible shift in the single most important type of response disposition, the electorate's enduring party loyalties," in "Some Dynamic Elements of Contests for the Presidency," *American Political Science Review*, Vol. LX (March, 1966), p. 27. However, Angus Campbell finds "indications in our survey data of a movement" toward party realignment in "Interpreting the Presidential Victory," in Milton C. Cummings, Jr., ed., *The National Election of 1964* (Washington: The Brookings Institution, 1966), p. 28. See also Philip Converse *et al.*, "Electoral Myth and Reality: The 1964 Election," *American Political Science Review*, Vol. LIX (June, 1965), pp. 321–36.

for great policy changes by government. Among these new initiatives are unashamed use of budget deficits to promote economic prosperity, new social welfare programs such as Medicare and the "war on poverty," full federal support of Negro voting and other civil rights, and a new American military involvement on the mainland of Asia. The future impact of the "black power" movement, the Vietnam war, deficit spending, and other developments is now uncertain, but they are most likely to upset, not reinforce, traditional alignments. Change, not continuity, seems evident.

THE EFFECTS OF PRESIDENTIAL ELECTIONS

The history of presidential elections indicates the impact of popular involvement in politics. The national vote is the means by which the scattered millions of the electorate come together symbolically to decide their political future. They choose not only a President, but a party. Majority action provides this party with the democratic legitimacy and political energy with which to pursue its programs.

One party usually is the normal majority party. Its policy emphases reflect the concerns and consensus of the dominant groups in the society. So long as it fulfills popular demands, it can expect to win the Presidency in Maintaining elections. When it temporarily fails in its task, a Deviating outcome occurs.

As individual campaigns pass into history, social tides are continuously changing the nation's political shoreline, eroding the size of some groups and adding to the mass of others, creating fissures in some regions and fusing political loyalties in others. In time, the parties react to these developments, sometimes to their own advantage as did the New Deal Democrats, sometimes disastrously, as did the Bryanites. The result is a Converting or Realigning election and a new political cleavage, providing the energy for new policy.

Unlike the tides of the sea, political tides are not easily predicted nor clearly distinct. Changes in voter loyalties do not fit any neat cyclical pattern, for the ebb and flow of party fortunes does not occur automatically after a fixed number of years. There is a tendency, it is true, for vital change to occur approximately once in every generation, but the length of time between these transformations varies considerably. The party system which became stabilized in 1876 lasted only until 1888, while the different party system which began to appear in 1928 still greatly affects politics today.

In another respect, however, political and natural events are similar. In both kinds of tides, change is typically neither unheralded nor precipitate. There is usually some rumbling before the wave breaks and considerable churning of the surf until the water is calm again. In presidential politics, there is not usually a single critical election, sandwiched between two periods of great stability. Rather, there are times of unease preceding the most crucial year and a period of assimilation after it. Secular realignment is more common and more basic than isolated party transformations. Typically, the most critical election represents a break in electoral continuity, but does not result in the immediate establishment of a new and persistent voter coalition. The tides of politics continue to flow. Persistence comes after the critical election, after the new party in power has had the opportunity to solidify its position through its policies in office.

The pattern of presidential elections provides additional evidence on the policy effects of popular decision. A change in voter loyalties does not result in direct control of policy. The voters alter their loyalties because of changing conditions, needs, and political stimuli, but they do not determine future action. The change in electoral cleavages is still crucial, for it affords the winning party an opportunity to deal with social problems of its time. Its specific actions in regard to these problems are not dictated by the electorate. If it is successful in meeting popular needs, however, it is likely to consolidate its power over a number of elections, as the voters give retrospective approval to its performance in office. "Unfavorable feeling toward a party that is being turned out of power may well be coupled with favorable feeling toward the party that follows it in office if the latter copes successfully with problems the public feels were mishandled by the preceding administration."[31] The electorate provides the occasion for action, but initiatives are the responsibility of the party in power.

The transition from one electoral era to another, resulting from considerable partisan movement by the voters, is an impressive manifestation of democratic intervention. Voters meddle decisively to change the political terms of reference. Party support and party programs become more congruent. Old policies and slogans are replaced by new, possibly more appropriate, appeals. The confusions of a waning order give way to the battle cries of an emergent party division.

In this century, alterations of the parties' bases twice have provided the political energy for alterations of policy. A decisive G.O.P. victory in 1896 provided the popular support for a period of Republican innovation. New social trends, and the failures of later Republicans, provided an opportunity for the Democrats in 1932. In each case, the victorious party's success in seizing its opportunity enabled it to dominate national politics for the succeeding generation. The great electoral changes of 1964 may have provided the energy for a new period of governmental innovation.

Our survey of national elections indicates an important but not omnipotent role for the voters. Citizens judge their satisfaction with the dominance of the majority party and its policy emphases. When social trends and popular feelings make the existing system outdated, party constituencies recombine into a new majority coalition. This coalition does not govern, but it provides the necessary popular support for a democratic gov-

[31] *The American Voter,* p. 554.

ernment. Its needs and demands condition the initiatives of those in power. Election victory does not provide detailed instructions for the winning party, but victory provides an opportunity to meet the new needs of the times and the desires of the new coalition. By expressing their satisfaction or discontent with measures and men, the voters can protect their vital interests. By acting to protect those interests, the parties link the voters to government.

The significance of elections, then, as discerned in presidential history, is retrospective judgment and prospective effect. This empirical result is consistent with the expectations of democratic theorists, the nature of American institutions, and the character of the voters, as previously discussed. Direct control of policy is not evident, but the citizenry indirectly affects policy by its approval or condemnation of the initiatives of politicians. To test this relationship again, we will now turn to state elections.

CHAPTER 6

GOVERNORS, MONEY, AND VOTES

STATE POLITICS affords another opportunity to discover the impact and significance of elections. In contests for the Presidency, the voters' intervention crucially affects the party balance, but their influence on governmental policy is neither direct nor obvious. Contests for governor involve fewer voters and more familiar issues. Perhaps the ballot has a more immediate impact in state elections. When government is close to the grass roots, politicians may be forced to keep their ears to the ground. In this chapter, we will test the existence of direct popular control of policy in postwar gubernatorial elections.

Voter control might be expected in regard to fiscal policy. State taxes and spending affect every voter in a very personal way. His income, purchases, and even fishing rights are taxed to provide his schools, roads, and license plates. Even before the United States came of age, the economic basis of politics had been evident to political theorists from Aristotle to Marx. In chapter IV, we also noticed the importance of material interests in American political attitudes. Most voters in the United States, we may recall, view the parties in terms of the group benefits they provide.[1] National balloting also has been

[1] See chapter IV, *supra,* and Angus Campbell *et al., The American Voter* (New York: Wiley, 1960), chap. 10.

found to be related to the swings of the business cycle. The party in power gains presidential votes and congressional seats in times of prosperity, but loses both in times of recession.[2]

A direct popular concern for fiscal policy is often posited in state politics. Taxes are seen as crucial to the voters. In particular, according to a widespread belief, the electoral fate of governors clearly follows from their budget practices: governors who increase taxes lose elections; governors who hold the tax line also hold their offices. If this relationship truly exists, the mystery of elections would be lessened considerably. Aware of the voters' demand, politicians would know how to behave and governmental policy would be popularly and directly controlled.

The presumed connection between taxes and votes has been emphasized recently, as both state taxes and spending have increased sharply. The states "face enormously increased demands for more and better schools, highways, welfare, recreational facilities, and so on—but most face them armed with very inadequate revenue sources. . . . The governor is to a great extent the most visible state official and therefore the logical scapegoat for the state's apparent inability to solve its problems."[3]

Many specific examples exist of the threat to governors from increased taxes. Before the 1960 election, Louis Harris found Democrat Albert Rosselini of Washington to be trailing in his bid for re-election. As one citizen complained, "I just think Rosselini is taking it out of the taxpayer's pocket. He raised the sales tax, and the tax on food, too—the poor man just can't make it. I say he's done a poor job." For similar reasons, Nebraska's Democratic governor was also found in danger. On the other hand, Democrats in Iowa and South Dakota, who had succeeded in restricting taxes, were seen as likely to be re-elected.[4]

[2] Louis H. Bean, *How to Predict Elections* (New York: Knopf, 1948), chap. 6.

[3] Austin Ranney, in Herbert Jacob and Kenneth N. Vines, *Politics in the American States* (Boston: Little, Brown, 1965), p. 91.

[4] "Why the Odds Are against a Governor Becoming President," *Public Opinion Quarterly*, Vol. XXIII (Fall, 1959), pp. 367–68.

Governors find it difficult to convince the public of the need for increased public services. As an aide to Governor Gaylord Nelson of Wisconsin despaired in 1960, "You can't get attention. You can't get attention for schools, or for taxes, for problems of aging, or mentally retarded children. . . . You can reach them one by one and make them understand. But how do you make them all understand?" His reporter, Theodore White, found it "noteworthy that the chief casualties in both parties in the fall elections later in 1960 were the governors beset by such problems as these." Half of the governorships changed party hands, "largely because of grass-roots tax revolts," while Nelson "squeaked through with 51.6 per cent."[5]

Presumed taxpayer resistance continues to worry government officials. Up to the present time, "as taxpayer resistance to state and local tax increases has stiffened, and as the demands of a burgeoning population for more governmental services has mounted, governors, mayors, and county supervisors alike have searched with mounting desperation for 'a way out.'"[6] Politicians evidently believe that voters seek direct control of policy through their ballots.

Although the relationship between taxes and electoral results is commonly assumed, it is not clearly proven. Obviously, many high-spending governors are politically successful. They gain enough support from the beneficiaries of state services to offset the lost votes of disgruntled taxpayers. This strategy, too, has some standing in the conventional wisdom of politics. Philosophers emphasizing direct control in elections feared that the populace would mandate high spending. In modern times, the opponents of Franklin Roosevelt complained, "You can't beat Santa Claus," as they explained the political success of vast increases in federal budgets. An apocryphal remark, erroneously attributed to Harry Hopkins, summarizes this tactic: "We shall

[5] *The Making of the President 1960* (New York: Atheneum, 1961), pp. 214–15.

[6] U.S. Advisory Commission on Intergovernmental Relations, *Eighth Annual Report* (1967), p. 4.

tax and tax, spend and spend, elect and elect."[7] Even on the basis of political aphorisms, therefore, there is reason to doubt the electoral consequences of state taxation.

Further skepticism about "tax revolts" is aroused when we consider the specific examples cited to demonstrate the theory. Governors Rosselini and Nelson won re-election in 1960, in the face of reported discontent with their financial records. Moreover, both ran ahead of their party's presidential candidate, John Kennedy, and both surpassed the national average vote for Democratic gubernatorial candidates in 1960. Contrary to Harris' expectations, moreover, the Democrats won in Nebraska, but lost in Iowa and South Dakota.

The superficially "obvious" relationship between taxes and elections is not so "obvious" when we begin to look at the contradictory strategies suggested by political folklore or at individual state results. The policy implications of state elections require more thorough exploration. It would therefore be useful to attempt more rigorous tests of the relationships between taxes, spending, and votes, through statistical operations performed on a computer.

Even if we find a statistical relationship, however, we still cannot be sure that we have found a direct causal relationship. At most we could conclude that tax increases and electoral losses are associated with one another. On the other hand, the absence of a statistical association would clearly disprove, or severely qualify, this alleged direct impact of voting. In a science of politics, disproving hypotheses is as important as their confirmation.

MONEY AND VOTES: TESTING HYPOTHESES

Three steps are needed to test an hypothesis through statistical methods: (1) State the hypothesis precisely; (2) define the terms

[7] Robert E. Sherwood, *Roosevelt and Hopkins*, rev. paper ed. (New York: Bantam, 1950), Vol. I, p. 124.

or variables quantitatively; (3) use an appropriate test for deriving a measure of association. The first step is simple and implicit in the previous discussion. Our precise hypothesis is that political success is associated with low tax increases. We will test this hypothesis by examining postwar elections in 37 states, excluding only the eleven southern states, which were overwhelmingly one-party, and the new states of Alaska and Hawaii.

In the second step, we must define political success and tax increases. Two different measurements of political success are used. It is first defined as *victory* for the incumbent party in a state, whether through the re-election of a governor or the victory of a new candidate of his party. This definition, however, may be too broad. An incumbent in one state might be re-elected in a runaway contest, while another governor won by a hair. A more precise indicator of political success would be the party's *vote change* from one election to the next. The most successful state party would show the greatest increase in its percentage of the vote since the last polling; the least successful would show the greatest decline.

To isolate the particular influence of state politics, we also must control the national trend. Therefore, for each candidate, the vote change is measured in comparison to all of his party's gubernatorial candidates.[8] The procedure is explained more fully in the Appendix.

Five measures of tax increases are used: (1) Absolute, or dollar, increase in per capita state taxes since the last election; (2) percentage increase; (3) annual percentage increase; (4) increase in "personal tax burden"—defined as per capita tax divided

[8] The voting data were obtained from Richard M. Scammon, ed., *American Votes 6: 1964* (Washington: Congressional Quarterly, 1966). Where 1944 figures were needed, they were obtained from New York World-Telegram, *The World Almanac and Book of Facts* (New York, 1945), pp. 721–45. Because Earl Warren won both parties' nominations in 1946, the California figures for this year are actually those from the 1942 election.

by per capita personal income; and (5) first-year taxes.[9] The last figure is the percentage of tax increases occurring in the first year of a governor's term. This measure is useful for testing another common political maxim, that new taxes should be concentrated at the beginning of an administration. By such action, governors presumably win time for the voters to forget their burdens before a new election looms. If this maxim is true, then governors who concentrate their tax increases in the first year should enjoy greater political success than those who follow a different course.

We now have two measures of relative political success and five measures of relative tax increases. The hypothesis to be tested is that they are inversely related, so that greater success will follow from lesser tax burdens.[10] For this test, each of the political measures is correlated separately with each of the tax indexes for the nine elections from 1948 to 1964.[11] The coefficient of association employed is known as the Goodman-Kruskall *gamma*. It can range as high as 1.0, which would fully support the folklore rule that political gains are related to limited new taxes. A coefficient of −1.0 would indicate that governors gain votes from large increases; lower coefficients would demon-

[9] The financial data were obtained from U.S. Bureau of the Census, *Compendium of State Government Finances*, published annually. The data for state spending and personal income, discussed subsequently, are also from this source. Per capita taxes include all sources of revenue. Calculations are based on the per capita tax in the fiscal year beginning in the same calendar year as a given election. The fiscal year begins for most states six months before the calendar year. Thus, for the election of 1964, the tax increases of greatest impact are those which begin July 1, 1964, the start of fiscal year 1965. The political assumption here is that voters will be most affected by recent increases in taxes, rather than by those already familiar to them, or only threatening in the future.

[10] The variations among states in the absolute level of taxes is not examined here. These differences result from many political and historical factors, fully considered by Clara Penniman, in Jacob and Vines, chap. 8.

[11] New Jersey and Kentucky, which hold gubernatorial elections in odd-numbered years, are included with the elections of the preceding years for purposes of analysis.

strate lower association. The statistical procedure used is explained in the Appendix.

The assumed relationships between money and votes concern expenditures as well as taxes. For a fuller test, state spending is also analyzed, using the same methods. Paralleling the analysis of taxes, the indexes of spending increases are: (1) Absolute increase in per capita general expenditure since the last election; (2) percentage increase; (3) annual percentage increase; (4) increase in "personal benefit"—defined as per capita spending divided by per capita personal income; and (5) last-year spending. The last figure is the percentage of the spending increase which occurred in the last year of a governor's term. If the voters indeed have short memories, it would be politically wise to concentrate new benefits in the period immediately preceding the balloting. Finally, the increases in spending and taxes are compared by the use of ratios. The *gamma* measure of association is used in all cases. A positive coefficient would indicate that restraints in spending lead to political success. A negative coefficient would suggest the opposite conclusion, that spending increases are more likely to yield electoral benefits.

MONEY AND VOTES: THE RESULTS

If citizens seek control of fiscal policy through their votes, our various statistical measures should reflect their concern. Association of the vote with gubernatorial taxing and spending programs will be evidenced by high correlations, within limits of 1.0 to −1.0. The lack of voter concern will be evidenced in lower coefficients. These are our standards. What are the results?

Table 6.1 summarizes the correlations obtained when we compare political success with increases in taxes and spending. The minus sign preceding the first figure in the 1948 column shows that low absolute tax increases in 1948 were associated not with victory, but with defeat. (Alternately, we can say victory was associated with high tax increases.) The second figure in the column indicates, however, that low absolute tax increases were associated positively with favorable vote change. In both cases, the low coefficients, −.16 and .27, indicate weak relationships.

Table 6.1 Political Success and Financial Policies

Political Variable	*Index of Increases*	*1948*	*1950*	*1952*	*1954*	*1956*	*1958*	*1960*	*1962*	*1964*
		Election Years (Coefficients of Correlation)								
Victory	Absolute Tax	−.16	.19	.21	.34	.00	.14	−.48	−.38	.26
Vote Change	Absolute Tax	.27	.29	.24	−.36	−.28	.13	.00	.00	.42
Victory	Absolute Spending	.30	.19	.21	.00	.17	−.29	−.46	−.42	−.26
Vote Change	Absolute Spending	.62	.14	.24	.15	.00	−.13	−.08	.19	.09
Victory	% Tax	−.31	.19	.41	.17	−.16	.14	−.32	−.38	−.26
Vote Change	% Tax	.14	.29	.30	−.41	−.28	.07	.08	−.07	.28
Victory	% Spending	.14	.19	.40	.00	.17	−.29	−.60	−.55	−.26
Vote Change	% Spending	.34	.14	.16	.15	.15	−.06	−.07	.14	.09
Victory	% Annual Tax	−.58	.19	.20	.00	.17	.14	−.28	−.14	.00
Vote Change	% Annual Tax	−.08	.44	.07	−.37	−.08	.00	.00	−.21	.26
Victory	% Annual Spending	−.46	.19	.21	.00	.17	−.14	−.48	−.55	−.26
Vote Change	% Annual Spending	.15	.14	.02	.22	.22	−.15	−.23	.14	.09
Victory	Personal Tax Burden	−.45	.38	.41	.17	−.35	.00	−.17	.29	.50
Vote Change	Personal Tax Burden	−.13	.56	.36	−.01	−.17	.15	.30	.25	.26
Victory	Personal Benefit	.00	.19	.41	.17	−.18	−.14	−.33	−.14	.00
Vote Change	Personal Benefit	.14	.13	.19	.20	.07	.28	.08	.26	.09
Victory	First-year Tax	.71	.72	.41	1.00	.34	.00	−.16	−.27	.23
Vote Change	First-year Tax	.26	.34	−.07	.00	.28	−.08	.08	.07	.26
Victory	Last-year Spending	−.30	−.54	.21	.00	−.51	.53	−.28	−.73	−.91
Vote Change	Last-year Spending	.14	−.49	−.42	.15	−.15	.20	−.24	.07	−.28
Victory	Absolute Ratio	.30	−.54	.00	.00	−.35	.14	−.17	.00	−.50
Vote Change	Absolute Ratio	.49	−.40	.28	.07	.09	−.07	−.08	.19	−.19
Victory	% Ratio	.14	−.54	.00	.00	−.35	.14	−.17	−.14	−.50
Vote Change	% Ratio	.28	−.40	.28	−.07	.23	.00	.15	.07	−.10
Number of States		28	28	26	28	27	28	24	28	22

The bulk of the table does not disguise the low coefficients obtained. The dominant impression from these figures is the absence of any meaningful association between these factors. The coefficients are rarely significant, and they are inconsistent in their direction (positive or negative). A coefficient of .30 would be about the minimum necessary to establish a relationship, but few of the statistics reach this level.

These results are contrary to all of the rules of political folklore. Governors who lead in increasing taxes do not suffer at the polls significantly. Conversely, governors who are cautious in their revenue programs in fear of a "tax revolt" are not particularly rewarded for their restraint. The impact of spending programs is also limited. Neither the relatively extravagant nor the comparatively penny-pinching state executives gain obvious electoral support for their labors. The voters do not express their financial demands by making consistent and meaningful distinctions among governors on the basis of state fiscal policies. The governors apparently have considerable discretion. While they cannot ignore the electoral impact of their budgets, they are not compelled politically either to restrict taxes or to expand spending.

The figures also provide some indication of the politically most desirable time to raise taxes or spending. Governors who concentrate their tax increases in the first year of their terms tend to be successful, confirming the hornbook rule, but the relationships are not strong or fully consistent. Contrary to the original supposition, however, it also appears best to concentrate spending increases in the earlier part of a gubernatorial term. Such action may be necessary for two different reasons. Early spending increases may be advantageous because time erases the voter's memories of the governor's extravagance. Alternately, the benefits of state spending may not become apparent to the voter for some time. An early sowing of increased governmental services may be necessary for state executives to reap the political harvest in the next election.

Though the over-all relationships are not convincing, there is a suggestive temporal shift in the electoral consequences of state fiscal politics. It appears that low taxes were politically profitable until 1956, while high spending has become more advantageous since 1958. However, because of the generally low level of the coefficients, the statistical evidence is not conclusive.

A temporal shift is indicated by the changing direction of the coefficients in Table 6.1. In the earlier period, positive correlations occurred more than twice as often as negative figures. Political rewards were associated with frugal government. In the contests beginning in 1958, the situation has become considerably different, and negative figures are more common than positive numbers. High taxers and spenders no longer seem vulnerable at the polls. Indeed, the simple factor of victory at the polls is particularly likely to be associated with a liberal fiscal policy in the later era.[12]

The apparent change in the political impact of governmental finances may result from new attitudes on the part of the voters. The electorate may well have become newly aware of the impact of state budgets, with rising governmental costs. While all of the states taxed 2.3 per cent of the gross national product in 1946, and spent but 1.8 per cent of the country's wealth, they received 3.7 per cent in 1962, and spent 3.8 per cent.[13] Yet even increased attention does not explain the greater electoral tolerance of spending governors.

The outcome of an election is only partially dependent on awareness of state finances. More decisive in determining victory is the general trend toward one of the parties. A Republican or Democratic swing elects both spenders and savers of the winning party, while the individual's record can have only a marginal effect. Nationwide trends explain the temporal shift in gubernatorial elections. As Table 6.2 evidences, the period from 1948 to 1956, when low-taxing governors were favored, was also a period of Republican dominance. In 1958, a period of Democratic supremacy began, coinciding with the success of high-spending executives.

Democrats are more prone to extend governmental programs, although not all spenders are Democrats, and not all Democrats

[12] There are more than twice as many positive as negative coefficients involving "victory" in the 1948–56 period. In the later time the positive coefficients are less than one-third the number of negative figures.

[13] Frederick Mosher and Orville Poland, *The Costs of American Government* (New York: Dodd, Mead, 1964), pp. 157, 165.

Table 6.2 Party Fortunes in Gubernatorial Elections of 37 States

	Number of Victories		*Median Vote (%)*	
Year	*Democrats*	*Republicans*	*Democrats*	*Republicans*
1948	14	14	49.2	50.8
1950	6	22	45.2	54.8
1952	6	20	45.5	54.5
1954	13	15	49.0	51.0
1956	13	14	49.6	50.4
1958	20	8	52.6	47.4
1960	12	12	50.1	49.9
1962	14	14	50.0	50.0
1964	14	8	54.0	46.0

are spenders.[14] The recent change to a Democratic advantage in state elections therefore largely accounts for the new relationship between increased spending and electoral victory. The earlier Republican dominance similarly accounts for the past success of governors who limited new taxes and spending. It is possible that the causal relationship should be reversed. Greater voter acceptance of state spending could lead to Democratic party victory, as earlier public support for low taxes might have brought Republican pre-eminence. This line of argument, however, seems to assume too much voter generosity and awareness to be plausible. The shift to the Democrats is almost certainly the result of party, not fiscal, factors.[15] The earlier discussion

[14] Although no detailed study is available, it may be significant that the range of annual per cent spending increases is greater for Democratic than Republican governors in three of the four elections since 1958, and similar to or higher than the Republicans' in all years except 1948. For national party differences consistent with this assumption, see Herbert McClosky *et al.*, "Issue Conflict and Consensus among Party Leaders and Followers," *American Political Science Review*, Vol. LIV (June, 1960), pp. 406–27; and Lewis A. Froman, Jr., *Congressmen and Their Constituencies* (Chicago: Rand McNally, 1963), chap. 9.

[15] The importance of national trends in congressional elections similarly is evidenced by Donald Stokes and Warren Miller, "Party Government and the Saliency of Congress," in Angus Campbell *et al.*, *Elections and the Political Order* (New York: Wiley, 1966), chap. 11, and Milton C. Cummings, Jr., *Congressmen and the Electorate* (New York: Free Press, 1966).

of the 1962 Wisconsin election reinforces the point.[16] Voters choose parties primarily and policies secondarily.

The results of state elections again demonstrate the pervasive influence of partisanship. Previously, we have learned how individual voters view the world of politics through partisan eyes and how the choice of party is crucial in the innovation of national policy. In gubernatorial politics as well, voters' preferences are channeled through parties. The direct control of government action is unlikely. Electoral influence must be indirect, through popular endorsement of policy-oriented politicians.

WHAT MAKES A DIFFERENCE?

Our general analysis indicates that there is no strong and unidirectional relationship between tax or spending increases and electoral results. Voters do not evidence a consistent concern for fiscal issues. Moreover, their party preferences complicate their policy choices. Within the general pattern, however, some factors may make a marginal difference. It would be useful, therefore, to separate or "control" some of these factors, to see if any stronger relationships become evident.

For this purpose, the states involved in each election were divided into two groups on each of the following dimensions: (1) Democratic or Republican governors at the time of the election; (2) competitive status;[17] (3) Democratic or Republican victory in the state in the current or preceding presidential election; (4) high or low personal income; (5) presence or absence of incumbent candidates; (6) two- or four-year terms; and (7) outcome of the previous election, either continuation of the same party in power or a party turnover. The relationship of politics and finances is then calculated separately for each group.

[16] See chapter IV, pp. 78–80, *supra*.

[17] The competitive states are those ranked 1 to 19 in gubernatorial competition by Richard Dawson and James Robinson, "Inter-Party Competition, Economic Variables, and Welfare Policies in the American States," *Journal of Politics*, Vol. 25 (May, 1963), pp. 265–87. Minnesota, which is not included in their study, is also considered competitive. The other states, as well as Nebraska, are considered less competitive.

Only one measure of each variable was used in this analysis. Political success was considered vote change, as previously defined. The index of tax or spending increases was the per cent annual increase. This measure was chosen as the one least affected by the wealth of the states or the differences between two- and four-year terms. The correlation coefficient is *Yule's Q*, explained in the Appendix, which varies from 1.0 to −1.0. The results are presented in Table 6.3.

Table 6.3 Political Success and Financial Policies: What Makes a Difference?

Variables	*1948*	*1950*	*1952*	*1954*	*1956*	*1958*	*1960*	*1962*	*1964*	*Total*
				Election Years (Coefficients of Correlation)						
Democrats: Taxes	.00	.85	−.38	−.33*	−.50	.00	−.14	−.38	−.28	−.09
Spending	.00	.85	−.38	1.00*	−.50	.00	−.14	.14	.28	.14
Republicans: Taxes	−.67	.14	.00	−.25	.00	.60	.78	−.14	.33	−.01
Spending	−.38	−.38	.00	.09	.47	−.60	−.50	−.14	.33	−.13
Competitive: Taxes	−.38	.60	−.72	.00	−.28	.60	.00	.00	−.90	−.17
Spending	.14	.60	−.72	.60	.28	.00	.00	.60	−.50	.11
Noncompetitive: Taxes	.45	.47	.00	−.47	−.14	.47	−.60	−.80	.20	−.08
Spending	.85	.00	.00	.47	.45	.00	.00	−.47	.78	.30
Dem. President: Taxes	−.38	.61	.00*	.00*	.00*	.00*	.38	.38	.28	.16
Spending	.14	.14	.00*	.00*	.00*	.00*	.88	.38	.28	.26
Rep. President: Taxes	−.14	.45	−.38	−.22	−.15	.14	−.72	−.60	.00*	−.22
Spending	−.14	−.14	−.08	.36	.15	−.14	−.72	−.22	.00*	−.08
High Income: Taxes	−.38	.89	−.28	.14	.14	.14	−.67	−.38	.60	−.05
Spending	−.76	.61	−.28	.61	−.38	−.40	−.67	.14	.00	−.13
Low Income: Taxes	−.67	.45	−.60	−.67	−.60	.14	−.50	−.14	−.38	−.37
Spending	.45	−.14	.00	−.14	.60	.45	.20	−.14	−.38	−.03
Incumbents: Taxes	−.38	.00	.22	−.92	−.38	.45	.20	−.25	.28	−.15
Spending	.00	.00	−.22	−.60	.61	−.22	−.50	.42	−.28	−.04
Nonincumbents: Taxes	−.80	.92	−.80	.00	.00	.22	−.14	−.33*	.00	.00
Spending	.00	.60	.00	.60	−.60	−.38	−.94	−.33*	.00	−.20
Two-year Term: Taxes	.50	.11	.71	−.11	−.22	.38	−.38	−.38	−.14	−.07
Spending	.50	−.30	−.11	−.11	.22	.00	−.38	.61	.45	.10
Four-year Term: Taxes	.80	.64	−.20	−.50	−.84	.00	−.20	−.14	−.84	−.15
Spending	.00	1.00	−.20	.20	.64	−.38	−.20	−.67	−.20	.04
Continuity: Taxes		.61	.85	−.50	−.11	.50	−.47	.00	−.50	.08
Spending		.28	−.14	−.18	−.54	−.30	−.80	.00	−.50	−.36
Reversal: Taxes		1.00*	1.00*	−.33*	−.38	.64	.50	−.47	−1.00	.33
Spending		1.00*	1.00*	−.33*	.38	−.20	1.00	.47	.78	.53

* Five or fewer states.

Financial policies affect governors of the two parties in a different manner. Although neither partisan camp is greatly affected by tax increases, a Democrat is more likely to run ahead of his party's national trend by limiting new spending. Republicans evidence the opposite relationship. They are more likely to run ahead of the national G.O.P. if their spending increases are relatively high.[18]

These results, although of a low magnitude, indicate similarities in the practical situation facing governors of both parties. To run ahead of his party, a governor should act contrary to the common public impression. A Republican, belonging to a party which is regarded as more concerned with economy, can lead his fellow partisans by being relatively generous with public monies. A Democrat, whose party is regarded as more extravagant, can exceed the national trend by frugality.[19]

The outcome of elections, as we have seen, is largely dependent on over-all swings. Marginal differences from these trends, however, can be gained by policies which broaden a state executive's coalition beyond that normally associated with the party. Frank Lausche established his position as Democratic governor of Ohio by his conservative fiscal policies, whereas Earl Warren twice won re-election as Republican governor of California by a liberal spending program. The relationships between the presidential vote in a state and taxation confirm this analysis. In states carried by Democratic candidates for the White House, governors surpass the national trend by frugal policies, while Republican states on the national level tend to give marginal support to more extravagant gubernatorial candidates.

[18] Even the total figures are still quite low, and the correlation could occur by chance more than one out of five times. These results, however, do indicate that the recent success of the Democrats is not due to voters deliberately casting their votes for high spenders.

[19] For images of the parties, see *The American Voter*, chaps. 3, 10, and Opinion Research Corporation, *Public Opinion Trends—Their Meaning for the Republican Party* (1965).

There are limited, but intriguing, differences between the more and less competitive states as well. Voters in the more competitive states are apt to support governors associated with larger tax increases and are not greatly troubled by spending increases. In the less competitive states, governors are barely affected by tax increases, but earn rewards for restrictions in state governmental expenditures. There is, in brief, a greater possibility of political gain for governmental welfare programs in competitive states.

These differences suggest alternative strategies for governors in varying political environments. In competitive states, politicians would seek votes by spending programs of mass benefit and devote less attention to the tax burden. Unsure of office, the parties would seek to appeal to the large number of lower-income voters in their fiscal programs. The costs of government will not be resented by the mass of voters if a substantial share is paid by the well-to-do. State spending will be of political benefit where the spending is widely distributed.

In the less competitive states, a different strategy would be appropriate. In these states, the "have-nots" of society have less opportunity for influence. The absence of two parties of relatively equal strength makes it difficult "to carry out sustained programs of action, which almost always are thought by the better element to be contrary to its immediate interests. This negative weakness thus redounds to the benefit of the upper brackets."[20] Politics in the less competitive states can be expected to be more controlled by economic elite groups, and successful politicians will be more prone to serve their interests. While these elites may not resent tax increases, which are often a re-

[20] V. O. Key, Jr., *Southern Politics* (New York: Knopf, 1949), p. 308. The argument was further developed by Duane Lockard, *New England State Politics* (Princeton University Press, 1959), chap. 12. It has since been criticized by Dawson and Robinson, *op. cit.* and Thomas W. Dye, *Politics, Economics and the Public* (Chicago: Rand McNally, 1966), and defended by John N. Fenton, *People and Parties in Politics* (Glenview: Scott, Foresman, 1966), chap. 2.

gressive burden on lower-income groups, they are more likely to seek and politically reward spending limits.

When we examine the states with wealth controlled, we find that low-income states are more willing to accept tax rises and high-income states are more receptive to spending increases. Because there are relatively fewer taxpayers in poorer states, these voters may be willing to support governors who raise taxes on other people. The leading, but clearly exceptional, example is that of Huey Long, who won strong popular approval of his "share the wealth" program. The tolerance for spending in high-income states may reflect the greater demands voiced by prosperous citizens with "rising expectations" of universal education, modern highways, and extensive recreational facilities. The outcry which greeted Ronald Reagan's effort to impose tuition in California's universities reflects the wealthier voters' concerns, and their pressures on governors to maintain public spending.

Correlations in the last three groupings provide some tentative guides to wise political action. Incumbents are better able to defend a record of tax increases, while new candidates are advisable for a party responsible for spending increases. There is apparently some political safety in a four-year term, for governors with longer tenure appear to benefit from higher taxes. Finally, governors of a party re-elected to office are most likely to succeed in future contests when they increase spending. State executives elected in a party turnover would be better advised to limit taxing and spending.

These differing strategies are of marginal, not overwhelming, importance. Our detailed correlations do not show direct voter control over state fiscal policy, even when important factors are analyzed separately. We find, rather, that governors have considerable discretion within the limits of the electorate's partisanship. The political situation of different states does make some strategies more attractive than others. The reactions of the electorate must be considered, for popular resistance to taxes or popular demands for new spending may have an effect at the polls. Still, these effects are neither obvious nor immediate, and politicians have considerable room for maneuver. There is no iron law of state politics or state finances.

THE MEANINGS OF STATE ELECTIONS

Clear electoral mandates are rare in gubernatorial contests. There are some technical reasons for the absence of any clear and direct relationship between fiscal policy and electoral success. By using a measure of total taxes, we lump together levies of greater and lesser political sensitivity. Voters may react to a state sales tax, while being hardly aware of minerals severance imposts. Similarly, some expenditures are more likely to win voter attention than others. State spending for welfare is widely distributed and debated, while the promotion of tourism is neither visible nor contentious. Our data may also be somewhat inaccurate, with items disguised or deferred through accounting devices.[21]

The fundamental problems involved in the explanation of state elections, however, are political, rather than technical. We have not found simple relationships because the relationships are not simple. The meaning of elections is complex, often contradictory, and can rarely be explained as a direct association between ballots and fiscal policy. The "buzzing, blooming confusion" of the political world is evident in institutions, in the voter's perceptions, and in campaigns.

The complexity of American institutions, as discussed in chapter III, limits governors and voters. State chief executives

[21] The statistical methods employed can also be criticized. Rank-order correlation is relatively simple, but it ignores the exact differences among the ranked data. Using only two or three categories for each variable also limits the degree of comparison possible. Because of the peculiarities of this method, a small change in the number of states in any cell can effect a drastic change in the coefficient of association. The small number of cases in any year also limits the generality of the findings.

do not fully control their own administrations. Separation of powers, decentralized administration, and the proliferation of public authorities create rival power centers. Their competition makes it difficult for the citizen to focus his attention and appropriately to distribute rewards and punishments for state taxing and spending. Institutional separations are often broadened by political fissures. A governor of one party may co-exist with a legislature and elected administrative officials of the opposition. Furthermore, at least until recent reapportionment, a governor might be more responsive to the urbanized areas of a state, while the legislature was biased in favor of rural districts. The responsibility for fiscal policies becomes quite clouded in these circumstances.[22]

At the same time, governors are in the middle of a complex federal system; they cannot isolate their states from the actions of superior and subordinate governments. National taxation limits the opportunities for state revenue; national fiscal policies stimulate or retard a state's prosperity; and national grants-in-aid allow increased state expenditure without increased internal taxation. Local communities collect a portion of state revenues and demand a rising proportion of state expenditures, while they increase their own taxes and spending. Governors are not formally responsible for national or local policies, but in the noncentralized American system of federalism, they cannot avoid involvement or some political culpability.

The chief executives are also involved, or entrapped, in a political party and will inevitably share in their party's electoral fate. National politics affects state elections, not infrequently overwhelming other influences. The fiscal records of the governors have only a marginal effect on the vote. National tides can sweep in or submerge both the frugal and the free-spending. An autonomous state politics does not exist.[23]

[22] See V. O. Key, Jr., *American State Politics* (New York: Knopf, 1956), chaps. 3, 7.

[23] See Key, *American State Politics*, chap. 2, and Judson L. James, "American Political Parties as Executive-Centered Coalitions" (mimeo, 1967).

Voter perceptions further complicate the governors' political problems. The most important political object to the electorate is the national party. The voter's reactions to the nature of the times or the provision of group benefits is commonly a broad and undifferentiated judgment on all politicians grouped under a partisan label. His fire is a fusillade of buckshot over the entire electoral terrain, not a rifle bullet precisely aimed at fiscal culprits. If unhappy with the Democrats, even economy-minded Democrats will not totally escape his wrath. Opposition to the Republican party will damage all of the G.O.P.'s candidates, whatever their fiscal policies.

The electorate, furthermore, cannot be expected fully to distinguish the different levels of the federal structure. The impact of taxes and spending is a total impact, not one in which the voter carefully separates national, state, and local finances. An increase in an individual's withholding tax may cause resentment of his state's governor, even when new taxes have actually been imposed by local or national governments. Conversely, the governor may receive credit for a new school or highway even when the major part of the cost has been paid by municipal or federal agencies.

Even if the voter does concentrate on state budgets, his goals are not necessarily constant nor coherent. He may wish tax relief in one year, but be more concerned with new state services at another election. In many cases, both goals are wanted. Thus, "taxation to finance welfare programs meets opposition among those who favor welfare programs even more frequently than among those who oppose them. . . . The same people simultaneously want increased expenditures and reduced taxes."[24] Given such contradictions, no clear electoral relationship is likely between political success and gubernatorial fiscal programs.

[24] V. O. Key, Jr., *Public Opinion and American Democracy* (New York: Knopf, 1961), pp. 168–69. See also Robert Axelrod, "The Structure of Public Opinion on Policy Issues," *Public Opinion Quarterly*, Vol. XXXI (Spring, 1967), pp. 51–60.

Finally, individual campaigns will affect the electoral importance of taxes and expenditures. In many state elections, these questions are not presented to the voters, or are not perceived by them. Attention may be limited to the personal character, associations, and abilities of the candidates. Any discussion of the incumbents' records may center on scandals or substantive policy, rather than on financial matters. National and even international issues may intrude. In the 1966 campaign, for example, news commentators stressed the importance of segregation in Alabama, scandals in Massachusetts, presidential politics in Michigan, and campaign funds in Pennsylvania.[25] While these may be appropriate issues, their emphasis clearly dilutes the impact of budgetary questions.

For these many reasons, tax and spending policies are not controlled through state elections. Even when they are important, there is no indication that popular resistance to taxes is the predominant fiscal consideration. The diversity of state politics is illustrated by the last three elections in our largest states, California and New York. In 1958, Democrat Pat Brown and Republican Nelson Rockefeller were elected governors of these two states, in each case reversing party control of the executive branch. In each case as well, their campaigns had been waged partially as attacks on the previous administration's extravagance, but largely on other issues. Brown was also aided by the strong Democratic tide created by the 1958 recession. Once in office, each of the governors adopted a budget of over $2 billion, balanced through some quarter-of-a-million dollars in new levies and increases in the state income tax. After compromises and amendments in the state legislatures, both governors' programs were adopted.

In 1962, Brown and Rockefeller were re-elected. California, soon to be the most populous state, had already become the nation's leader in spending. The state's campaign, however, centered not on finances, but on Richard Nixon's presidential

[25] American Broadcasting Company, *Factbook: Elections 1966.*

ambitions, other national issues, and political extremism. In New York, Rockefeller's tax record was a more central issue, but its impact was reduced by such personal questions as his divorce and remarriage. To meet the criticisms of his financial record, the Governor pledged no new taxes in his second term.

In the following four years, the budgets of the two states rose considerably, to $3.9 billion in New York and $4.6 billion in California. Rockefeller withdrew his no-tax pledge and resorted to bonds, accelerated tax payments, and eventually a state sales tax. Brown also made use of extensive borrowing and accelerated payments and sought a withholding system for income levies as part of a program of "fiscal reform."

Each governor ran for a third term in 1966, and each defended his past budgets by pointing to achievements such as the Feather River water project in California or the Medicaid program of New York. Finances were an issue in each state, but there were other factors. In New York, Rockefeller apologized to the voters for the "blooper" of his no-tax pledge, and attributed the deficit in state revenues to a lagging national economy. Narcotics control, "bossism," and splinter parties complicated the situation. In California, the candidates' personalities, student activity at Berkeley, and race relations received predominant attention in an election seen as a national test of conservative sentiment. While taxes were debated, the focus was on local, rather than state, revenues. In November Rockefeller won, but Brown was defeated.

These two cases illustrate the difficulty in interpreting gubernatorial elections in a single-minded way or finding them a "mandate" for lower taxes or increased spending. Simple relationships and simple explanations are restrained by the diversity of American institutions, the national tides of party politics, and the multiplicity of state issues. Complexity is created as well by the voter, who does not mechanically respond to financial allurements. The conventional assumption is that taxes are particularly unpopular and politically dangerous. The record indicates, however, that the electorate can understand and accept the need and uses of public revenues and spending. An account of a Rockefeller street campaign speech is enlightening:

> As the Governor spoke, a man in his shirtsleeves came out of a tavern, The Inn, and called: "I want to know what you're going to do about the state income tax. It's bad news."
>
> "Let me tell you about pure water. I know you don't bother with it," Mr. Rockefeller said, as the crowd laughed.
>
> "Taxes, taxes!" the man continued to shout.
>
> The Governor said that the taxes paid by the man helped children go to school, and the crowd applauded. The man retreated to The Inn. He declined to give his name.[26]

Voters will often bear taxes when they are convinced of the value of state services, just as they will often reject state services when they appear wasteful. To return to our original hypothesis, there is no inevitable "taxpayers' revolt," if we judge by the empirical evidence presented here. Limits on state taxation are not necessarily imposed by the voters. In fact, the opposite relationship is quite common. High spending can be politically advantageous.

Even if invalid, however, the belief in a taxpayer revolt can still be important in restricting state action. Politicians necessarily must make some assumptions about the electoral consequences of their behavior. Their commitments and actions are conditioned by the reactions they expect from the voters. If governors believe they will be electorally punished for taxing and providing services, they will not tax nor provide services. The governor's reading of the public will is as vital as the true content of that testament.

The politician is the crucial link in voter influence over public policy. The electorate does not mandate policy, but it accepts

[26] *The New York Times*, September 21, 1966, p. 37. The account of the Brown and Rockefeller administrations is drawn from various articles in the *Times*.

or rejects the officials who initiate policy. Politicians are not severely restricted by decisions at the polls, but neither can they fail to protect the voters' vital interests. In state politics, governors have discretion to limit or raise taxes and spending, as their conception of the public's needs and desires indicates. The electoral consequences are uncertain, depending on the governors' commitments, the voter's changing concerns, and the quality of party competition. If this uncertainty prevents any simple explanation of politics, it does provide an opportunity for meaningful dialogue between elected and electors.

The evidence of state elections is consistent with our earlier discussions of theory, institutions, and voters. Empirical evidence from presidential and gubernatorial contests is similar. On neither level do the voters prescribe specific governmental action. Initiatives in public programs do not follow directly from popular mandates. The impact of elections on policy, therefore, must be sought through their indirect effects. If the voters do not determine policy, they still may influence it through their choice of candidates and parties. Our evidence indicates that the crucial decisions are made by the elected, not the electors. The actions of these officials, in turn, may be related to their campaign pledges, as stated in party platforms. We will explore the meaning and fulfillment of these pledges in the next two chapters.

CHAPTER 7

"IF ELECTED, I PROMISE"

AN ELECTION rarely is a policy referendum or a mandate for designated future actions. The voters largely make their decisions on the basis of party loyalties rather than issues. Direct control over policy is therefore unlikely. Indirect influence on policy is still possible, through voters' judgment of party performance. There is an inevitable fusing of party and policy, and therefore an inevitable programmatic result from elections. Voters cannot choose either a program or a party alone, but must select both simultaneously, even unwittingly or unwillingly.

Parties are the crucial links between the voters' interests and the activities of government. The electorate approves or disapproves of policy by its choice of a party. Democrats and Republicans support particular programs in their quest for office and become identified with particular actions through their conduct in office. In our studies of presidential and gubernatorial elections, we found that the initiatives and commitments of parties and candidates are vital in the determination of public policy.[1] We may now focus on these commitments as found in the national platforms. Adopted by their only general bodies, the

[1] A good treatment of the effect of commitments is Norton Long, "After the Voting Is Over," *Midwest Journal of Political Science*, Vol. VI (May, 1962), pp. 183–200. See also Theodore Sorensen, *Decision-Making in the White House* (New York: Columbia University Press, 1963).

nominating conventions, and presented to the voters as the presidential election approaches, they most fully represent the parties' intentions.

Indirect voter influence over policy can be facilitated in two ways through the platforms. First, the documents may provide a means by which the voters choose parties and their policies. The electorate makes its judgments on the basis of the past performance of the parties and their promised group benefits. Meaningful platforms would aid such decisions. Secondly, the platform may be significant even if not widely read. The campaign manifesto may reflect program initiatives made by parties in anticipation of voter needs and demands. If the platform commits politicians to relatively specific actions, the electorate's choice of a party would also become a choice of policies.

In both cases, platforms must be specific, policy-oriented, and relevant to the voters' concerns. The conventional view, however, is that platforms are meaningless, and the party document has received more scorn than attention. According to one hoary cliché, "A platform is to run on, not to stand on." The classic condemnation of platforms is Ostrogorskii's:[2]

> The platform, which is supposed to be the party's profession of faith and its programme of action is only a farce—the biggest farce of all the acts of this great parliament of the party. The platform represents a long list of statements relating to politics, in which everybody can find something to suit him, but in which nothing is considered as of any consequence by the authors of the document, as well as by the whole convention. . . . The platform has just as little significance and authority for Congress. Its members consider themselves in no way bound to the programs laid down in the convention, for they know perfectly well under what circumstances and with what mental reservations it has been promulgated.

[2] M. Ostrogorskii, *Democracy and the Organization of Political Parties*, Vol. II (Garden City: Doubleday Anchor, 1964), pp. 138–39.

If platforms are indeed meaningless, it seems odd that they should occasion, as they have, severe intraparty disagreement, and the attention of interest groups, mass media, and practical politicians. There was far more dispute among the 1964 Republican convention delegates, for example, over the platform than the prospective candidates. Similarly, in the 1948 convention, southern delegates left the Democratic convention in a dispute over platform provisions. Rather than neglecting the platforms, politicians appear to regard them as significant factors in the quest for voter support.[3]

THE RATIONAL PLATFORM

One means of exploring the impact of platforms would be an assessment of their *rational* character. Defined in instrumentalist terms, rationality is any means which furthers the goals of voters and parties. Traditional critics of platforms consider them nonrational because they do not contribute to the realization of voters' goals. The party documents, it is claimed, do not help the voter to make informed policy choices and are unrelated to the party's policy positions. Conversely, a platform which is rational would provide a guide to party commitments, help the voter in making his decision, and link the programmatic appeals made in campaigns to the actions of government. By examining platform rationality, we can test these assertions and the policy significance of party manifestos.

Two kinds of rationality are involved. Derived from the theory of Anthony Downs,[4] they can be designated voter-rationality

[3] Among the limited number of studies of platforms are Edward F. Cooke, "Drafting the 1952 Platforms," *Western Political Quarterly*, Vol. 9 (September, 1956), pp. 699–712, Paul T. David *et al., The Politics of National Party Conventions*, 1960), esp. pp. 407–9, and Paul Tillett, ed., *Inside Politics: The National Conventions, 1960* (New Brunswick: Rutgers, The State University, 1960), chaps. 6–9.

[4] *An Economic Theory of Democracy* (New York: Harper, 1957). Related, important works include J. M. Buchanan and G. Tullock, *The Calculus of Consent* (Ann Arbor: University of Michigan Press, 1962); Duncan Black, *The Theory of Committees and Elections* (Cambridge University Press, 1958), and Donald E. Stokes, "Spatial Models of Party Competition," *American Political Science Review*, Vol. LVII (June, 1963), pp. 368–77.

and party-rationality. Platforms provide for voter-rationality if they help an individual to select the party that will bring him the greatest individual benefit or "utility income." The voter's concern for individual protection and gains has been noted in chapter IV. Benefits are not only material gains, but all things valued by the voter, such as psychic satisfactions or altruistic actions. Platforms promote party-rationality if they contribute to the victory of their authors. Considerations of the wisdom or morality of individual benefits or party actions are not independently involved in this model—although wise and moral actions are likely eventually to have an effect.

A particular action may serve neither, either, or both of these kinds of rationality. For a party to ignore its pledges consistently, for example, serves neither end, because it confuses the voters and also results in distrust of the party, to its ultimate detriment. Honoring of pledges, by contrast, in most cases is rational for parties and an aid to voters. To take a different situation, it may be rational in a two-party system for a party to be vague on important issues, for it can thereby gain support from diverse groups in the electorate. However, such vagueness does not contribute to voter-rationality, since electors will find it difficult to make an informed choice.[5]

Let us specify some of the qualities of a party platform that would aid the voters. A rational platform would have five qualities:

1. It would be concerned, in considerable degree, with questions of public policy and would be precise enough to be meaningful to the voter.

2. Since voters tend to make their party choices on the basis of performance, it would facilitate a comparison of the two parties' past positions and actions, with special attention to the merits and defects of the incumbents' record. The platform would thereby provide a judgment on the "nature of the times."

[5] Downs, pp. 135–39.

3. It would indicate future positions of the party, specifically enough to be meaningful to the voter, particularly in policy areas of greatest benefit to the voter. Such statements are needed partially as an aid to voting in the impending election, providing a guide to the group benefits available through each party. Statements on future policy also are needed for the next election, as a means of judging the party's reliability in keeping pledges.[6]

4. The party would be highly consistent in its positions from one platform to the next.

5. If victorious, the party would carry out its indicated platform positions to the best of its ability.

Platforms would need to meet a somewhat different set of standards if they were to be considered a contribution to the party's rational goal of election. The parties would attempt to anticipate the voters' policy interests. For a two-party system, we can suggest the following criteria:

1. The content of the platform would vary in accord with the party's campaign strategy. It would deal with policy questions only insofar as this discussion contributed to victory.

2. The past records of the parties would be presented as a favorable comparison of the party with its opposition, to win voters concerned with the "nature of the times."

3. In regard to future policies, the party would promise group benefits, but its pledges would vary in specificity according to the political situation. In detail: (a) The party would specifically accept any policy known to be intensely favored by a majority of voters. (b) The party would specifically accept any policy favored by a minority of voters and not opposed by a substantial minority. (c) Where voter preferences are uncertain or politically

[6] Downs, especially in chap. 3, emphasizes that the voter must rely on past actions of the parties, rather than future promises. If future pledges are relatively specific, and discounted by the voter, it is then rational for him to consider them in making his choice. In any case, Downs sees a need (on p. 106) for future promises so that the party can be measured in the next election as a faithful or faithless keeper of its word.

unimportant, the party position would tend to be vague. (d) Where opposing positions on an issue are held by two or more minorities of voters, the party position would tend to be vague. (e) In certain cases, despite the foregoing propositions, the party might specifically accept a minority position on an issue. This action would occur if the party were attempting to enlist the support of a "passionate minority," i.e., a minority for which support on one particular issue was more important than the party's stands on all other issues. Party-rationality would also require consistency and party performance, as in propositions 4 and 5 above.[7]

It is important to realize that it is not necessary to the achievement of either kind of rationality that there always be differences between the parties, as advocated by proponents of "responsible party government."[8] Complete disagreement would be nonrational, for it would lead to the collapse of the political system, a disadvantageous result for almost all voters. Disagreements on issues on which there is a decided majority preference would also not be rational. It would lead either to the selection of a party opposed to most voters' wishes or to the continuous defeat of one party, and the foreclosure of choice.

For the parties, issue differences where there is an intense majority preference would be nonrational, probably resulting in defeat of the party sponsoring the minority position. On other issues, differences result from uncertainty or from dissimilar strategies. Uncertain of public preferences, the parties may advance differing positions, hoping they have correctly gauged public sentiment. Alternately, the parties may be aware of preferences but attempt to appeal to different or opposed "passionate

[7] These propositions are derived, with some modification, from Downs, propositions 2, 3, 4, 8, 14, 15, 23, and 24 and from chaps. 3, 4, 7, 8, and 13. Cf. Robert Dahl's brilliant analysis, *A Preface to Democratic Theory* (Chicago: University of Chicago Press, 1956), particularly chaps. 3–5.

[8] See American Political Science Association, Committee on Political Parties, *Toward a More Responsible Two-Party System* in *American Political Science Review*, Vol. XLIV (September, 1950), Supplement, and James MacGregor Burns, *The Deadlock of Democracy* (Englewood Cliffs: Prentice-Hall, 1963).

minorities," again resulting in conflicting policies. This can be a rational course, but it is also logical for the parties to agree in their appeals to minorities, as well as to majorities.

Do American platforms fit this "model" of rationality? Through analysis of major party platforms from 1944 to 1964,[9] it is possible to test some of these propositions and thereby gain an indication of the policy significance of platforms. The propositions on party performance are considered in chapter VIII. It is not necessary to substantiate in detail the propositions on the consistency of party platforms. There is a manifest continuity in each party from one election to the next. Changes of emphasis and of specificity, as noted below, are evident, but there is no important change in direction. Indeed, entire sections are sometimes carried over (and probably copied) from one quadrennium to the next. Even the unusual 1964 Republican document, though different in many respects from the 1960 platform, incorporated "as pledges renewed those commitments which are relevant to the problems of 1964."[10] We will confine our analysis to the first three major propositions on both voter and party responsibility, as revealed in the twelve major party platforms of the postwar period.

The method used for this purpose is content analysis. "Content analysis is a term used to describe a wide variety of research techniques, all of which are used for systematically collecting, analyzing, and making inferences from messages."[11] The purpose of these methods is to reduce the multiplicity and ambiguity of verbal communications to a relatively small number of comparable categories. Quantitative techniques can then be applied to reveal patterns and trends. There are three major steps in this technique: (1) Selecting a unit of analysis; (2) estab-

[9] The platforms were obtained in Kirk H. Porter and Donald B. Johnson, *National Party Platforms, 1840–1964* (Urbana: University of Illinois Press, 1966).

[10] *Ibid.*, p. 683.

[11] Robert C. North *et al.*, *Content Analysis* (Evanston: Northwestern University Press, 1963), p. 50.

lishing categories; and (3) providing clear standards for classification within these categories.[12]

The unit of analysis selected here is the sentence in the platform. (In other cases, words, or paragraphs, or inches of printed material might be used.) Where distinct ideas are included in a compound sentence, each idea is counted separately, and transitional sentences are excluded. There are some possible distortions in this method, for important qualitative differences may be disregarded. One sentence explicitly pledging "We will repeal the draft" is considered equal to one of vague rhetoric, such as, "America is the land of opportunity." College students would probably dispute the equivalence. These distortions are acceptable, however, for pledges tend to be short, and rhetoric to be long-winded. We are therefore making it more difficult to show policy significance in platforms.

Each sentence was placed in one of three principal categories, which were then further divided into eleven minor categories. These categories follow the typical organization of platforms, which proceed from the general to the specific, and from discussion of the past to proposals for future action. The categories used are listed below, together with examples from the 1964 platforms.[13] Specific standards of definition will be found in the Appendix.

1. *Rhetoric and Fact*

   "The American free enterprise system is one of the great achievements of the human mind and spirit." (Dem.)

[12] Content analysis is discussed further in Bernard Berelson, *Content Analysis in Communications Research* (Glencoe: The Free Press, 1962); and Ithiel de Sola Pool, *Trends in Content Analysis* (Urbana: University of Illinois Press, 1959). Among recent works using this method in the study of American politics are: Elmer E. Cornwell, *Presidential Leadership of Public Opinion* (Bloomington: Indiana University Press, 1965); John W. Ellsworth, "Rationality and Campaigning: A Content Analysis of the 1960 Presidential Campaign Debates," *Western Political Quarterly*, Vol. 18 (December, 1965), pp. 794–802; and Ira Sharkansky, "Four Agencies and an Appropriations Subcommittee," *Midwest Journal of Political Science*, Vol. IX (August, 1965), pp. 254–81.

[13] Porter and Johnson, pp. 641–90, *passim*.

"It is a high mission of government to help assure equal opportunity for all." (Rep.)

2. *Evaluations of the Parties' Records and Past Performances*
   - *(a) General Approval*
     "The many achievements of the Eisenhower Administration in strengthening peace abroad and the well-being of all at home have been unmatched in recent times." (Rep.)
   - *(b) General Criticism*
     "At the onset of 1961, America was in the depths of the fourth postwar recession." (Dem.)
   - *(c) Policy Approval*
     "In the Nuclear Test Ban Treaty, we have written our commitment to limitations on the arms race." (Dem.)
   - *(d) Policy Criticism*
     "[The Administration] has burdened this nation with four unbalanced budgets in a row, creating deficits totaling $26 billion." (Rep.)

3. *Statements of Future Policies*

There are six minor categories, intended to be arranged in increasing order of commitment and specificity. A rational voter should find it increasingly easy to understand the party's intentions as he progressed through the pledges in the different categories.

- *(a) Rhetorical Pledges*
  "We pledge wise, firm and responsible conduct of the nation's foreign affairs." (Rep.)
- *(b) General Pledges*
  "The antitrust laws must be vigorously enforced." (Dem.)
- *(c) Pledges of Continuity*
  "We pledge continued Federal support for a sound research program aimed at both the prevention and cure of diseases." (Rep.)
- *(d) Expressions of Goals and Concerns*
  "We will encourage the resettlement of Arab refugees in

lands where there is room and opportunity." (Dem.)

(e) Pledges of Action

"We pledge tax incentives to encourage modernization of fishing vessels." (Rep.)

(f) Detailed Pledges

"The security of American trade unions must be strengthened by repealing section 14(b) of the Taft-Hartley Act." (Dem.)

The pledges of future action were also classified separately by topic, as well as by content. Nine policy areas were distinguished and are detailed in the Appendix. The topics are: (1) foreign policy, (2) defense, (3) economic policy, (4) labor, (5) agriculture, (6) resources, (7) social welfare, (8) government, and (9) civil rights and ethnic policy.

JUDGMENTS OF THE PARTY RECORDS

We are now able to assess the rational quality of platforms. A basic concern of voters is the past performance of the parties. In judging the "nature of the times" a party manifesto which consisted only of rhetoric would be of little help to the electorate. It would derive more benefit from the documents if they concentrated on evaluations of the parties, particularly the incumbents' record of performance. Table 7.1 summarizes the percentage distribution of platform statements, with evaluations of the parties' records further subdivided into the four minor categories.[14] This distribution of platform statements indicates a greater contribution to voter-rationality than is commonly supposed. Platforms are not principally vague paeans to God, mother, and country. The first category, including factual state-

[14] In 1964, the Democrats issued two platforms. The first was a conventional platform, the second a long "Accounting of Stewardship, 1960–1964," detailing and praising the record of the Kennedy-Johnson administration, and comparing its achievements to the platform promises of 1960. Because of this separation, the percentage of statements of policy approval is markedly above normal, and that for future policies is markedly below normal. If the first platform alone is analyzed, the percentages, reading vertically in Table 7.1, would be: 25, 7, 2, 8, 1, 56.

Table 7.1 Content Distribution of Party Platforms
(In Percentages of Designated Platform)*

	Dem. 1944	*Rep. 1944*	*Dem. 1948*	*Rep. 1948*	*Dem. 1952*	*Rep. 1952*	*Dem. 1956*	*Rep. 1956*	*Dem. 1960*	*Rep. 1960*	*Dem. 1964*	*Rep. 1964*
Category												
Rhetoric	22	11	12	23	18	9	14	15	20	21	20	11
Evaluations												
General Approval	23	3	11	3	11	3	5	15	4	7	14	5
General Criticism	0	7	3	4	1	18	11	4	7	1	1	12
Policy Approval	13	2	10	8	16	11	9	26	4	13	48	2
Policy Criticism	0	10	8	1	3	14	17	2	11	1	1	25
Future Policy	42	68	56	61	51	45	44	38	53	56	15	44
Number of Statements	92	177	205	159	419	345	596	538	795	519	941	414

* Percentages add vertically to 100%, except for variations due to rounding. Percentages are of the number of statements in each platform.

ments as well as "hot air," always comprises less than a quarter of all statements, and the average is approximately one of six statements.

Two of every five platform statements represent evaluations of the parties' records, providing abundant material for those crucial voters who cast their ballots on the basis of past performance. In their manifestos, the parties respond to the electorate's concern for past performance. The patterns in this general category are further indications of the rational character of the platforms. Statements relating to policy actions always predominate over general approvals and criticisms. This pattern holds for each party in each of the six election years. In reading the platform, therefore, the citizen would be able to make comparisons of the parties on the basis of the issues and actions of the preceding period. Its relatively specific statements on past policy also commit a party to future action.

The discussion of the past centers around the actions of the incumbent party in the White House. Less attention is given the actions of the party out of the Presidency, even when it controls Congress, as in 1948 and 1956–60. In Figure 5, we compare the approvals and criticisms of the incumbents and their opponents. The frequencies of platform statements assume the following order: approvals by the in-party, criticisms by the out-party, approvals by the out-party, and criticisms by the in-party. The debate is one over the record of the executive party. It is not a contrast between two different sets of policies argued during the past four years.[15] A further indication of the emphasis

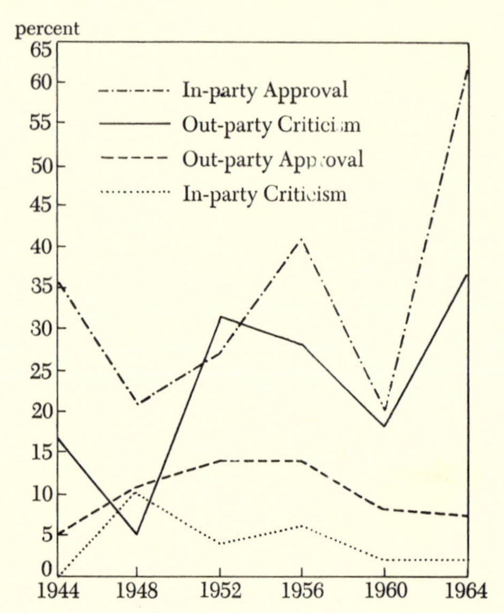

Figure 5. Distribution of Platform Statements on Parties' Records

on the in-party's record is the greater frequency with which the in-party makes any policy evaluations, whether approving or disapproving. These patterns are in accord with the voters' own emphasis on the incumbents' record, as discussed in chapter IV.

[15] The only important exception to this ordering comes in the 1948 Republican platform, where the party disdainfully declared, "We shall waste few words on the tragic lack of foresight and general inadequacy of the Democrats; they have lost the confidence of all parties"—Porter and Johnson, p. 451. In 1948, it may be recalled, the Republicans were so certain of victory that they allocated Cabinet positions before the election. Their platform, perhaps, is therefore more typical of an in-party. More typical behavior is described by Cooke, p. 706, who reports that the incumbent Democrats in 1952 deliberately discarded statements critical of the opposition from the original platform drafts, and instead concentrated on approval of their own records.

A focus on the record of the incumbents is further promoted by the nature of the American political system. Presidential government and the lack of an authoritative spokesman for the other party focus attention on the chief executive's program. A two-party system, moreover, tends to reduce political conflict to a simple alternative of continuity or change in present policies without equal consideration of the opposition's alternatives. It is also simpler to concentrate on the known record of the incumbents than on the hypothetical performance of the opposition.

Platforms also serve the cause of party-rationality. Democrats and Republicans anticipate the voters' reactions in their campaigning, seeking to emphasize electoral perceptions of partisan benefit. Without direct control, the voters are thereby influencing politicians' behavior. The distribution of statements is not random but in accord with the apparent strategy of each party in the campaign. Three platforms, illustratively, are prominent in the emphasis given to statements of rhetoric and general approval of the party: the Democratic in 1944, the Republican in 1956, and the Democratic again in 1964. In each, the party attempted (successfully) to win on the strength of the personal popularity of the incumbent. In each year, the opposition party presented a sharply contrasting platform, emphasizing partisan and policy criticism, and future policies. Accepting the incumbent's popularity, the opposition sought to shift the focus of the campaign.

Parties also devote varying proportions of their platforms to evaluations of the past, depending on the course deemed most likely to succeed. Opinion polls provide some guide to public sentiment and the likely outcome of the election. If the record of the party has been well-received and victory seems likely, it will tend to emphasize that record. If the public is dissatisfied with past action, even if the record is "objectively" good, the rational course for the party is clearly to neglect the "nature of the times" and make more promises or resort to vagueness.

The distributions of platform statements conforms to these expectations of party strategy. In the elections of 1944, 1952, 1956, and 1964 the winner was predicted early in the campaign. The underdogs, possibly in an attempt to overcome their disadvantage, put less emphasis on their record and more on what they would do in the future. The 1960 election was generally expected to be close, and the distribution of platform statements was similar for the two parties. In 1948, an exception, the Democrats were universally expected to lose, but still stressed the past record more than the Republicans. This discrepancy was offset by the greater specificity of Democratic pledges, discussed below.

FUTURE PLEDGES IN PLATFORMS

The future pledges in platforms can also be examined to assess their contribution to rationality. Voter-rationality and indirect policy influence would be promoted if the large proportion of citizens concerned with group benefits could find some guide to these benefits in the platforms. Alternately, by making meaningful promises of future action, the parties would be initiating proposals to protect the electorate's vital interests. Victory for the party would then mean endorsement as well of a set of programs.

Analysis of the 2,245 future pledges in the twelve platforms reveals some meaningful patterns. The topical distribution, presented in Table 7.2, is largely the result of the definition of the topics. There is a concentration in the areas of foreign policy, economic policy, and social welfare, because these topics are broadly defined. Variations among the topics are more significant and reveal the responsiveness of the parties to voter concerns. Over the two decades, there has been a definite decline in the attention given to issues of general economic policy and to agriculture, an indication of the decreasing salience of the New Deal ideological division between the parties, and of the reduced political importance of the farm vote. Greater stress has come to be placed on issues of defense and welfare, as they have become more important to the voters and more politically profitable to the parties.

The degree of specificity evident in future pledges varies considerably among topics and platforms. The content distribution of future pledges is presented in Tables 7.3 and 7.4. An inspection of the two tables demonstrates that, although there

Table 7.2 Topical Distribution of Future Pledges, by Platforms

(In Percentages of Designated Platform)*

Topic	*Dem. 1944*	*Rep. 1944*	*Dem. 1948*	*Rep. 1948*	*Dem. 1952*	*Rep. 1952*	*Dem. 1956*	*Rep. 1956*	*Dem. 1960*	*Rep. 1960*	*Dem. 1964*	*Rep. 1964*	*Total*	*(N)*
Foreign	18	17	18	22	15	19	13	15	19	14	11	26	*17*	(378)
Defense	8	6	5	6	4	8	4	10	4	10	10	20	*7*	(170)
Economics	23	18	17	20	16	12	12	15	15	14	13	11	*15*	(328)
Labor	5	9	7	2	4	2	6	5	5	5	11	3	*5*	(115)
Agriculture	18	14	12	7	11	10	12	17	7	9	6	7	*10*	(226)
Resources	8	11	10	9	14	14	16	11	13	8	9	5	*11*	(257)
Welfare	8	8	17	12	17	10	17	6	18	19	24	8	*15*	(335)
Government	8	11	8	17	8	17	11	12	10	10	8	13	*11*	(246)
Civil Rights	5	7	6	5	11	8	11	8	7	11	8	7	*9*	(190)
Number of Pledges	39	120	114	97	213	154	261	205	425	289	145	183		(2,245)

* Percentages add vertically to 100%, except for variations due to rounding. Percentages are of the number of pledges in each platform.

Table 7.3 Content Distribution of Future Pledges, by Topics

(In Percentages of Designated Topic)*

Category	*Foreign*	*Defense*	*Economic*	*Labor*	*Agriculture*	*Resource*	*Welfare*	*Government*	*Civil Rights*	*Total, (N)*
Rhetorical	31	25	15	6	17	10	13	29	25	*20* (438)
General	12	26	31	21	17	18	12	16	15	*18* (408)
Continuity	15	12	9	4	18	11	9	4	8	*11* (241)
Goals	16	11	17	17	13	18	17	22	18	*17* (377)
Actions	15	18	13	30	20	24	26	16	19	*19* (434)
Details	11	9	14	23	15	18	23	14	14	*15* (347)
N Topic	378	170	328	115	226	257	335	246	190	(2,245)

* Percentages add vertically to 100%, except for variations due to rounding.

Table 7.4 Content Distribution of Future Pledges, by Platforms
(In Percentages of Designated Platform)*

Category	Dem. 1944	Rep. 1944	Dem. 1948	Rep. 1948	Dem. 1952	Rep. 1952	Dem. 1956	Rep. 1956	Dem. 1960	Rep. 1960	Dem. 1964	Rep. 1964	Total	(N)
Rhetorical	18	23	11	20	22	30	18	23	22	12	17	16	*20*	(438)
General	23	11	19	34	20	16	16	13	16	18	21	22	*18*	(408)
Continuity	8	4	15	4	15	4	13	21	7	12	16	6	*11*	(241)
Goals	26	24	7	16	8	19	14	16	19	22	19	15	*17*	(377)
Actions	20	18	24	21	23	20	22	14	18	17	16	23	*19*	(434)
Details	5	19	24	5	11	11	16	13	18	19	11	17	*15*	(347)
N Platform	39	120	114	97	213	154	261	205	425	289	145	183		(2,245)

* Percentages add vertically to 100%, except for variations due to rounding.

are many rhetorical and vague statements, a majority of pledges almost invariably fall in the four more specific categories, giving some meaningful guide to future action. It is also apparent that the degree of specificity varies by topic and platform. To make comparisons simple, it is helpful to have a single measure of specificity.

A "pledge weight" has been constructed for this purpose. This figure is simply a weighted average of the pledges in any platform and topic.[16] If all pledges were rhetorical, the figure would be 1.0. If all promises were detailed, it would be 6.0. The average for all pledges is actually 3.4. The data are presented in Table 7.5.

This measure shows platform pledges to be politically rational. Specificity in platform pledges is particularly conducive to voting on the basis of promised group benefits, the most common criterion employed by the voters. The parties in turn construct

[16] The method is simple. The content categories, from "rhetorical" to "detailed," are assigned arbitrary weights from 1 to 6. The number of pledges in each category is then multiplied by the appropriate weight, and the total of the products is divided by the total number of statements. Algebraically, f_1, f_2, etc., being the number of pledges in each category:

$$\text{“Pledge Weight”} = \frac{\Sigma f_1 + 2f_2 + 3f_3 + 4f_4 + 5f_5 + 6f_6}{N}$$

Table 7.5 "Pledge Weights," by Topics and Platforms

Topic	*Dem. 1944*	*Rep. 1944*	*Dem. 1948*	*Rep. 1948*	*Dem. 1952*	*Rep. 1952*	*Dem. 1956*	*Rep. 1956*	*Dem. 1960*	*Rep. 1960*	*Dem. 1964*	*Rep. 1964*	*Topic Mean*	*(N)*
Foreign	3.8	2.4	3.8	2.2	2.9	2.5	3.2	3.3	2.8	3.0	3.5	3.7	*3.0*	(378)
Defense	3.7	2.6	2.2	3.0	1.5	2.0	3.3	2.9	3.3	3.3	2.9	3.5	*3.0*	(170)
Economic	2.4	3.9	2.4	2.7	2.9	2.8	3.4	3.5	3.5	3.4	2.4	3.3	*3.2*	(328)
Labor	3.5	3.4	5.2	3.0	4.1	4.3	4.9	3.9	3.9	4.0	3.8	3.8	*4.1*	(115)
Agriculture	3.4	3.8	3.9	3.0	3.3	3.9	3.8	2.9	3.2	3.8	3.7	3.9	*3.5*	(226)
Resources	3.0	4.5	4.2	4.0	3.4	4.1	3.3	3.3	3.9	4.1	3.8	4.0	*3.8*	(257)
Welfare	3.3	4.0	4.6	3.3	4.1	3.6	4.3	3.6	4.2	4.2	3.3	4.4	*4.0*	(335)
Government	3.3	3.8	2.7	3.0	2.8	3.1	2.8	3.8	3.0	3.7	2.9	3.0	*3.2*	(246)
Civil Rights	3.0	4.0	4.7	4.4	3.0	3.3	2.6	2.7	3.8	4.1	2.8	2.2	*3.3*	(190)
Platform Mean	*3.2*	*3.6*	*4.0*	*3.0*	*3.2*	*3.2*	*3.6*	*3.2*	*3.5*	*3.7*	*3.3*	*3.6*	*3.4*	(2,245)
N Platform	39	120	114	97	213	154	261	205	425	289	145	183		2,245

their platforms in order to appeal to these popular interests.

There are two distinct groups of topics, as measured by the "pledge weight." There is a relatively low degree of specificity in the areas of foreign, defense, and economic policy, and of government and civil rights. Labor, resources, and welfare evidence more detailed promises, and agriculture tends in the same direction. These clusters are significant, for they reflect the voters' knowledge and interests and the parties' attempts to respond to the concerns of the voters.

On topics in the first group, the voter is likely to be uninformed. Vague platform pledges are a sufficient appeal in these cases. In the second group of topics, however, voters are more likely to be knowledgeable. Pledges dealing with these topics consequently must be specific to convince the electorate. The gains to be obtained from a given foreign policy, for example, are usually cloudy, but a "senior citizen" is apt to have the skill of an actuary in calculating the advantage of a change in old-age retirement provisions. Parties respond to these differences by being more or less explicit in their promises.

Variations in specificity are also related to the voters' interests and political perceptions. We have learned that relatively few voters are concerned with issues of general policy or ideology.[17] Platform provisions dealing with such issues are likely to receive less popular attention. While the topics evidencing low specificity are of general importance, the special advantage to particular individuals or groups is uncertain. Thus, all voters certainly gain from a successful foreign policy, or honest government, but the advantage to a particular voter is difficult to see. The benefits are general, or "nondistributive" to individuals. In the absence of some obvious failure, a voter need not be too concerned about party policy in these areas. The social benefits of government action will probably occur without his attention, and he will gain as much as others. Since voters are not apt to be concerned about these topics, the parties need be less concerned about popular reactions and can resort to vagueness.

A minority of voters, however, are concerned with general questions. Pledges even to these voters need not be specific. The satisfactions to voters in such cases are psychic and ideological, not personal, and promises to them can be hazy but still effective in winning their loyalty. If a voter considers foreign policy, defense, or economic issues important, he is likely to be satisfied with general commitments such as mutual security, American nuclear superiority, or maintenance of the free-enterprise system.[18]

The bulk of the electorate is concerned with narrower policies and group benefits. Republican and Democratic candidates are evaluated according to the particular or "distributive" benefits they seem to offer farmers, workers, or businessmen. Pledges to win these voters must be specific to be effective. The advantages of higher minimum wages to a worker or of depletion

[17] See Angus Campbell *et al.*, *The American Voter* (New York: Wiley, 1960), and chapter IV, *supra.*

[18] A similar analysis is applied to incentives in organizations by Peter B. Clark and James Q. Wilson, "Incentive Systems: A Theory of Organization," *Administrative Science Quarterly*, Vol. 6 (September, 1961), pp. 129–66; and by Wilson in *The Amateur Democrat* (Chicago: University of Chicago Press, 1962).

allowances to an oil company are quite definite. They are of decided interest to those affected and are likely to have a direct influence on their electoral decisions.[19]

The parties respond to the particular interests of the voters by including specific pledges on these topics in their platforms. Such pledges are the documentary expression of their concern for popular needs. Not all, but some voters are likely to become aware of these pledges. Evasive statements are difficult in regard to distributive benefits. Because of the importance of these pledges to those involved, they will be more knowledgeable about the topic and able to demand more from the parties. The writers of the campaign manifesto will act to win this support, even anticipating group demands before they arise. Moreover, an organized interest group is likely to exist, making explicit demands on the party's platform drafters, who in turn are quite receptive to any group with a plausible claim on voter loyalties. For all of these reasons, specificity increases on those issues of distributive benefit. Voters indirectly affect policy through partisan pledges of group gains.

Even within the topics of relatively low specificity, there are some more detailed pledges. It seems significant that these latter pledges also tend to emphasize distributive benefits, their focus evidently on a specific group. Thus, half of the foreign policy pledges in 1948, in the third through sixth categories, and large proportions in later years, deal with United States relations toward Israel, in obvious attempts to win the votes of American Jews. Specific pledges on defense or government often relate to the living or working conditions of servicemen or civil servants, rather than the broader issues within the policy area. Similarly, specific economic pledges are directed toward discrete groups, such as shipbuilders, small businessmen,

[19] For similar reasons, Downs, pp. 254–56, observes that the tangible interests of producers are likely to be preferred in democratic government over the more generalized interests of consumers.

airlines, or retailers. More basic issues of government regulation of the economy are dealt with vaguely.

Party strategy also accounts for these differences in specificity, as campaigners react to their perceptions of the electorate. The rational party will specifically support any policy definitely favored by a majority of voters or by an unopposed minority, while it will be less specific when it deals with issues on which voter opinion is unknown, unimportant, or divided. The issues on which we have found low specificity are of the latter variety. Aside from ideological positions, there is no clear consensus among American voters on issues such as foreign policy, economic controls, and government. On other questions, such as territorial government, the group affected is politically unimportant. In another group of issues, such as regulation of the economy, opinion exists but is divided. In all of these cases, a political party will commonly seek to appeal to all views, the necessary result being an unspecific pledge.

However, even within policy areas of low specificity, some pledges will be detailed, where an apparent majority opinion exists or where there is an unopposed minority. Although foreign policy planks tend to be vague, both parties have specifically and continuously pledged nonrecognition of Communist China in the belief this was the strong preference of a voting majority. Similarly, voter opinion since 1944 has clearly favored the social security system. Acting rationally in response to a majority preference, both parties have continuously pledged highly specific improvements in benefits. On issues such as agriculture and resources, or support of Israel, a highly interested minority has not been strongly opposed, and party pledges could be relatively precise.

Labor represents a different case. Pledges on this topic are highly specific even though opinion is often strong and conflicting. Specificity here is the result of the alliance of each of the parties to one or the other of the opposing camps. The Democratic identification with labor unions, and Republican estrangement, has been so strong that neither party has attempted to muddle its positions on these issues.[20]

Civil rights is a unique topic. The "pledge weight" here lies between the two groups, although closer to that of lower precision. The variation in specificity from one election to the other, however, is extremely high, indicating its unusual character. As an issue, civil rights is peculiarly tangible as well as ideological, involving both distributive and general benefits. Some voters may be satisfied with imprecise statements, such as praise of equality; others demand detailed pledges, such as the abolition of literacy tests for voting. Neither the nature of the subject nor the expectations of the voter provide a sure guide to the parties.

Civil rights is also peculiar in the nature of voter opinion on the subject, and the consequent influences on party strategy. Aside from a shared ideological commitment to "equality," citizens have been divided and have felt more intensively on both sides of this issue than on any other topic.[21] Parties can attempt to appeal to both sides by taking an ambiguous position. Thus, in reacting in 1956 to the school desegregation decisions, the Democrats merely recognized "the Supreme Court of the United States as one of the three Constitutional and coordinate branches of the Federal Government," while the Republicans were so bold as to declare that "the supreme law of the land is embodied in the Constitution, which guarantees to all persons the blessings of liberty, due process and equal protection of the laws."[22]

[20] Cooke, p. 704, notes the different reception given to labor and business representatives in the platform-drafting committees. The difference between the parties on issues of labor regulation is also evident in Congress. On the House vote to repeal section 14 (b) of the Taft-Hartley Act, the Democrats voted in favor, 200 to 86, while the Republicans were opposed, 117 to 21: *Congressional Record*, Vol. 111, 89th Cong., 1st sess. (July 28, 1965), p. 18646.

[21] See Herbert McClosky, "Consensus and Ideology in American Politics," *American Political Science Review*, Vol. LVIII (June, 1964), pp. 361–82; William Brink and Louis Harris, *Black and White* (New York: Simon and Schuster, 1967).

[22] Porter and Johnson, pp. 542, 554.

However, because opinion is so intense, a party can also attempt to win a "passionate minority" to its side by clearly endorsing its position. If one party takes a specific position, the most rational course for the other party is also to take a precise position, or else lose votes from both sides. Thus, in 1948 and 1960, both parties took highly detailed and similar stands on civil rights.[23] These similarities are further indications of the parties' rational attempt to capture votes on these issues and of the consequent indirect influence of voters on policy.

PARTY VARIATIONS

In the previous sections, we have seen that platforms often can serve as an aid to voter-rationality and thereby help to provide an indirect policy influence to elections. Platforms aid a retrospective judgment on past performance and provide indications to the voter of the benefits he may expect in the future, especially those benefits of a distributive character.

The actions of the party are crucial in providing these aids to the voter. In writing their platforms, the parties respond to the perceived political demands of the electorate. Both Democrats and Republicans adjust their strategy to the peculiarities of each election, evaluate the past records of the parties, and promise definite gains to identifiable interests. There are also variations between the parties in the specificity of their pledges. These differences also can be related to the parties' perceptions of the demands of the voters.

We have earlier found that the party trailing in a particular campaign tends to emphasize future pledges. Similarly, the party

[23] See Downs, pp. 55–56. If the two "passionate minorities" were of equal voting power, it would be rational for both parties to take specific but opposing positions. The stances of the candidates, but not the platforms, were such in 1964 on civil rights. The election results were in direct response to these strategies, Johnson winning 94 per cent of the Negro vote and Goldwater carrying five states of the Deep South. In electoral payoff, however, the former was more important and the Goldwater strategy was therefore irrational. Changing opinions on the issue—the "white backlash"—may lead to different strategies in the future.

expected to lose the presidential election is always more specific. It is as if the underdog, trailing in polls and predictions, attempts to win converts by making more detailed promises. The leading party needs only to protect its advantage, which can be done best by not antagonizing any group and by holding to relatively ambiguous positions. The best example of these presumptive strategies is the 1948 campaign, in which the two parties produced both the most and least specific platforms.

The Democrats under Truman, facing apparently inevitable defeat, perhaps attempted to recoup by a variety of explicit promises, particularly of distributive benefits. The Republicans and Dewey, confident of victory, suppressed controversy and stressed unity. Though the Democrats had a smaller proportion of pledges in the total platform, their promises were far more specific. The greater specificity of the likely losers is evident as well in 1944, 1952, 1956, and 1964. The relationship is less clear in 1960, when no winner could be predicted confidently in advance. Perhaps the greater precision of the Republican platform was due to Nixon's attempt, as a minority party candidate, to win crucial marginal support.[24]

Further variations attributable to party strategies may be sought by examining the stress placed on different topics. In seeking support through its pledges, a party could devote a larger proportion of its platform to those policy areas it believes politically profitable. A second tactic would be greater specificity in these pledges. To gain a general measure of the emphases of the parties, therefore, we must combine the adjusted percentage share of each policy area with its "pledge weight." The resulting figure is called an index of "attention." In general, this figure is comparable to the "pledge weight."

[24] Nelson Rockefeller's intervention persuaded Nixon to add several more specific sections to the platform. In judging the rational character of the platform, the significant point is that such provisions were considered necessary to Republican victory. See Karl Lamb, in Tillett, ed., chap. 6, and Theodore H. White, *The Making of the President 1960* (New York: Atheneum, 1961), chap. 6.

It can vary from 2.0, the lowest degree of specificity, to 7.0, the level of the most detailed pledges.[25]

The graphs of Figure 6 picture the "attention" given by the parties to the various topics. They also serve to summarize much of the previous discussion. Taken as a whole, the slope (upward or downward) of the graphs is an indication of the changing importance of different topics. Measured against the average of all indexes, 4.5, each graph also indicates the relative specificity of the topic depicted.

Party differences also become evident. Republicans are seen to place more emphasis on defense and governmental issues, and Democrats on labor and welfare. In the terms used earlier, the G.O.P. relies more on nondistributive benfits, whereas the Democratic emphasis is on those issues of differential significance to social groups and individuals. These variations are in accord with the images of the parties held by the voters. Although there have been some recent changes, Republicans have tended to be regarded as better managers of the government and to be more trusted on issues of war and peace. Democrats have been regarded more highly in terms of domestic policy and group benefits.[26] The parties emphasize their areas of strength. By responding to voter preferences, they again demonstrate the impact of elections on policy. Republican victory will mean more emphasis on nondistributive issues; Democratic success will bring particularistic gains.

In any given year, rather than all years, the parties usually differ in their relative emphasis, as each stresses those topics it

[25] The percentage devoted to each topic is greatly dependent on the way in which the categories have been constructed. To adjust the percentage in a given year, we divide it by the percentage devoted to that topic in all years. If no particular emphasis is placed on this topic in the given year, the resulting ratio will be 1. Increased or decreased emphasis will be reflected in ratios, above or below 1. This ratio is then added to the "pledge weight" for that year to obtain the index of "attention."

[26] *The American Voter*, chap. 3. Increased support for the 1964 Democrats on foreign policy questions and reduced support on issues of group benefits are shown in Donald E. Stokes, "Some Dynamic Elements of Contests for the Presidency," *American Political Science Review*, Vol. LX (March, 1966), pp. 19–28. Further changes are likely in 1968.

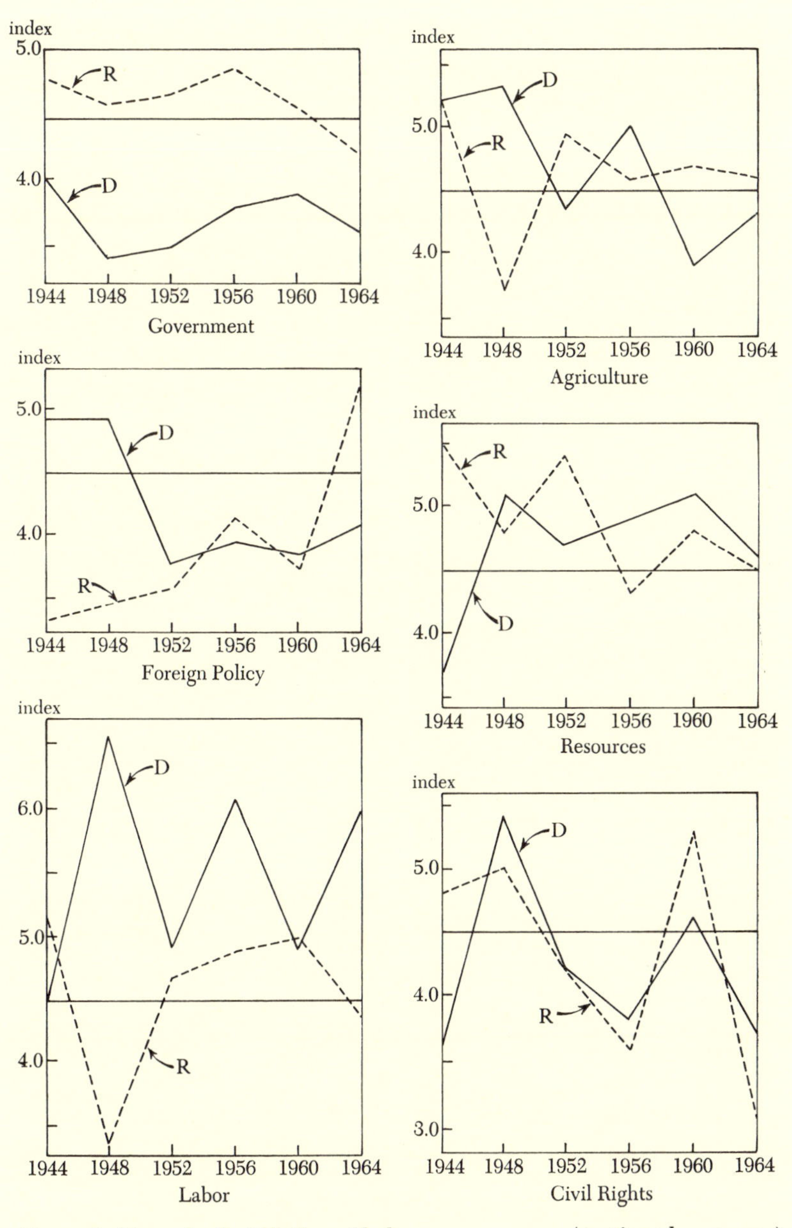

Figure 6. "Attention" of Platform Pledges **(continued next page)**

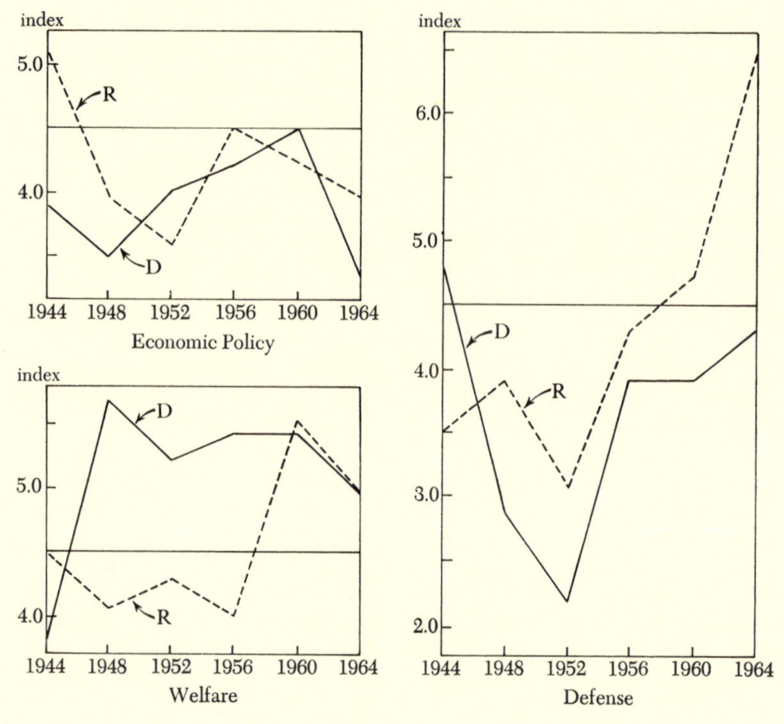

Figure 6 (cont.). "Attention" of Platform Pledges

finds to its advantage. A party's stress is related to its campaign strategy in a particular election. Thus, the Democrats were attentive in their 1944 pledges to foreign and military questions in an effort to win support on the basis of their wartime leadership. The alleged evils of the Taft-Hartley Act occasioned stress on labor in the 1948 Democratic manifesto, while the Republicans that year and in 1952 were concerned with the conduct of government, in reaction to the alleged Democratic "mess in Washington."

The Republican campaign of 1964 differed from past patterns. Some particular pledges of the past were discarded. High levels of specificity were achieved in six of the nine topics. Moreover, the amount of attention devoted to different subjects was quite at variance with the past. Less attention was devoted to all forms of distributive benefits than in 1960, and the civil rights plank drew the least notice of all twelve studied.[27] Foreign policy and defense questions reached unequaled levels of both percentage of the total platform (a combined total of 46 per cent) and "attention" (5.2 and 6.4, respectively). This platform, like the Goldwater campaign, may have been directed either at previous nonvoters who might be stirred by a changed content, or at creating a winning coalition of "passionate minorities," each willing to support the party on the basis of its most intense beliefs.[28] The measurement of "attention" thus confirms the peculiar character of the 1964 Republican effort.

THE INFLUENCE OF PLATFORMS

We have attempted to gauge the contribution platforms make to voter-rationality and party-rationality. Platforms can aid the voter's retrospective judgment and his quest for governmental benefits. They include considerable discussion of policy questions, often with a meaningful degree of specificity. They also include, however, a great share of rhetoric and vagueness. As a summary measure of voter-rationality in platforms, it is useful to combine categories. Rhetorical statements, general approvals and criticisms, and rhetorical or general pledges will be considered "nonrational" elements in the platform (from the voter's viewpoint). The remaining statements, since they have some meaningful content, will be considered "rational." Of the twelve platforms, as indicated in Table 7.6, only four had a majority of "nonrational" statements. The distribution between these two

[27] Civil rights drew little notice only in the platforms adopted. Of course, it drew considerable attention in the convention and in the campaign. As an indication of G.O.P. strategy, however, the low index of attention is the significant finding.

[28] On the 1964 Republican effort, see Richard Rovere, *The Goldwater Caper* (New York: Harcourt, Brace & World, 1965), and John Kessel, *The Goldwater Coalition: Republican Strategies in 1964* (Indianapolis: Bobbs-Merrill, 1968).

groupings is fairly constant over time, with most platforms tending toward a slight predominance of "rational" statements. Although much in platforms is not helpful to the rational voter, there would appear to be sufficient material to help him to make an informed choice.

Table 7.6 Percentage Distribution of All Platform Statements

	Dem. 1944	*Rep. 1944*	*Dem. 1948*	*Rep. 1948*	*Dem. 1952*	*Rep. 1952*	*Dem. 1956*	*Rep. 1956*	*Dem. 1960*	*Rep. 1960*	*Dem. 1964*	*Rep. 1964*	*Total*
"Rational"	38	56	57	38	48	50	55	52	48	54	59	55	*52*
"Nonrational"	62	44	43	62	52	50	45	48	52	46	41	45	*48*

In judging the past records of the parties, platforms are again of partial assistance. The record of the incumbent party, the one more crucial to the voter, is roundly debated, and this debate is conducted principally in terms of policy actions. The alternative policies of the opposition, however, are not given the same consideration. A rational choice on the basis of the incumbents' record is facilitated, but a true comparison of the two parties is not feasible.

The parties present rather full descriptions of their future policy objectives and intentions and tend to be relatively specific. Their future pledges are most explicit in those policy areas, involving distributive benefits, of most interest to voters with limited time and knowledge. The platforms also match the images voters hold of the parties in terms of "group benefits" and the "nature of the times," the most common voter conceptions. They are therefore a contribution to voter-rationality. However, the parties do not stress the same issues in most elections, and direct comparison of their positions becomes difficult. Although not overwhelming, the considerable proportion of meaningless pledges is also an impediment to the voter.

The platforms fall short of the full standards of voter-rationality because they are party instruments, serving the cause of party-rationality. The content of the platform varies with the strategy of the party. A policy emphasis and specificity in future pledges is sometimes consonant with partisan success. In such cases, platforms serve both party-rationality and voter-rationality. At other times, when a party is relying on the personality of its candidate, the party loyalty of the voters, or an apparent tide in its favor, it will have less cause to detail its policy actions and intentions.

In choosing their issues, parties act rationally, emphasizing the policy areas of their strength and neglecting the strong points of their opponents. They tend to be specific on these issues of direct, distributive benefit to the voters and to resort to rhetoric or vagueness where the voters are unclear, uninterested, or divided. Policies favored by a majority of the voters are endorsed by the parties, as are those supported by an unopposed minority. Where opposing minorities exist, the party rationally evades a policy choice. The parties do not often disregard majority preferences in an appeal to "passionate minorities." When they do make such appeals, as in civil rights, the parties are likely to imitate one another in the specificity and direction of pledges. These responses probably contribute to political stability by deemphasizing the most intense social conflicts.[29]

Rationality is evident in platforms. They provide one means by which a party can pursue victory while serving popular interests. To be sure, convention delegates do not consciously consider platforms in these terms, or calculate "pledge weights." The significant finding, however, is that there are logical explanations to behavior which outwardly resembles only a circus —and one at which all the animal cages have been unlocked.[30] Similarly, platforms promote voter-rationality, although it would be foolish to claim that more than a small minority reads the entire document. The statements made in the platform reach the voter less directly, through interest groups, mass media, candi-

[29] See Dahl, pp. 90–105.

[30] For an analysis of the logic of national nominating conventions, see Nelson Polsky and Aaron Wildavsky, *Presidential Elections*, 2nd ed. (New York: Scribners, 1968), chap. 2.

dates' speeches, party controversy, and incomplete popular perceptions. A campaign is a contest for incremental votes, not for total support, and the platform is one of the means by which marginal voters make decisions. Interested "issue publics" may become aware of salient points, and an alleged broken promise may affect voters of even limited conceptual insight sufficiently to turn an election.[31] Even if the electorate does not read it, the platform functions to shape future action. The party becomes identified with certain policies, although all voters do not recognize the identification. In foreseeing the interests of voters and making appeals to these interests, the parties provide an indirect means of electoral influence on policy. Voters do not control government, but parties are restrained in their actions by their need to win votes.

The platform is a campaign document. Its characteristics are rationally derived from the party's goal of victory. In order to win elections, the party must also promote, in part, the cause of voter-rationality. The attention to the presumed interests of voting groups in the platforms provides a policy significance to elections. These documents are reasonably meaningful indications of the party's intentions. By their strictures about the past and pledges for the future, a party becomes committed to particular policies. The voter, by conferring legitimacy on these programs, intervenes significantly in the process of government. Platforms provide assistance to voters and indirect policy influences on the parties. Platforms indeed are to run on, not to stand on—but they also can reflect and affect the pace, direction, winner, and meaning of the race.

[31] See Philip E. Converse, "The Nature of Belief Systems in Mass Publics," in David E. Apter, ed., *Ideology and Discontent* (London: The Free Press, 1964), pp. 245–46; *The American Voter*, pp. 234–49.

CHAPTER 8

THE FULFILLMENT OF PLATFORMS

THE PROOF of the pudding remains in the eating. It may be true that platforms are prepared well, consist of the right ingredients in proper proportions, and seem palatable to the voters. But, how are they digested? After the elections, do platforms prove to be attractive but insubstantial, like empty pastry shells, or is there some filling inside?

Indirect influence of voters on public policy is possible if two conditions are met. First, there must be some meaningful identification of parties with specific programs. The evidence of the last chapter indicates that this condition is generally satisfied. Second, the parties must fulfill their pledges to a reasonable extent. The platforms would be useless to voters in promoting their specialized interests unless the party documents actually presaged action. Similarly, the parties would not be truly anticipating and meeting voter needs if their pledges were unredeemed. Popular support of a party is a meaningful intervention only when this support has observable policy consequences.[1] In this

[1] Performance of pledges is also necessary to achieve both party-rationality and voter-rationality, as discussed in the last chapter. See pp. 153–54, *supra*, and Anthony Downs, *An Economic Theory of Democracy* (New York: Harper, 1957), pp. 103–9.

chapter, we will examine the parties' performance on their pledges. A high degree of fulfillment of platforms will be a further indication of the indirect effects of elections.

Platforms are usually considered unrelated to government action. As David Truman authoritatively writes, "The platform is generally regarded as a document that says little, binds no one, and is forgotten by politicians as quickly as possible after it is adopted. . . . Considered as a pledge of future action, the party platform is almost meaningless and is properly so regarded by the voters."[2] Since platforms are allegedly unimportant, much of the effort to reform our parties has been directed toward increasing their importance and the degree of fulfillment.[3]

There are many reasons to expect platforms to be disregarded. Written as electoral documents, they are obviously different from a legislative program. Often, platforms represent only the view of the victorious faction at a national convention. Opponents may be defeated at the convention, but still retain the power to block implementation of party promises. The many checks and balances of American government are a further restriction on platform fulfillment.

Given these obstacles, it is noteworthy that politicians do in fact devote some attention to their platforms. In House debate on the Medicare bill in 1965, for example, party spokesmen agreed that election commitments had decided the issue. Democrat Ray Madden concluded, "The greatest testimonial for this legislation, coupled with the educational legislation passed several weeks ago, was the returns of the recent election of November 5, 1964. By a majority of over 15 million, President Johnson and Vice-President Humphrey won an unprecedented victory

[2] *The Governmental Process* (New York: Knopf, 1951), pp. 282–83.

[3] See American Political Science Association, Committee on Political Parties, "Toward a More Responsible Two-Party System," *American Political Science Review*, Vol. XLIV (September, 1950), Supplement. Proposals made in this report include biennial conventions, shorter platforms, a small party council to interpret the document, and mandatory acceptance of platform pledges by party candidates.

and the principal plank in their platform was education and medicare."

Regretfully, Republican Thomas Curtis agreed to the potency of platform pledges: "It is obvious that this House is not in a mood to deliberate. The decision which was made outside of the well of the House, outside the deliberative process, is going to prevail. . . . Is it not obvious, Mr. Chairman, what has happened? The Congress of the United States has become a rubber-stamp."[4] A party victory in the 1964 election was interpreted as an endorsement of party program. Indirect voter influence over policy was achieved.

Platforms are also used as standards by which parties approvingly measure their own performance and condemn that of the opposition. A generation of Republican speeches has been based on a comparison of New Deal deficit spending to the Democrats' 1932 promises to reduce federal expenditures and balance the budget. More recently, Democrats have found their platform a source of pride rather than embarrassment. At the close of the 89th Congress in 1966, the party published a list of 28 major statutes which fulfilled 1964 promises. Ranging alphabetically and ecologically from air pollution to water pollution, the list clearly included the most important legislation of the previous two years.[5]

These partisan evaluations are obviously self-serving and cannot be accepted without more thorough analysis. Nevertheless, they do demonstrate that parties at least place some importance on claims that they have fulfilled or neglected the platform. Politicians perceive their electoral interest to lie in performing on their promises—or at least appearing to perform. Other factors may prevent fulfillment, but apparently some efforts will be made. We must now try to judge to what extent these efforts succeed.

[4] *Congressional Record,* Vol. 111, 89th Cong., 1st sess. (April 7, 1965), pp. 6947, 6976.

[5] Democratic National Committee, *The Democrat,* Vol. 6 (October, 1966), p. 3.

TESTING PARTY PERFORMANCE

We begin by stating a precise hypothesis, "Platform pledges are fulfilled."[6] As a second step, we define (or "operationalize") our terms specifically, in order to curtail ambiguity or inconstancy in our language. We must specify the meaning of both "pledges" and "fulfillment."

Platform pledges will be defined as all statements in the third through sixth categories of future promises. As designated in the last chapter, these include pledges of continuity, expressions of goals and concern, pledges of action, and detailed promises. For all of the twelve platforms, this definition provides 1,399 pledges, which is 62 per cent of all commitments and 27 per cent of all statements in the platforms. National policy also is affected by the general social values included in rhetorical and general statements and by party evaluations of the past. However, since it is difficult to see the detailed policy implications of these provisions, we will confine our analysis to the specific commitments.

To explore fulfillment, our other term, is even more difficult. A promise and an action are inherently different. In an ideal world of platform fulfillment, each pledge could be matched to a specific action. In reality, pledges and actions are too discrete for such simple matching. Platforms, lengthy and specific though they may be, are unrelated to a large proportion of governmental actions. The parties deliberately evade pledges on some issues; others require knowledge too specialized for either politicians or voters; and others arise only after the presidential election.

[6] In this case, we are dealing only with a statement of association. If we were dealing with a causal statement, i.e., "Platforms lead to party unity," it would be best to cast our statement in such a way that we prefer it to be disproven. In social science we can rarely expect to prove a statement. The best we can usually do is to disprove an opposite statement. We can then console ourselves that we have increased the probability that our preferred statement is true. See Morris Cohen and Ernest Nagel, *An Introduction to Logic and Scientific Method* (New York: Harcourt, Brace, 1943). For application to statistical tests of significance, see Linton Freeman, *Elementary Applied Statistics* (New York: Wiley, 1965), pp. 149–56. See also chapter VI, *supra*, p. 129–30.

Much of Congress' output, such as street franchises in the District of Columbia, is too limited to receive attention from a national convention. Important measures also are considered in the absence of relevant platform pledges. Congress created the Communications Satellite Corporation, passed the 1965 Voting Rights Bill, and condoned expansion of American troop landings in Vietnam, although none of these actions were specifically supported in the party manifestos. The President and bureaucracy are even more active than Congress, and most of their work is necessarily independent of platform provisions.

In testing fulfillment, there are questions of degree as well. Must a pledge be kept in full to be considered kept at all? The Democrats in 1964 pledged to extend the minimum wage law to all industries "affecting interstate commerce." Was this pledge kept by the 1966 law extending coverage to 8.1 million workers, or was it violated because other millions of workers remained outside of the law's protection? This is a question of definition, less legal than methodological.[7] Similarly, the means of fulfillment may vary. Passage of one law may make another unnecessary, or a presidential action may be substituted for legislation.

Fulfillment is here considered some substantial governmental action of the kind and in the direction promised. There must be realization of a pledge, not only an attempt, and the achieved result must be clearly akin to the promise. No judgments are made of the adequacy or desirability of the action taken.

Fulfillment can be achieved in one of four ways. (1) *Full action* is the passage of a law (or section of a law) directly related to the platform provision. A very close correspondence must exist between the promise and the statute. Compromise legislation which differs significantly from an explicit pledge, as in the case of minimum wage coverage, is not included. (2) Another means of fulfillment is presidential or other *executive actions* which

[7] Legally, the pledge was kept, because extensions of coverage are made by changing the definition in the law of "interstate commerce." In one sense, therefore, the pledge was only a truism: the law would cover those who were covered.

directly accomplish commitments. (3) Pledges may not be directly fulfilled, but *similar actions* may be taken by either Congress or the executive branch. (4) Finally, there is a category of *negative fulfillment*. An important proportion of promises are pledges *not* to act, to maintain the status quo. Where the party has been true to its promise to leave a situation completely undisturbed, this is also considered adequate performance.[8]

There are two means by which a pledge may be unfulfilled. In one situation, an attempt may be made to accomplish the goal, but it is *defeated*. Such results occur when a presidential measure is killed in committee, a proposal loses in a floor vote, or the President successfully vetoes a bill. Second, platform commitments may fail of accomplishment simply because there is *no action*. The pledge is ignored or, in rare instances, completely opposite action is taken. This last category also includes non-presidential bills which are buried in committee.

Judgments on fulfillment were made after comparing the pledges in both party platforms for a given election to the legislation and other action of the following four years. (For the 1964 platform, only the events of 1965 and 1966 are included.) This task involves the separate organization of platform promises and official policies and then itemized comparisons between the two categories. The procedure, along with other methods employed in this chapter, is detailed in the Appendix.

The judgments used may become clearer through the following examples of pledges from the 1964 Democratic platform and corresponding governmental responses:[9]

[8] In the previous chapter, such pledges were considered in the same manner as those promising some innovative action. "Negative fulfillment" does not apply to situations where an existing law must be extended to remain in force, and the law then is continued without change. Where any activity is required, such action falls outside of this category, which is reserved for promises literally to do nothing. For those satisfied with the status quo, such promises are significant and often crucial.

[9] All statements from the 1964 platforms are from Kirk H. Porter and Donald B. Johnson, *National Party Platforms 1840–1964* (Urbana: University of Illinois Press, 1966), pp. 641–49, 677–90.

Full Action

Platform: Increase minimum wage.

Action: Minimum wage increased to $1.60.

Executive Action

Platform: Develop potential of the armed forces for training deficient persons.

Action: The Defense Department established a program to induct up to 100,000 youths ordinarily unqualified for military service.

Similar Action

Platform: Extend coverage of minimum wage to all workers in industries affecting interstate commerce.

Action: Coverage extended to 8.1 million new workers.

Negative Fulfillment

Platform: Oppose racial quotas or preferential practices.

Action: No action.

Defeated

Platform: Eliminate section 14(b) of Taft-Hartley Act.

Action: Cloture on repeal bill failed in the Senate, after House passed appropriate legislation.

No Action

Platform: Legislation for full equality of women.

Action: No action.

THE RECORD OF FULFILLMENT

Tables 8.1 and 8.2 present the degree of fulfillment of party pledges by election years and by topics. Separate columns are provided for promises by the Democrats and Republicans, by both parties, and by the faction in and out of the White House.[10]

The most important conclusion to be derived from the mass of figures is that pledges are indeed redeemed. Even if we consider only commitments which are met by direct congressional or executive action, we find that slightly over half of the pledges are fulfilled. If we relax our standards and include similar actions

[10] For the definition of bipartisan pledges, see pp. 281–82, below.

Table 8.1 Fulfillment of Platform Pledges, by Election Years
(In Percentages)*

Election Year	*Democratic*	*Republican*	*Bipartisan*	*In-Party*	*Out-Party*	*Total*
1944: Full Action	11	33	66	11	33	40
Executive	0	3	7	0	3	4
Similar	45	17	0	45	17	15
Negative	0	14	7	0	14	10
Total Action	*56*	*67*	*80*	*56*	*67*	*69*
Defeated	33	24	20	33	24	24
No Action	11	9	0	11	9	7
1948: Full Action	48	10	58	48	10	46
Executive	4	0	11	4	0	6
Similar	6	30	4	6	30	9
Negative	7	5	4	7	5	6
Total Action	*65*	*45*	*77*	*65*	*45*	*67*
Defeated	27	45	23	27	45	28
No Action	8	10	0	8	10	5
1952: Full Action	28	45	67	45	28	43
Executive	3	8	0	8	3	3
Similar	10	16	8	16	10	11
Negative	12	11	0	11	12	9
Total Action	*53*	*80*	*75*	*80*	*53*	*66*
Defeated	29	10	18	10	29	21
No Action	18	10	7	10	18	13
1956: Full Action	32	42	53	42	32	42
Executive	3	4	8	4	3	5
Similar	13	19	7	19	13	13
Negative	6	18	12	18	6	10
Total Action	*54*	*83*	*80*	*83*	*54*	*70*
Defeated	28	13	14	13	28	20
No Action	18	4	6	4	18	10
1960: Full Action	46	31	69	46	31	51
Executive	14	5	7	14	5	9
Similar	16	16	10	16	16	13
Negative	5	6	6	5	6	7
Total Action	*81*	*58*	*92*	*81*	*58*	*80*
Defeated	14	24	7	14	24	14
No Action	5	18	1	5	18	6
1964: Full Action	54	12	79	54	12	40
Executive	10	6	0	10	6	6
Similar	14	15	6	14	15	13
Negative	5	7	15	5	7	7
Total Action	*83*	*40*	*100*	*83*	*40*	*66*
Defeated	16	21	0	16	21	16
No Action	1	39	0	1	39	18
Total: Full Action	40	30	64	46	26	45
Executive	8	5	6	9	4	6
Similar	14	17	7	16	15	13
Negative	6	10	8	8	8	8
Total Action	*68*	*62*	*85*	*79*	*53*	*72*
Defeated	22	21	13	16	27	18
No Action	10	17	2	5	20	10
Number of Pledges	(517)	(418)	(464)	(432)	(503)	(1,399)

* Within years, last three figures in each column add vertically to 100%.

or appropriate inaction, nearly three-fourths of all promises are kept. Perhaps most comforting to those who believe in party integrity is that only a tenth of the promises are completely ignored.

The bipartisan aspects of American government are evident. When the parties agree in their positions, some action is almost certain. Seven of ten bipartisan pledges are redeemed by direct congressional or executive action, and 85 per cent are fulfilled in one way or another. It is also noteworthy that the party out of power, even though without the resources of the executive branch, has been able to achieve about half of its own pledges, while also sharing in performance on bipartisan planks. A party will not be completely frustrated even if it loses the Presidency. The lowest out-party figure is for the Republicans after 1964. This result is a reflection of the unusual character of their platform and of their reduced representation in the 89th Congress.[11]

Winning the Presidency, however, does make a considerable difference in platform fulfillment. In all categories, the in-party achieves about four-fifths of its program, half again as much as the losers. The difference is even greater if we consider only direct actions. The winners directly realize five of every nine promises, but the opposition gains less than a third and must make its record on the realization of programs similar but not identical to its promises, and on "negative fulfillment."

The record of the in-party is superior after all elections but 1944, in which the winning Democrats made only nine specific pledges, too small a number for meaningful analysis. The importance of the White House is also evident in the topical distributions. In each policy area, the in-party achieves a substantially greater proportion of its pledges. Moveover, in each topic but foreign policy, the difference between the in-party and out-party is greater than that between Democrats and Republicans over the entire time period, a further indication that control of

[11] The low out-party proportion after the 1948 election is probably a reflection of the vague Republican platform, which contained only 20 specific pledges. Republican gains in the 1966 congressional election did not result in the later passage of the party's program, but rather in the blocking of new Administration programs.

Table 8.2 Fulfillment of Platform Pledges, by Policy Topics

(In Percentages)*

Policy Topic	*Democratic*	*Republican*	*Bipartisan*	*In-Party*	*Out-Party*	*Total*
Foreign						
Full Action	33	20	66	33	23	46
Executive	27	4	12	25	11	15
Similar	14	16	13	13	17	14
Negative	2	7	5	5	2	4
Total Action	*76*	*47*	*96*	*76*	*53*	*79*
Defeated	14	11	4	15	12	9
No Action	10	42	0	9	35	12
Defense						
Full Action	43	31	78	59	18	49
Executive	21	12	8	14	15	12
Similar	14	14	0	9	16	9
Negative	8	5	0	9	4	4
Total Action	*86*	*62*	*86*	*91*	*53*	*74*
Defeated	14	10	14	9	12	12
No Action	0	28	0	0	35	14
Economic						
Full Action	40	40	89	52	31	51
Executive	4	5	0	6	2	3
Similar	16	10	0	19	8	10
Negative	8	11	6	7	12	9
Total Action	*68*	*66*	*95*	*84*	*53*	*73*
Defeated	22	21	5	10	31	18
No Action	10	13	0	6	16	9
Labor						
Full Action	24	11	64	24	13	34
Executive	5	0	0	6	0	2
Similar	10	11	0	18	0	7
Negative	0	28	0	6	13	7
Total Action	*39*	*50*	*64*	*54*	*26*	*50*
Defeated	37	28	22	43	22	30
No Action	24	22	14	3	52	20
Agriculture						
Full Action	47	45	68	59	36	53
Executive	0	0	0	0	0	0
Similar	10	14	12	14	10	12
Negative	12	17	20	18	11	16
Total Action	*69*	*76*	*100*	*91*	*57*	*81*
Defeated	23	14	0	5	31	13
No Action	8	10	0	4	12	6
Resources						
Full Action	47	27	71	48	28	48
Executive	8	2	5	9	3	5
Similar	10	20	4	14	11	11
Negative	19	23	16	19	20	20
Total Action	*84*	*72*	*96*	*90*	*62*	*84*
Defeated	11	14	0	4	29	9
No Action	5	14	4	6	9	7
Welfare						
Full Action	46	31	88	54	33	55
Executive	4	0	0	5	0	2
Similar	14	19	3	12	18	11
Negative	2	6	6	2	3	4

Table 8.2 (continued)

Policy Topic	*Democratic*	*Republican*	*Bipartisan*	*In-Party*	*Out-Party*	*Total*
Total Action	66	56	97	73	54	72
Defeated	23	37	3	25	30	21
No Action	11	7	0	2	16	7
Government						
Full Action	33	24	31	43	11	28
Executive	3	7	0	8	4	4
Similar	15	25	7	20	25	18
Negative	3	4	6	3	3	5
Total Action	54	60	44	74	43	55
Defeated	31	26	50	22	32	32
No Action	15	14	6	4	25	13
Civil Rights						
Full Action	17	20	25	20	17	22
Executive	4	19	19	20	7	16
Similar	25	23	13	27	23	18
Negative	4	0	6	0	3	4
Total Action	50	62	63	67	50	60
Defeated	37	28	31	20	40	32
No Action	13	10	6	13	10	8
N. Total	(517)	(418)	(464)	(432)	(503)	(1,399)

* Within topics, the last three figures in each column add vertically to 100%.

the White House is crucial. Voter endorsement of one party in presidential elections thus makes a significant difference in future policies, providing the power necessary for governmental action. This finding is consistent with the conclusions of our historical study in chapter V.

Accomplishment varies considerably by policy topic. Performance is notably poor in three areas: labor, government, and civil rights. In these cases, legislation directly to redeem a platform pledge has been particularly unlikely, with executive, similar, and negative actions more feasible. In all three cases as well, bipartisan pledges have fared badly in comparison to the record on other topics. These similarities are due both to the nature of the issues and to the structure of American government.

In each of these areas, the parties tend to appeal to distinct and recognizable minorities, such as unions, governmental reformers, and Negroes. When pledges are made, they are often in response to and in imitation of an interest group appeal. To win the support of unions, the Democrats will endorse repeal of the Taft-Hartley Act. To indicate their support for reduced spending, the Republicans will propose a constitutional amendment for an item-veto on appropriations bills. To appeal to the urban North, both parties will back a strong civil rights program.

These specific platform pledges are made to enhance the party's electoral appeal. However, the interests involved are too weak to ensure fulfillment. In some cases, opposing groups resist the platform provision. Although these issues are contentious, the parties do not resort to platform vagueness in an effort to satisfy the contending groups. Some definite appeals are made to one interest or another. The existence of opposition, however, can make fulfillment more difficult.

Conflict tends to be particularly intense on labor and civil rights, for these issues raise both material and ideological stakes. Pledges appealing to one group are likely to arouse vehement opposition from another, so that action is prevented. The same fact is evident on some governmental issues, such as home rule for the District of Columbia. However, on most issues of government the problem is quite different. Because issues such as an item-veto or electoral college reform are abstract, supporters are unlikely to be intense, and these proposals are most likely to be simply presented and then forgotten.

Opposition on these three issues, moreover, tends to be concentrated at strategic points in Congress. Labor and civil rights bills are particularly prone to delay by the House Rules Committee and to destruction by a Senate filibuster. During the postwar period, southerners have often held strategic positions as committee chairmen and party leaders and, in a series of shifting alliances with members of both parties, have been able to prevent many of these measures from becoming law. On governmental issues, southerners have been influential in preventing passage of statehood and District of Columbia bills, but other measures have been defeated through opposition by a variety of factions.[12]

In these cases, none of the contending groups is sufficiently powerful to win its program, and the chances of fulfillment of any party's pledges are consequently reduced. These pledges become electoral appeals without great chance of legislative action.

What does this degree of fulfillment indicate? Is it significant that nearly three-fourths of all pledges are kept in some way? Or is it more significant that over a quarter of all pledges are not redeemed? Whatever the exact measurement employed, it is notable that platforms are considered at all, for the party manifestos have usually been scorned, not respected. To find any fulfillment of party pledges is rather remarkable, in the light of the conventional wisdom.

There is no absolute standard with which to compare party performance. Even the promises of the Delphic Oracle were subject to interpretation, and human vows are necessarily less reliable. All married persons have solemnly pledged to "love honor and cherish," but a fourth of all marriages end in divorce. Should parties be more faithful?

If platform pledges were only endorsements of undisputed values, such as Motherhood and Country, fulfillment would not be significant. We have therefore restricted our attention to the more specific statements. However, parties may not be promising and accomplishing important programs. Legislating a raft of trivia does not compensate for failure to deal with the vital issues of the time. And an over-all and impressionistic reading of platforms indicates that they deal with specific important issues.

Moreover, we have also found distinctly superior performance by the party in the White House. The power of the Presidency is

[12] For the record in the 81st Congress, see David Truman, *The Congressional Party* (New York: Wiley, 1959).

not needed to accomplish bland programs. It becomes valuable only when a party seeks to accomplish policies in dispute. We have also found that there are variations in fulfillment by topic, with lessened achievement in policy areas in which positions are most conflicting and entrenched. Such opposition would not exist unless vital interests were at stake in attempts to redeem platform pledges.

THE CHARACTER OF THE PARTIES

In choosing a party to control the government, the voters can influence official action. The character of the winning faction is crucial, for its concerns and initiatives form the basis for governmental programs. Through further analysis of platforms, we are now in a position to assess the character of American parties.

There are two different models of what the parties are or should be. According to one model, Democrats and Republicans are virtually identical, one "Tweedledee" and one "Tweedledum." They say the same things to the same people, and there is no real basis for policy choice between them. Moreover, the parties are weak, decentralized, and undisciplined. "The parties are unable to hold their lines in a controversial public issue when the pressure is on. This condition," wrote the dean of American students of politics, "constitutes the most important single fact concerning the American parties. He who knows this fact, and knows nothing else, knows more about American parties than he who knows everything except this fact."[13] Partisanship therefore will have little relation to government, and party pledges, particularly on the most contentious issues, are unlikely to be fulfilled.

[13] E. E. Schattschneider, *Party Government* (New York: Holt, Rinehart & Winston, 1942), pp. 131–32. These sentences are italicized by Schattschneider. Other writers defend this model. See Herbert Agar, *The Price of Union* (Boston: Houghton Mifflin, 1950); Pendleton Herring, *The Politics of Democracy* (New York: Norton, 1940); and Edward C. Banfield, "In Defense of the American Party System," in Robert A. Goldwin, ed., *Political Parties U.S.A.* (Chicago: Rand McNally, 1964), pp. 21–37.

Other writers wish the situation were different. The model they would prefer is one of "party government," in which there are clear programmatic differences between Democrats and Republicans. The differing policies would then provide the voter with "a choice, not an echo." Strong centralized and disciplined parties would direct governmental action. The platform of the majority party would constitute the agenda of the President and Congress, and its pledges would be redeemed by a cohesive national organization.[14] Platforms provide material for judging the empirical reality of those opposing models. We shall examine the degree of similarity and conflict in platform pledges, party action in Congress, and fulfillment of conflicting commitments.

If the parties are duplicates of one another, a large proportion of their pledges will be similar or bipartisan promises. If they are fit for "party government," a large proportion of pledges will be in conflict. Fitting neither model would be a situation where the promises of Democrats and Republicans were neither identical nor conflicting, but only different. To resolve the question, the 1,399 relatively specific pledges were compared. The percentage distribution of pledges, by election year and policy topic, is presented in Table 8.3.

There is only limited conflict in the planks, while there is greater, but still only moderate, bipartisan agreement. For the most part, the parties are simply different and fit neither of the two models. The parties do not duplicate one another, but appeal to distinct groups of voters. On infrequent occasions, their varying appeals bring them into direct opposition. About a tenth of all pledges involve party conflict. These occasions are important, but they do not constitute all or even the major proportion of American party activity. Only in the intense campaigns of 1952

[14] Schattschneider has been one of the foremost advocates of "party government." For similar views see "Toward a More Responsible Two-Party System," and Harvey Wheeler, *The Restoration of Politics* (Santa Barbara: Center for the Study of Democratic Institutions, 1965). For a fuller discussion of party models, see Judson L. James, *American Political Parties and Democratic Government* (New York: Pegasus Press, forthcoming, 1969), chap. 2.

Table 8.3 Similarity and Conflict in Platform Pledges
(In Percentages of Pledges of Designated Year or Topic)*

Year or Topic	*(N)*	*One-party Pledge Only*	*Bipartisan Pledges*	*Conflicting Pledges*
Election Year				
1944	(102)	70	28	2
1948	(124)	51	42	7
1952	(205)	52	29	19
1956	(302)	61	34	5
1960	(464)	51	39	10
1964	(202)	70	19	11
Policy Topic				
Foreign	(216)	47	47	6
Defense	(84)	65	33	2
Economic	(177)	62	22	16
Labor	(84)	42	33	25
Agriculture	(150)	56	33	11
Resources	(185)	63	26	11
Welfare	(255)	60	27	13
Government	(136)	76	24	0
Civil Rights	(113)	40	60	0
All Pledges	(1,399)	57	33	10
N. Total	1,399	799	464	136

* Rows add horizontally to 100% for the three columns.

and 1964 did the proportion of conflicting pledges approach the proportion of bipartisan commitments.

Conflict between the parties varies among the topics. In general, conflict is higher on issues in which the benefits are divisible and tangible, and contending groups exist. These are material issues in the broad sense, including benefits to specific groups involved in economic policy, labor, agriculture, resources, and social welfare. Even in these categories, bipartisan pledges still predominate, but there is a greater likelihood that the parties will clash directly. The parties react to the voter's stress on their particular interests. Competition in the form of conflicting pledges is greatest on those issues we have found to be most important in influencing the electorate. A similar stress in the specificity of pledges was observed in the last chapter.

Bipartisan agreement on platform pledges is exceptionally high only on issues of foreign policy and civil rights. On the former, bipartisanship is partially the result of necessity. Diplomacy can be conducted more assuredly if there is unity between the parties. Since treaties require ratification by two-thirds of the Senate, the minority party also must be drawn into policy-making. Party agreement on civil rights is principally the result of political factors. Democrats and Republicans have followed similar platform strategies on this issue, as we have seen in the previous chapter. Recognizing that "passionate minorities" exist on this issue, the parties have imitated one another's appeals, in both form and content.[15]

Further evidence on the applicability of the two models of parties is possible through analysis of performances on conflicting pledges. If the parties have any meaningful identity, we would expect them to display their character on these questions. If, to the contrary, the parties are shapeless, they would be unable to present a united front on the most contentious issues. Analysis of congressional roll calls was employed to assess the degree of party solidarity. Through procedures detailed in the Appendix, 70 roll calls were selected as directly related to the issues presented by platform conflicts.[16]

If the platforms have any significance in Congress, we would expect the parties to differ on these "conflict roll calls." They would then constitute party-unity votes, in which a majority of Democrats take a position in opposition to a majority of Republicans. In all three of the postwar administrations, this expectation is largely met. Of the relevant roll calls, 89 per cent in the

[15] In the future, if racial tensions continue to increase, it is possible that conflicting pledges on civil rights will be frequent.

[16] There were 45 issues involved in the 136 conflicting platform pledges. In other words, because of duplications, there was an average of three platform provisions to every issue.

Truman years and 87 per cent in both the Eisenhower and Kennedy-Johnson periods were of this type.

By comparison, of all congressional roll calls in this period, only about half split the two parties. Specifically, 58 per cent of the roll calls in the Truman years, 46 per cent in the Eisenhower administration, and 49 per cent in the Kennedy-Johnson sessions found a majority of the parties in opposition to each other.[17] The parties' representatives and senators act in accord with their national pledges, resulting in greater conflict than is normal for Congress. Election disputes are not forgotten when Congress convenes, but carry over into legislative voting.

We can also measure the degree of unity within each party on these roll calls and the extent of similarity between Republicans and Democrats. Internal solidity is gauged by an "index of cohesion," which varies from 100, when the party is completely united, to 0, when it is completely divided. Similarities between the parties are shown by an "index of likeness," which varies from 100, when the parties duplicate one another, to 0, when they are completely opposed. For purposes of comparison, these measures are calculated both for "conflict roll calls" and for all congressional votes. The latter roll calls are also divided into party-unity votes and bipartisan votes, in which a majority of both parties takes the same position. Table 8.4 presents the average indexes of cohesion and likeness for each presidential era.

The degree of cohesion on the controversial platform pledges is similar to that which exists in Congress generally. The most relevant comparison is that between "conflict roll calls" and all party-unity votes. Both are cases of partisan conflict, and the degree of party cohesion is similar. Unity of the parties does tend to be somewhat higher on the platform votes, and this finding is

[17] The percentage of party-unity votes among all roll calls is taken from the relevant volumes of *Congressional Quarterly Almanac*. All roll calls in the congressional sessions in which platform votes occur were used for this comparison. There were no "conflict roll calls" in 1945–47, 1951–52, 1960, and 1964. Consequently, these years are not included in calculations of general congressional voting.

significant. Given the visibility, pressures, and importance which attach to these votes, relatively high party solidarity indicates that a large proportion of the party does stand behind its pledges. Party unity does not melt in the heat of controversy. It is maintained, and even some increased fusion of the party can be observed. At the same time, to change the image, platforms are seen as one sector in a general field of party battle, for cohesion on these issues is quite similar to that on all party votes. The platform conflicts are not special cases. They are, rather, the most obvious and dramatic instances of larger differences between the parties.

Table 8.4 Party Cohesion and Likeness
(Average Indexes for Presidential Terms)

	House Cohesion		*Senate Cohesion*		*Likeness*	
	Democrats	*Republicans*	*Democrats*	*Republicans*	*House*	*Senate*
Period						
1948–50						
Conflicts	54	86	39	45	30	64
All Roll Calls	63	67	60	55	68	64
Party Unity	60	64	60	54	38	43
Bipartisan	66	70	60	56	98	98
1953–59						
Conflicts	66	66	66	67	35	37
All Roll Calls	60	64	56	65	74	77
Party Unity	56	60	52	62	42	43
Bipartisan	64	68	60	68	98	96
1961–66						
Conflicts	56	74	58	50	35	50
All Roll Calls	73	67	60	62	66	74
Party Unity	64	64	56	58	36	43
Bipartisan	82	70	64	66	94	99

The parties also vote differently from one another. The index of likeness is usually lower for platform conflicts than for all votes in Congress, indicating greater differences between the parties on these issues. The typical platform vote would find the two parties opposed, with somewhat less than a fifth of each faction joining the opposition. In all congressional votes, however, the parties would be relatively similar to one another, and actually in agreement on half or more of the roll calls.

Roll calls on conflicting pledges are again found to be similar to all party-unity votes. Whenever the parties differ, the extent of their difference is comparable to their differences over platform issues, and there is actually somewhat greater conflict in the votes related to party promises. The platform is again seen as related to congressional behavior. It is associated with party conflict and is seen as an indication of the character of this conflict, rather than being an independent source of contention. "Conflict roll calls" relate to fundamental group differences.

A final test of the two models is the fulfillment of conflicting pledges. Parties which are only "Tweedledee" and "Tweedledum" could not be expected to redeem controversial promises, while performance would be more likely in a system of "party government." The conflicts between the parties involved 45 distinct issues. For each of these issues, a judgment was made of the degree of fulfillment. This record is summarized in Table 8.5, where a comparison is made of the performances of the in-party and out-party as well as of the Democrats and Republicans.

The party in power actually does somewhat better on the most contentious issues than it does generally. Performance on these pledges is especially marked in regard to full legislative action, and only one issue was not acted upon at all. Despite their controversial nature and the lack of bipartisan support, the President's party does redeem its disputatious promises. Differences between the in-party and out-party are far greater than those between Democrats and Republicans. The disparity shows the policy significance of electoral victory.

By contrast, the out-party is almost completely stymied in accomplishing its most controversial pledges. Only two opposition measures ran the full gamut of obstacles. The out-party was able to bring most of its proposals to a vote in Congress, but was unable finally to accomplish much of its program. In all years and on all topics, the in-party has a far better record. When the in-

Table 8.5 Party Performance on Conflicting Issues
(In Percentages of Conflicting Issues)*

	In-Party	*Out-Party*	*Democrats*	*Republicans*
All Issues (N = 45)				
Full Action	58	4	38	24
Executive	4	0	4	0
Similar	14	9	14	9
Negative	4	7	2	9
Total Action	*80*	*20*	*58*	*42*
Defeated	18	69	40	47
No Action	2	11	2	11
Total Action: Election Years				
1944	100	0	100	0
1948	100	25*	100	25*
1952	87	27*	27	87*
1956	50	25	25	50
1960	62	23	62	23
1964	100	0	100	0
Total Action: Policy Topics				
Foreign	100	50*	100	50*
Defense	100	0	0	100
Economic	100	0	56	44
Labor	70	0	56	14
Agriculture	86	14	57	43
Resources	62	38*	62	38*
Welfare	67	11	45	33
Government	. . .	. . .	. . .	. . .
Civil Rights	. . .	. . .	. . .	. . .

* Each percentage represents the proportion of issues on which conflicting pledges were fulfilled by the designated party. On three issues, both parties' pledges are considered fulfilled because of compromises of divergent party positions. In these cases, the total percentage of the two parties may be greater than 100%.

party failed, it did not necessarily mean that the out-party succeeded. In some cases, such as the Taft-Hartley Act, Medicare before 1965, and aid to education, neither party was able to accomplish its objective. Only occasionally do the contending factions compromise their differences. Conflicts in platform pledges persist in congressional action.

The dominant position of the in-party is particularly marked in regard to tangible and material policies. Almost all victories on conflicting issues in regard to economic policy, labor, agriculture, and welfare are won by the group occupying the White House. (The topic of resources is an exception.) The difference between Democratic and Republican success in these areas is not great, but there is a vast disparity when the parties are considered in terms of control of the administration. On the other hand, there are fewer conflicts and more minority party influence in the less concrete areas of policy, such as foreign affairs.

In general, our evidence indicates that neither model fits American parties well. Pledges do not duplicate one another, nor are they commonly conflicting. Party lines hold in Congress on votes relating to platform conflicts, but many congressmen and senators cast their ballots with members of the opposition. Platform pledges, particularly those of the party in power, are redeemed, but there are many opportunities for the minority to win on some issues, or to block all action. Democrats and Republicans are not "Tweedledee" and "Tweedledum," but neither are they practitioners of "party government."

PARTIES, PLATFORMS, AND POLICIES

The evidence of this and earlier chapters suggests another model, that of parties as competing coalitions. These coalitions are not under the discipline of a centralized leadership, but neither are they meaningless entities. Parties are social formations which are united to a noticeable extent in the quest for victory.[18] The quest for victory becomes involved with issues of public policy in two ways. Party leaders and candidates have their own programmatic objectives, and their election will mean popular endorsement of their aims. In addition, parties use

[18] See Neil A. McDonald, *The Study of Political Parties* (Garden City: Doubleday, 1955), chap. 2.

programs and issues as one of the means of attracting the votes necessary to win office. In responding to popular demands, or anticipating them, politicians provide a means for indirect popular influence on governmental action.

The platform may be seen as a useful indicator of the nature of the party coalition. The parties do not copy each other's pledges, but make divergent appeals, thereby pointing to the differences in their basic composition. Union support for the Democrats is reflected in pledges to repeal Taft-Hartley, while business endorsement of Republicans is evidenced in G.O.P. support for tariff protections. Party voting in Congress on platform issues is another indication. The degree of internal cohesion and interparty difference on "conflict roll calls" is quite similar to that on other contentious issues. Attitudes on platform issues reflect the more general attitudes of the parties.

The platform is important, but not as an inspired gospel to which politicians resort for policy guidance. It is important because it summarizes, crystallizes, and presents to the voters the character of the party coalition. Platform pledges are not simply good ideas, or even original ones.[19] In their programs, Democrats and Republicans are not typically breaking new paths; they are promising to proceed along one or another path which has already become involved in political controversy. The stands taken in the platform clarify the parties' positions on these controversies and reveal the nature of their support and appeals.

Thus, the party manifesto is Janus-like, both retrospective and prospective. After issues have already arisen, the platform indicates the party's future intentions. If victorious, the party coalition will pursue its programs. Endorsement of a proposal in the platform provides evidence of its suitability for governmental action and an argument in its behalf. The many obstacles of American institutions, however, may prevent action. Fulfillment of platform pledges is common, but it is not required.

[19] Minor parties are often credited with originating new ideas, but the evidence is mixed. See V. O. Key, Jr., *Politics, Parties and Pressure Groups* (New York: Crowell, 1964), 5th ed., chap. 10, and William Hesseltine, *Third-Party Movements in the United States* (Princeton: Van Nostrand, 1962).

The pattern of Medicare is illustrative. National health insurance had been proposed during the Truman administration, but was defeated in Congress. Proposals for a more restricted program of hospital insurance for the aged through social security began to be heard in the mid-1950's. It became an important issue in Congress, but the House Ways and Means Committee, which had jurisdiction over the measure, refused to approve it. Supporters then sought its endorsement in party platforms. The Democrats included Medicare in their 1960 platform, and it became a primary item on the agendas of Presidents Kennedy and Johnson. The Senate voted on the measure three times, finally approving it in 1964, but the House still refused to act. In 1964, the Democrats again endorsed Medicare and, following the Johnson victory, it became law in 1965. The platform did not force party action immediately, but it did indicate the character of the Democratic coalition.

The party coalition needs popular support in order to accomplish its aims. Our findings on the fulfillment of platforms demonstrate the superior position of the victorious party in regard to policy achievement. The in-party is better able to meet its platform commitments, particularly on those issues in dispute with its opposition. Popular intervention provides the lever of power for a group of politicians which seeks to move the government.

To win power, parties must also serve the interests of voters. Party responsiveness to or anticipation of popular desires can provide a means of indirect electoral influence over policy. Such influence requires both meaningful platform commitments and the fulfillment of these pledges. We have found that platforms are relatively specific. Moreover, and contrary to the conventional wisdom, these platform pledges are redeemed. Legislation or executive action directly fulfills more than half of the planks, and some definite action is taken in nearly three-fourths of the cases. Achievement is even greater for the party in the White House. The vote for party is also a vote for policy.

The influence of the electorate is most evident in regard to the voters' particular material and tangible interests. The political theorists defending elections were most concerned with the protection of personal interests. The evidence in this and the last chapter consistently indicates that elections are in fact most likely to provide such protection. The platforms' most specific appeals are related to tangible and distributive rewards, and conflict between the party pledges is most common on such issues. The parties are relatively coherent and distinct in fulfilling these pledges, and the effect of party victory is particularly evident in fulfilling tangible promises. In giving their support to one party, the voters are bringing to power a group with a definable set of policies which are especially significant in relation to the personal interests the voter wishes to protect and promote.

Popular intervention in government does not mean direct and complete control over policy. The parties are insufficiently cohesive, and American institutions insufficiently centralized to permit even a good imitation of "party government." Elections do make a difference, however, by installing a coalition with specific commitments, relevant to the voters' interests, and likely of fulfillment. The voter can make a more meaningful choice than that between "Tweedledee" and "Tweedledum," and also can serve his own interests and secure his own protection.

Platforms, then, are a meaningful guide to party action, not because of their binding quality, but because they contain the commitments and appeals of the parties, and thereby permit indirect voter influence. We should therefore take platforms seriously—because politicians appear to take them seriously. Responding to critics of his program in 1966, President Johnson declared: "I made it abundantly clear that I ran on a platform that contained my commitments; that I expect to carry them out to the extent of my ability; that I appreciated their cooperation to the extent that they could in good conscience give it to me."[20] Surprisingly, American party leaders usually agree.

[20] The President was replying to criticisms by Democratic governors after the party's election defeats—*The New York Times,* December 22, 1966, p. 24.

CHAPTER 9

"TO SECURE THESE RIGHTS"

OUR STUDIES to this point have indicated the indirect influence of elections on government. An important indirect effect of elections may be the protection of the voters. The subject has arisen a number of times in previous chapters. We now turn to a more focused discussion of this vital function of elections.

The protection of citizens has been regarded by political theorists as the most important benefit of elections, as seen in the analysis of chapter II. This belief is also a basic American tenet. In the Declaration of Independence, Thomas Jefferson declared the protective functions of elections. To secure man's unalienable rights of life, liberty, and the pursuit of happiness, he wrote, "governments are instituted among men, deriving their just powers from the consent of the governed." Natural rights could be guaranteed in practice only by a government held responsible through the political process.

The evidence of political protection, however, is difficult to establish, much like the presence of physical health. Both qualities are often defined negatively. The nature of protection becomes most evident when men are oppressed, just as the nature of health is most evident when men are diseased. In the absence of actual oppression, we cannot be certain that voters are protected, for it is impossible fully to know what governments did not do, nor why they were restrained.

Even if protection can be defined and located, its causes are not easily isolated. Elections do not alone provide protection. Tyranny may be restrained by the moral values of a community, the personal code of ruling classes, or by a group's ability to defend itself by means of its prestige, economic wealth, or even physical force. "It must be said that the vote is only one weapon amongst many which are available to groups. At the same time, it has to be admitted that many of these alternative devices (e.g. lobbying, press campaigns) derive much of their value from the existence of the vote. . . . But even if the vote occupies a place of importance among weapons of the group, it still remains a question how far a group requires defense at all."[1]

A crucial test of the protective value of elections would be provided by the history of American Negroes, particularly in the South. Both in 250 years of slavery and in the past century of discrimination, this group surely has needed whatever weapons of self-defense were available. Despite this need, Negroes have had few social, material, or physical means for their protection. Lacking other resources, they could not supplement the power of their ballots with different forms of influence.

Even the value of the vote has been peculiarly limited for colored Americans. By virtue of their color, the status of blacks was literally visible and therefore potentially disturbing to others. In most political situations, one group's interests do not clearly conflict with the demands of other large factions. On racial questions in the United States, by contrast, whites have often been as intensely involved as blacks.[2] Even when they voted freely, blacks have been a minority in virtually all areas and therefore subject to defeat by a white majority. Where a

[1] W. H. Morris-Jones, "In Defense of Apathy: Some Doubt on the Duty to Vote," *Political Studies,* Vol. II (February, 1954), p. 30.

[2] See V. O. Key, Jr., *Public Opinion and American Democracy* (New York: Knopf, 1961), p. 218, and William Brink and Louis Harris, *Black and White* (New York: Simon & Schuster, 1967).

majority of the population has been black, they have often been disfranchised or manipulated. These factors have operated to blunt the vote as a protective weapon, particularly in the South, where black population and needs have been greatest.

Any evidence of Negro protection from the vote would be persuasive evidence of the efficacy of elections. If self-defense through the ballot can be found in the instance of this most disadvantaged group, it is even more likely to exist for others. Protection for Negroes would indicate that politicians anticipate and defend the interests of the enfranchised, even when the vote is not fully informed and independent.

The South offers a semiexperimental situation for assessing the impact of elections. In this region, Negro voting has been discontinuous. Disfranchised until the Civil War, black Americans gained the vote with the onset of congressional Reconstruction in 1867. They retained the suffrage, at least in part, until the passage of new state constitutions around the turn of the century. In the last two decades, southern Negroes have been slowly regaining the vote. In three different historical periods, therefore, we can appraise and compare the position of the Negro with and without the protection of the ballot.

An immediate problem is to separate the influence of the vote from many other important factors. Even if the existence of a Negro electorate appears related to changes in the Negro's life, we cannot be sure a causal relationship exists. These changes might result from such influences as new attitudes on the part of whites or economic growth. Independent causes might account for both the existence of the Negro vote and the modification in the race's social position. Furthermore, political factors other than votes may be involved. In a federal system, the actions of the national government may be decisive. As discussed in chapter III, the decisions made through elections may be limited through the actions of the courts and the bureaucracy. The vast changes in the South which followed the Supreme Court's desegregation decision of 1954 are obvious illustrations of the nonelectoral means of political change.[3]

In an attempt to assess the impact of the ballot, we will rely on historical and comparative analysis. The time sequence of events is an important indication. If Negro voting precedes Negro social gains, and Negro nonvoting precedes Negro social losses, it is reasonable to conclude that voting affects social position. Comparative studies may also be used, specifically: (1) Comparison of the same states at different times, to control the effect of environmental factors, such as the economy, attitudes, and history; (2) comparison of different states at the same time, to control temporal factors, such as migration, attitude change, and economic growth; (3) comparison of blacks and whites, to isolate racial differences in the effects of previous factors. With these controls, it becomes reasonable to associate changes in black protection with the franchise.

Our analysis necessarily will involve detailed examination of Negro history and of the character of race relations in the United States. These subjects are clearly important in their own right and deserve much fuller study than is possible here. Our purpose, however, is not an historical account. Rather, the changes in the status of Negroes are of interest to us as a case study in the influence of voters on government. By focusing on a group which has needed protection, and which has won, lost, and then regained the franchise, we hope to demonstrate the general protective qualities of elections.

Protection remains to be specified. What is the political meaning of the intangible goals of life, liberty and the pursuit of happiness? Only partial and tentative definitions can be pursued

[3] These methodological problems are ably discussed by William R. Keech in "The Negro Vote as a Political Resource: The Case of Durham" (Ph.D. dissertation, University of Wisconsin, 1966), and "Some Conditions of Negro Influence over Public Policy through Voting," a paper delivered at the 1966 meeting of the American Political Science Association. Professor Keech is now preparing a fuller study of this subject for publication.

here. Protection should be seen in relative terms. The quality of the Negro's status must be judged against that of southern whites. In regard to the relative protection of life, we will concentrate on the cases in which political authorities are involved in the taking of life, such as lynching and capital punishment. While liberty is an ambiguous term, to Negroes it has surely involved the absence of state-supported segregation. The degree of legal separatism will therefore be treated here as an index of the relative restriction of Negroes. The meaning of the pursuit of happiness is still more vague. It would be generally agreed, however, that government can promote individual welfare through public education. Relative equality in Negro schools will be defined here as protection of this third inalienable right.

FROM SLAVERY TO RECONSTRUCTION

While slavery existed, even free Negroes were denied the vote throughout the South and in all of the nation but five states of New England. The freedmen did not gain the suffrage immediately after the end of the Civil War. Reconstruction first proceeded under lenient presidential direction. The defeated states were permitted to establish new governments upon the petition of only a tenth of the former voters. Power was quickly regained by the defeated slaveowners, who excluded Negroes from the franchise through the "Black Codes."

Black entrance into southern politics was delayed until 1867, when Radical Republicans gained control of Congress. This group was inspired both by an idealistic desire to help the freedmen and by a practical desire to win their votes and insure party dominance in the South.[4] The Radicals overturned the existing white governments, imposed military rule on all of the Confederate states but Tennessee, and required new constitutions, black suffrage, and the acceptance of the Fourteenth and Fifteenth amendments to the federal Constitution.

[4] See David Donald, *The Politics of Reconstruction* (Baton Rouge: Louisiana State University Press, 1965).

The Reconstruction governments were neither dominated by Negroes nor dominant for long in the South. Negroes alone never controlled a single state, and no Radical rule of any color ever existed in Tennessee or Virginia. In the other states, the Republican majority soon collapsed. Whites came to be solidified in the reviving Democratic or Conservative parties of the region. By congressional action in 1872, political rights were restored to all but 600 former Confederates. As white Redemption progressed, various means of fraud, intimidation, and violence were used to bar Negroes from the polls. "Within ten years after the surrender at Appomattox—including two years of native white rule—eight states had been 'redeemed' and their redemption had been effected within a range of a few months to seven years after their readmission to the union."[5] After the disputed election of 1876, the Republican party consented to the removal of the last troops from the South, in return for southern acquiescence in the election of Hayes as President. White supremacist governments were fully established.[6]

The fruits of black voting after the Civil War cannot be attributed simply to the fact that blacks or their white sympathizers controlled southern state governments for long periods of time with the force of federal guns. Even without control, however, blacks did enjoy the vote during Reconstruction, and this resource did contribute a degree of protection.

The life of Negroes was imperfectly assured under slavery. Having the legal status of property, the slave enjoyed the security equivalent to that of a valuable machine. A master was considered unlikely to destroy his property, and any damage to a slave by others required financial compensation. Although some 300 persons were lynched in the South from 1840 to 1860, only

[5] John Hope Franklin, *Reconstruction* (Chicago: University of Chicago Press, 1961), p. 197, and chap. 11.

[6] See Paul Lewinson, *Race, Class and Party,* paper ed. (New York: Grosset and Dunlap, 1965), chap. 3, for a general history, and C. Vann Woodward, *Reunion and Reaction* (Garden City: Doubleday Anchor, 1956), for the Compromise of 1877.

about a tenth were Negroes.[7] No meaningful protection, however, was provided against the violence of masters. The number of unnatural slave deaths, though unrecorded, was undoubtedly very high. "Without the power to punish, which the state conferred upon the master, bondage could not have existed. By comparison, all other techniques of control were of secondary importance."[8]

Black lives were endangered during both presidential and congressional Reconstruction. An authoritative estimate is that 5,000 blacks were killed during the entire period.[9] Lynching came to be directed against the freedman, for "with the abolition of legal slavery his immunity vanished. The economic interest of his former protectors, the master class, now stood the other way about—required that he should be promptly disabused of any illusion that his liberty was real, and confirmed in his ancient docility. And so the road stood all but wide open to the ignoble hate and cruel itch to take him in hand which for so long had been festering impotently in the poor whites."[10]

A considerable proportion of this violence was concentrated in the period immediately after the war, when white supremacist governments held sway, and in the years in which the Redemption parties were gaining control. Some improvement in the protection of life apparently occurred during the intervening period of Radical rule. Federal Force Acts and anti-Klan measures, state laws, and the arming of Negro militiamen contributed to a decline in anti-Negro violence in 1870–74. Still, the continued existence of the Klan and its clandestine support by most whites limited the effect of such measures.[11]

[7] W. J. Cash, *The Mind of the South* (New York: Knopf, 1941), Doubleday Anchor ed., p. 56.

[8] Kenneth M. Stampp, *The Peculiar Institution* (New York: Knopf, 1956), p. 171.

[9] Gunnar Myrdal, *An American Dilemma* (New York: Harper, 1944), McGraw-Hill paper ed., Vol. I, p. 450.

[10] Cash, p. 123.

[11] See Vernon L. Wharton, *The Negro in Mississippi 1865–1900* (Chapel Hill: University of North Carolina Press, 1947), p. 221, and Joel Williamson, *After Slavery* (Chapel Hill: University of North Carolina Press, 1965), pp. 259–73.

Liberty clearly increased for Negroes during this period. While slavery was the most obvious restriction on freedom, the Negro's status did not improve greatly upon emancipation. The reinstated white governments passed a series of "Black Codes," so that freedmen "should to the utmost extent practicable be limited, controlled, and surrounded with such safeguards as will make the change as slight as possible both to the white man and to the negro."[12] Under the Codes, Negroes were required to be attached to a master, who could hold them to service and could punish them through control of their wages. The freedman's travel, occupations, and property rights were restricted. Details of personal conduct were prescribed for Negroes, while they were denied the use of the courts to enforce proper behavior on the part of whites. In addition, every southern government in this period rejected the Fourteenth Amendment adopted by Congress, which provided for citizenship, "due process of law," and "equal protection of the laws" for all persons in the states.

The Radical governments, elected with new black votes, reversed this course. Not only were the Black Codes repealed, but attempts were made to further racial integration. The courts were opened to both races. Desegregated schools were mandated in the new Louisiana constitution and were implied in the South Carolina charter. Many states passed laws requiring nondiscrimination in the use of public facilities, such as railroads, hotels, and restaurants. In most instances, these laws were not employed or enforced. Nevertheless, the statutes did provide some measure of formal liberty for blacks during the period.[13]

The greatest achievements of the Radical governments, and their greatest contrast with the period of black disfranchisement, related to public education. Under slavery, instruction

[12] Williamson, p. 75.

[13] See George B. Tindall, *South Carolina Negroes 1877–1900* (Columbia: University of South Carolina Press, 1952), pp. 293–300. The definitive account of the history of segregation is C. Vann Woodward, *The Strange Career of Jim Crow*, 2nd rev. ed. (New York: Oxford University Press, 1966); for this particular period, see pp. 22–29.

even of free Negroes was illegal. The restored white regimes did little to provide schooling for whites and did nothing at all for Negroes. By contrast, the Radicals established the principle of free education in all of the Confederate states. Furthermore, they extended this means for the pursuit of happiness to blacks as well as whites, provided definite tax sources in all states, and established a minimum school term in almost all of the rebel territories. The number of students actually enrolled in school increased toward the established goals. In South Carolina, for example, no more than 20,000 white children had been enrolled in the free schools before the war. In 1870, only 8,000 of each race were enrolled. By 1876, there were 50,000 whites and 71,000 blacks attending school for four to five months of the year, a long term for the era. A similar development occurred in North Carolina.[14]

Widespread hostility to public education and the depressed economic conditions of the South kept the region's educational systems highly deficient by modern standards. Whatever the deficiencies, however, they tended to be shared by the races. In Mississippi, teachers of both races received the ludicrous salary of $53 a month. State school spending in Alabama was distributed fairly on the basis of per capita population, and South Carolina provided $1.85 a year for both black and white students.[15]

As Radical Reconstruction ended, Negroes were clearly in a better position than their voteless fellows during slavery and presidential Reconstruction. Life was insecure, but political authorities attempted some protection. Personal liberty had been provided in law, if not in fact. A system of public education was developing. These improvements had been furthered by the presence of northern troops, congressional intervention, and the new legal guarantees of the Constitution. Negro voters, moreover, were often manipulated by whites and clearly were not

[14] Edgar W. Knight, *The Influence of Reconstruction on Education in the South* (New York: Teachers College, 1913), pp. 89–94.

[15] Wharton, p. 246; Horace Mann Bond, *Negro Education in Alabama* (Washington: Associated Publishers, 1939), chap. 7; Tindall, p. 212.

well versed in politics. Negro citizens, therefore, did not control policy, but the behavior of government appears to have been affected by their presence. Officials anticipated Negro demands and provided protections. Apparently, the simple existence of a large Negro electorate had wrought changes in the actions of southern politicians.

PROTECTION AND DISFRANCHISEMENT

The successes of the Redeemers, completed by 1877, left the blacks without direct political power, but not without at least indirect political influence. The new political order in the South did not immediately and universally mean black disfranchisement. The black vote declined, but did not disappear for about two decades. It is an indication of the importance of the vote alone that black interests continued to be considered even after white supremacists returned to power.

In South Carolina, for example, Redeemer Wade Hampton made and fulfilled pledges to Negroes of "Free Men! Free Ballots!! Free Schools!!!"[16] In other states, white factions came to rely on black votes, courting Negro support with both corrupt and conscionable appeals. Economic pressure and outright bribery were used to win some of these votes, but general political benefits were also provided. As one observer put it, "They are just as ready to conciliate the Negro as the Northern politician to flatter the Irishman." As a result, "the Negro was both hated and cajoled, both intimidated and courted, but he could not be ignored as long as he voted."[17]

Full Negro disfranchisement began with the Mississippi constitutional convention of 1890. The process was substantially completed by 1903, when every former Confederate state had adopted either a new constitution or the "white primary," to bar Negroes from the nominating contests of the dominant Democratic party. The legal devices included poll taxes and record-

[16] Tindall, chap. 2.

[17] Woodward, *The Strange Career of Jim Crow*, p. 54.

keeping requirements, literacy and "understanding" tests, property and residence qualifications, "grandfather clauses," registration provisions, and disfranchisement for minor criminal offenses. Any remaining loopholes were closed by discriminatory administration, fraud, and intimidation. The purpose of these restrictions was candidly declared—"universal white manhood suffrage, and the exclusion from the suffrage of every man with a trace of African blood in his veins."[18] The movement achieved its aims. In Louisiana, where statistics are most reliable, there were 130,000 registered Negroes in 1896, and these voters were a majority in 26 parishes. Four years later, under a new constitution, there were only 5,000 Negroes registered, and they constituted a majority in no parish.[19]

Disfranchisement was the result of an unfortunate combination of circumstances. The movement developed because Negro suffrage itself became the principal issue of southern politics and brought the white majority of the region to unite against the Negro. From Redemption until the 1890's, the position of the colored race was not a major question. Negro suffrage did not appear to threaten the direct interests of any large and influential group, but was rather a convenient source of support for some whites. In the last decade of the century, however, the racial question came to the fore, primarily because of the Populist groundswell.

Populism introduced a distinct class conflict into southern and national politics. As whites divided along lines of economic self-interest, the Negro became a potential ally, pawn, or balance of power. An alliance between low-income whites and blacks was promoted in such states as Georgia and Texas and actually achieved considerable gains in North Carolina.[20] Subordinating

[18] The President of the Louisiana constitutional convention of 1898, quoted in U.S. Commission on Civil Rights, *Report* (1959), p. 33. The history and effect of these provisions are elaborated by V. O. Key, Jr., *Southern Politics* (New York: Knopf, 1949), chaps. 25–29.

[19] Lewinson, p. 81.

[20] See Helen G. Edmonds, *The Negro and Fusion Politics in North Carolina 1894–1901* (Chapel Hill: University of North Carolina Press, 1951), chaps. 3–5.

racial differences, the Populists emphasized class unity, "an equalitarianism of want and poverty, the kinship of a common grievance and a common oppressor."[21] Under these circumstances, black suffrage became a distinct threat to the wealthy and conservative Bourbons of the South, who had formerly accepted and controlled black votes.

To other Populists, however, the black vote was to be feared rather than welcomed. Many low-income whites felt economically competitive with blacks. Their racial antipathies increased when the Bourbons bought or bargained for black votes. So long as these votes were available, Populists such as South Carolina's Ben Tillman argued, they could be turned against the interests of poor whites. Only black disfranchisement could guarantee success.

For their different reasons, the opposing white factions came to agree that the Negro vote was dangerous. Whether conservative or radical, "the groups on top at the moment, whatever their political orientation, feared that their opponents might recruit Negro support."[22] To avoid placing the Negro in the crucial balance-of-power position, the white factions united in the disfranchisement movement.

The potential significance of the vote was perversely demonstrated by these attempts to deprive the Negro of its protection. So long as the Negro possessed the ballot, whites recognized that racial advantages might follow. As Henry Grady rationalized, "Let the whites divide, what happens? Here is this dangerous and alien influence that holds the balance of power. It cannot be won by argument, for it is without information, understanding or traditions. . . . It must be bought by race privileges, granted as such, or by money paid outright."[23]

The disfranchisement experience certainly shows that "the vote alone—*without* other sources of power, *without* education or wealth or status, and *without* armed support is not a sufficient

[21] Woodward, *The Strange Career of Jim Crow*, p. 61.
[22] Key, p. 550.
[23] Quoted by Lewinson, pp. 88–89.

resource for effective citizenship."[24] The franchise, by itself, was an insufficient weapon to defend even the very right to vote. Nevertheless, the franchise did make a difference. Before as well as after 1903, Negroes were impoverished, uneducated, despised, and unarmed in the South. These qualities always made them highly vulnerable to attack. When the issues and events of the Populist period made Negroes visible and threatening, the overwhelming power of the united whites led to the loss of suffrage. Until this time, and despite their other disadvantages, Negroes were able to employ their modest measure of political power to gain some definite protections.

The Negro's right to life was insecure even in the early period of Redemption. In North Carolina and other states, a convict lease system was developed, under which Negroes were given inequitably long prison sentences and then hired to railroad companies for the construction of new lines.[25] Lynching reached one of its infamous peaks in 1884, when 160 Negroes were murdered by mobs, primarily in the South. On the other hand, action to curb lynching was taken in some states, promises to this effect were included in the programs of both major parties, and opposition to racial attacks was a major appeal of the Populists to Negroes.

Disfranchisement loosed these restraints on anti-Negro hatreds. Lynchings, riots, and private murders followed the adoption of new constitutional restrictions. In South Carolina, Tillman's Negrophobia had particularly enraged feelings:

> While the state had accustomed itself peacefully to dozens of Negro postmasters before, the appointment of one in 1898 at Lake City touched off a mob that burned the postmaster up in his own house and shot down his family as they escaped. The same year mobs of "white cap" raiders ranged over the

[24] Donald Matthews and James Prothro, *Negroes and the New Southern Politics* (New York: Harcourt, Brace & World, 1966), p. 15. Italics in the original.

[25] Frenise A. Logan, *The Negro in North Carolina 1876–1894* (Chapel Hill: University of North Carolina Press, 1964), chap. 18.

> countryside of Greenwood County shooting and hanging an undetermined number of Negroes. . . . The more defenseless, disfranchised and intimidated the Negro became, the more prone he was to the ruthless aggression of mobs.[26]

The white racist sentiments which generated these outrages undoubtedly existed before disfranchisement and, indeed, inspired the political as well as the physical attack on the blacks. It is important to realize, however, that the loss of the ballot removed one of the restraints on this cruel behavior. Political power was no longer even a possible defense, and the increase in violence evidenced the change.

Protection, whatever its meaning, surely must include governmental defense of the life of citizens. Association of the franchise with personal security would be a meaningful indication of the effects of electoral power. Moreover, this demand need not be explicitly presented by the voters. An official surely knows that they want their lives protected. If he is concerned at all with a group of the population, he will act in its defense.

Trends in lynching provide a general index of blacks' right to life before and after disfranchisement. We cannot prove causation, but an association of lynching and disfranchisement would indicate the influence of the ballot. Although an illegal act, it is difficult for a lynching to occur or to remain unpunished without the knowledge and acquiescence of public officials. Since law enforcement officials are elected locally, their actions or inactions may be affected by their political prospects. One authoritative estimate is that police negligence contributed to 95 per cent of lynchings. "It can hardly be doubted that political considerations were largely responsible for the neglect and indifference characteristic of officers and courts in these cases. The members of the mob were nearly all actual or potential voters; the victim and most of his race, disfranchised by social pressure or other means, were politically impotent." As one Texas sheriff

[26] Woodward, *The Strange Career of Jim Crow*, p. 87.

who permitted a lynching explained, "I handled the thing the best I knew how, and undoubtedly it suited the people of the county, for I was re-elected by a great majority shortly after the affair."[27]

Lynching has steadily declined and virtually disappeared in this century. Vast social changes, not the vote, are the basic causes of this improvement. The crime is associated with a rural population, economic depression, and a lack of recreational facilities. Consequently, the spread of cities, prosperity, and mass media have reduced lynching in all parts of the nation.[28] To isolate the effect of political factors, we must compare the relative decline for each race in the South to that in other areas. A crucial comparison is with the Border states, which shared slavery, distrust of the Negro, and a rural economy with the Confederacy, but which did not fully join in disfranchisement.

The incidence of lynching is shown in Table 9.1, with comparisons made for each race and region. The first of two periods extends from 1882, when the first reliable figures were collected, to 1903, the year in which Southern Negro disfranchisement was completed. The second period extends to 1927, after which time the crime began to disappear.[29]

The number of lynchings declined in all regions and among both races. Yet, southern blacks received comparatively less

[27] Arthur Raper, *The Tragedy of Lynching* (Chapel Hill: University of North Carolina Press, 1933), pp. 13–14, 359.

[28] A clear statistical correlation between cotton prices and the incidence of southern lynchings is found by Buell F. Gallagher, *American Caste and the Negro College* (New York: Columbia University Press, 1938), Appendix A. In a fuller analysis, Walter White also found relationships to the native-born white proportion of the population, the general homicide rate, and the Methodist and Baptist proportion of the church-going population. See *Rope and Faggot* (New York: Knopf, 1929), pp. 227–51.

[29] The figures are derived from White, pp. 254–59, who in turn relied on the authoritative figures collected by Tuskegee Institute. The conservatism of the Institute probably results in an underestimate of Negro lynchings in the later period. More recent figures would only further strengthen the argument. From 1927 to 1956, there were 190 lynchings in the nation, all but 18 of Negroes, and predominantly in the South. See U.S. Bureau of the Census, *Historical Statistics of the United States, Colonial Times to 1957* (1960), p. 218.

protection than any other group. Even while they had the suffrage, they were the principal targets of mob rule. With the loss of the ballot, the blacks of the old Confederacy became almost the exclusive victims. White southerners, living in the same violent environment, fared better. Perhaps in part because they retained their political power over sheriffs, they were largely relieved of the grim sentences of "Judge Lynch."

In other areas, where blacks could vote, they also were less likely to be brutalized. As seen in Table 9.1, the number of lynchings declined considerably and at a faster rate than in the South, both in the border states and in the rest of the nation. This relative improvement occurred, moreover, despite the tensions arising from vastly increased black migration. While the number of lynchings of southern blacks fell by less than a third after 1903, there was a 37 per cent decrease in the border states, and a 50 per cent decline in the rest of the nation. The significant comparison is not in the absolute numbers, which reflect population totals, but in the relative declines.

Data on the prevention of lynchings, though scant, confirms the regional differences. In 1903–31, blacks were brutalized in 23 different incidents, while mobs were thwarted in 62 cases in the South. There was one lynching of a white man, and 9 prevented attacks. Outside of the former Confederacy, 5 blacks

Table 9.1 Lynchings, by Region and Race, 1882–1927

Region and Race	*1882–1903*		*1904–27*	
	No.	*%*	*No.*	*%*
Southern Negroes	1,795	53	1,227	78
Southern Whites	466	13	100	6
Border-state Negroes	198	6	125	6
Border-state Whites	222	7	28	3
All Other Negroes	68	3	34	3
All Other Whites	594	18	33	3
Totals	3,343	100%	1,547	100%

were lynched and 15 were protected, while among whites the numbers were one and 7.[30] The figures are small, but there was an evident tendency for blacks to be more secure against mobs outside the South, and for a lesser disparity in white and black safety.

To be sure, other factors were involved in lynching than the franchise. Even without the vote, mob violence against Negroes did decline in the South. Strikingly, the same South Carolina constitution which disfranchised Negroes also provided for the removal of any sheriff negligent in preventing a lynching and for the payment of damages by the county government to the victim's family.[31] Protection might come in other ways, but it is also evident that the vote tended to be associated with the reality of the right to life. No better example exists than that of Georgia Populist Tom Watson. While he sought black votes Watson condemned lynching and mobilized white men to prevent a threatened black lynching. After disfranchisement, Watson openly wrote of the black man, "We have to lynch him occasionally, and flog him, now and then, to keep him from blaspheming the Almighty, by his conduct, on account of his smell and his color."[32] The loss of the vote was significant, indeed, when it exposed the Negro's very life to these sentiments.

SEGREGATION, EDUCATION, AND THE VOTE

The loss of the vote was also associated with declines in the protection of the Negro's right to liberty and the pursuit of happiness. Restrictions on liberty were most evident in the growth of mandatory, legal segregation. There was no immediate movement toward separatism upon the defeat of the Radical Republi-

[30] Raper, Appendix B. Among the prevented southern Negro lynchings were some in which the trial amounted to a legal lynching, such as the notorious Scottsboro case, *Powell* v. *Alabama*, 287 U.S. 45 (1932).

[31] White, chaps. 8, 9.

[32] C. Vann Woodward, "Tom Watson and the Negro in Agrarian Politics," in Charles E. Wynes, ed., *The Negro in the South since 1865* (University: University of Alabama Press, 1965), p. 61.

cans, nor even after the Supreme Court invalidated federal civil rights laws in 1883.[33] The bulk of the segregation laws was not passed until the turn of the century—significantly, after the Negro had lost his vote.

As Woodward has proven, "In the earlier part of the period reviewed, the Negro could and did do many things in the South that in the latter part of the period, under different [and nonvoting] conditions, he was prevented from doing."[34] Before 1900 the majority of southern states legally required segregation only in railroad cars. Georgia alone also applied the doctrine to other transportation such as street cars and the extreme statutes mandating separate drinking fountains, textbooks, circus entrances, and cemeteries were the product of an era when Negroes were politically powerless. Even the white primary was not generally adopted until the states had first passed the constitutional provisions sufficient to eliminate black voting.

The relationship between disfranchisement and the passage of Jim Crow laws was not always direct. Some segregationist laws were passed in the earlier years, and some non-Confederate states legislated segregation but not disfranchisement. The associations between the two phenomena are persistent enough, nevertheless, to support the belief that the existence of even a weak black electorate provided some safety for the race.

In South Carolina, all attempts to repeal civil rights laws were repelled until 1889, and white legislators from black areas were prominent in the defense of these Reconstruction acts.[35] In North Carolina as well, state civil rights acts remained on the books—and were employed—throughout the nineteenth century. The turning point did not come in the Tarheel state until 1899, when a legislative majority elected on a white supremacy platform eliminated Negro suffrage and then enacted the state's first Jim Crow laws.[36] Mississippi prohibited racial intermarriage in 1880

[33] *Civil Rights Cases*, 109 U.S. 3.

[34] Woodward, *The Strange Career of Jim Crow*, p. 105.

[35] Tindall, p. 293.

[36] Logan, chap. 17; Edmonds, chap. 12.

and required railroad segregation in 1888, but most other separatist statutes were passed after the 1890 constitution was adopted. Legal segregation first came to railroad depots in 1892, to street cars in 1906, and to state charity hospitals in 1910.[37]

The Negro's position in the South was never a happy one, but until the loss of the vote, it did generally lack the indignity of official sanctions of racial separation and suppression. "Exploitation there was in that period, as in other periods and in other regions, but it did not follow then that the exploited had to be ostracized. Subordination there was also, unmistakable subordination, but it was not yet an accepted corollary that the subordinated had to be totally segregated and needlessly humiliated by a thousand daily reminders of their subordination."[38]

Exclusion from the polls brought a relative deterioration as well in education, the blacks' means for the pursuit of happiness. The Redeemers had promised to maintain the system of public education. Said Mississippi Governor Stone in 1877, "Our prosperity and greatness as a state, and happiness as a people, depend upon free and liberal education of the youth of both races."[39] The pledge of racial equality was generally kept so long as blacks retained the vote. Although the schools were quite poor, the quality of black schools did not worsen substantially in comparison to those of whites. Promises were also made to Negroes at the time of disfranchisement. North Carolina Governor Aycock in 1900 declared, "We must not only educate ourselves, but see to it that the Negro has an opportunity for education."[40] Booker T. Washington in turn accepted the loss of suffrage and urged his race to concentrate on self-improvement through education. Without the franchise, however, these promises and hopes were not fulfilled.

[37] Pauli Murray, ed., *States' Laws on Race and Color* (Woman's Division of Christian Service, 1950), pp. 237–50. See Wharton, chap. 15.

[38] Woodward, *The Strange Career of Jim Crow*, p. 44.

[39] Stuart G. Noble, *Forty Years of the Public Schools of Mississippi* (New York: Teachers College, 1918), p. 49.

[40] U.S. Commission on Civil Rights. North Carolina Advisory Committee, *Equal Protection of the Laws in North Carolina* (1963), p. 131.

Various legislative schemes had been offered in the earlier period to deprive Negroes of educational opportunities. A favorite proposal was to segregate taxes, so that only the direct taxes paid on Negro property would be available for the colored race's schools. Such plans were consistently defeated while the Negro remained at least a potential voter. Then, "Disfranchisement made the Negro vote negligible and stripped Negro school funds of what meager protection they had earlier enjoyed. In states where the change was made by constitutional convention, educational law was altered at the same time to make easier the diversion of Negro school funds to white schools at county or district levels."[41] State payments were no longer made on a per capita basis, but county officials were given, and used, discretionary powers to provide funds for whites and to deny them to blacks.

Educational statistics for this period are scarce, but consistent. The data on school attendance, summarized in Table 9.2, are illustrative. In 1880, there existed disparities between the races, but the inequities were not peculiar to the former Confederacy. In six of these eleven states, including Alabama and Louisiana, the proportion of blacks in school was greater than or similar to that of enrolled whites. In all of the border states, by contrast, the proportion of blacks in school was at least 10 per cent less than that of whites. There is no indication, there-

Table 9.2 Persons Five to Eighteen Enrolled in Common Schools
(In Percentages)

	Southern and Border States		
Year	*Whites*	*Blacks*	*U.S.*
1880	56	43	63
1889–90	66	52	69
1899–1900	72	58	72
1908–9	75	56	72

[41] Louis R. Harlan, *Separate and Unequal* (Chapel Hill: University of North Carolina Press, 1958), p. 40.

fore, that acceptance of Negro education was traditionally greater in these states.

Black enrollment worsened in relation to that of whites after disfranchisement, and the deterioration was clearly peculiar to the former rebel states. By 1909, in each of them but Arkansas, the proportion of blacks in school was at least 10 per cent below the registration of whites. In the border states, where inequality had been greatest, the deficiency of Negroes was this high only in one state, and in West Virginia, a greater proportion of Negroes was enrolled.[42]

Deterioration was also evident in pupil-teacher ratios, another measure of educational quality. In 1889, for all former slave states, there were 43 enrolled pupils for every white teacher and 54 black children for every teacher of that race. The disparity was less than suggested by these figures, because some white teachers still worked in black schools. In 1900, when segregation was virtually complete, the ratio was still 43 for whites but had risen to 58 for blacks. By 1908–9, the gap had increased to 40–57.[43] In Virginia, the difference ranged as high as 36 whites to a teacher, compared to 75 blacks.[44]

Public education was obviously deficient throughout this period, and the black child bore more than his share of these deficiencies even before his parents lost the vote. In 1900, the federal Office of Education estimated that a black student received half as much school aid as a white child in both southern and border states.[45] He attended a school further from his home, with a shorter term and poorer equipment, and staffed by fewer and less able teachers than his white contemporary.[46] But the

[42] These paragraphs, and Table 9.2, are based on: U.S. *Report of the Commissioner of Education for the Year 1880* (1882), pp. xii, lvii; *Report for Fiscal Year Ended June 30, 1910* (1911), Vol. II, pp. 670, 1260.

[43] U.S. Commissioner of Education, *Report* (1911), Vol. II. p. 1261.

[44] W. E. B. DuBois and A. G. Dill, *The Common School and the Negro American* (Atlanta: Atlanta University Press, 1911), p. 41.

[45] *Report* (1901), Vol. I, pp. 99–100.

[46] Harlan, pp. 12–13.

worst discrimination did not occur until after disfranchisement. By 1910, the Negro child received only a fourth as much aid as the Caucasian. His teachers' salaries had been reduced, both absolutely and relative to those of whites. While the region began a vast program of educational expansion in the first decade of the twentieth century, almost all of these new facilities were reserved for the children of white electors. Virginia alone built 325 high schools in six years, but not a single Negro student entered one of them. In the entire South in 1910, there were only 88 Negro high schools, seven *fewer* than in 1905.[47]

Educational disparities increased in individual states as well. In Mississippi, for example, teacher salaries remained equal for both races until 1886. By the time of the new constitution of 1890, white salaries were $33 a month, and black $23. By 1905, Negro remuneration was actually reduced to $20, while white payments reached $42. An initial pupil-teacher disparity of 34 whites to 51 blacks became a difference of 36 to 67. The quality of Negro teachers declined as well, at least according to local certification standards. Where 40 per cent of black instructors were on the lowest level of certification in 1890, 52 per cent fell into this category in 1910. The apparent decline in quality was probably related to the ending in 1890 of most state support for Negro normal schools.[48]

Education in North Carolina had remained relatively equal during the nineteenth century. In 1880, state annual per capita aid amounted to $1.47 for each white pupil and only nine cents less for blacks. By 1894 the disparity had widened only slightly, to $1.93 to $1.72. Five normal schools were established for Negroes, as well as a Negro college, in the decade before 1897. Some whites expressed concern that "the Negroes are improving in education faster than the whites, which is a sad state of things," but the political climate did not permit action to deprive them of their opportunities.[49] After disfranchisement, "what

[47] Dubois and Dill, pp. 122–34.

[48] Noble, pp. 76, 88.

[49] Logan, pp. 141–52.

may properly be described as the rape of the Negro school fund occurred every day and under the process of law." From an equitable 28 per cent of the school funds in 1900, the Negro share dropped to 13 per cent in 1915. High schools, transportation, and other educational features were monopolized by whites.[50]

The same pattern was found in Alabama. After Redemption, white enrollment had increased from 91,000 to 160,000, but black enrollment more than kept pace with an increase from 55,000 to 99,000 by 1888. State aid to the schools continued to be provided on an equal per capita basis until 1891, and black political influence was directly responsible for the establishment of Tuskegee Institute. In 1891, Wilcox county, in the heart of the Black Belt, reported spending 50 per cent more on the salaries of black than white teachers. By 1908, however, spending for blacks had declined from 65¢ to 37¢ per pupil, while expenditures for white pupils had increased to $12.20 each.[51] In South Carolina, racial differences in spending were as high as 60–1 in the Black Belt, and 12–1 for the entire state. The school term was lengthened from 105 to 133 days for whites, while it decreased for blacks from 75 to 67 days.[52] Although Florida doubled its expenditure for black children in the 1899–1909 decade, it tripled the greater spending for whites.[53]

The fruits of educational discrimination can be seen in the course of illiteracy in the South during these years. From 1870 to 1890, the Confederate states made considerable progress in eliminating Negro ignorance. In eight of the eleven areas, progress exceeded the national average. In the border states, only three of five states did as well. From 1890 to 1910, there was less progress. Only two of the Confederate states surpassed

[50] Harlan, p. 131 and chap. 4.

[51] Bond, p. 162 and chaps. 10–12.

[52] Harlan, chap. 6.

[53] Dubois and Dill, p. 68; Dubois, *The Negro Common School* (Atlanta: Atlanta University Press, 1901), p. 71.

the national average in the increase of Negro literacy, compared again to three of the five border states.[54]

The relative position of Negroes in regard to literacy worsened after 1900. Although literacy increased absolutely among both races, comparison of persons educated before and after the loss of suffrage shows that ability to read increased faster among whites than blacks. The comparative position of the younger colored generation, in school after disfranchisement, was actually worse than that of their elders, leaving them less fit to compete in a modern civilization. In Mississippi, for example, there was eight times as much illiteracy among blacks than whites in the older generation and over nine times as much among younger Negroes. The proportions of white illiterates in the younger generation was reduced to 5 per cent in all states but Louisiana, while black illiterates constituted 15 per cent of their age group in all but three states. In the border region, by contrast, both the absolute and relative position of younger Negroes was better than that of their elders in all states but Maryland, and only in the latter state was the proportion of young Negro illiterates greater than a tenth.[55]

The conditions of southern Negro life before and after the turn of the century suggest a definite association between the right of suffrage and the protection of vital interests. Voting alone does not protect these interests. Even when admitted to the polls, Negroes were liable to lynching, segregation, discrimination in public spending, and eventually to disfranchisement itself. Even when voteless, there was an absolute decline in lynching and some improvement in education. In relation to whites and to voting members of his race in other regions, however, the

[54] Dubois and Dill, p. 16.

[55] The comparison is made of persons aged thirty-five to forty-four in 1920 with those aged fifteen to twenty-four. The older group would have attended school before 1900, since formal education usually ended by the age of fifteen. The younger group would have had its opportunity for schooling after 1902, when its senior members reached the age of six. See U.S. Bureau of the Census, *Fourteenth Census of the United States, Taken in the Year 1920* (1922), Vol. II, pp. 1161–80.

southern black suffered most when he was without recourse to the ballot. His race became the predominant target of lynching; his inferior status was underlined through legal segregation; and his children bore the costs of a comparatively worsening education. The ballot could not guarantee his life, liberty, and happiness, but the absence of the vote made these rights far more difficult to secure.

THE REVIVAL OF NEGRO VOTING

Black voting remained low in the South through the first four decades of this century. Renewed political participation by colored southerners began with the Supreme Court's abolition of the white primary in 1944.[56] In the following years, civil rights movements spurred an irregular growth in Negro voting. The legal manifestation of these movements was the passage of five federal civil rights acts concentrated on assuring racial access to the ballot box. By 1966, as seen in Table 9.3, nearly a third or more of adult blacks had registered to vote in all southern states but Mississippi.[57]

The revival of the black vote offers a third opportunity to analyze the differences in racial conditions associated with the right to suffrage. However, many factors other than the exercise of the franchise undoubtedly had an effect on these conditions. Emigration by blacks reduced their perceived threat to white southerners. Improved economic conditions contributed to more equal treatment of the races in public spending. Attitudes of racial tolerance grew, stimulated by resistance to the racist ideology of nazism, competition with the egalitarian appeal of communism, and concern over the emergence of African and Asian nationalism. Within the United States, judicial action was

[56] *Smith v. Allwright,* 321 U.S. 649 (1944).

[57] Table 9.3 is derived from Matthews and Prothro, p. 148, and supplemented by figures in *The New York Times,* May 15, 1966, section IV, p. E-3. The Tennessee 1958 figure is estimated.

a potent stimulant of racial equality.[58] Such independent factors, as well as changed black attitudes, might account for both increased black voting and improved racial conditions.

Table 9.3 Negro Registration in the South, 1940–66
(In Percentages of Adult Negroes Registered)

State	*1940*	*1947*	*1952*	*1958*	*1960*	*1964*	*1966*
Alabama	*	1	4	15	14	19	31
Georgia	2	20	23	26	29	27	46
Louisiana	*	2	25	26	31	32	39
Mississippi	*	1	4	5	6	7	14
South Carolina	*	13	20	15	16	37	38
Virginia	5	11	16	21	23	34	49
Arkansas	3	21	27	33	38	40	54
Florida	3	13	33	31	39	51	62
North Carolina	10	14	18	32	38	47	49
Tennessee	16	25	27	48	59	73	72
Texas	9	17	31	39	35	58	59

* Less than 0.5.

Even when electoral politics contributed to change in the Negro's status, its impact was national as well as southern. The federal government, particularly the executive branch, became increasingly active in the cause of civil rights. The acts of the President and the bureaucracy were surely stimulated by the importance of Negro votes in the North, which were increasingly numerous, freely cast, and strategically located for victory in the Electoral College. Even in 1942, Myrdal predicted, "The Northern vote might become the instrument by which the Negroes can increasingly use the machinery of federal legislation and administration to tear down the walls of discrimination."[59] In time, the parties came to make specific appeals for this vote.[60]

[58] For a general review, see Woodward, *The Strange Career of Jim Crow*, chaps. 4, 5.

[59] Myrdal, Vol. I, p. 440.

[60] See chapter VII, *supra*, pp. 169–70, and Henry Lee Moon, *Balance of Power: The Negro Vote* (Garden City: Doubleday, 1948).

The unique influence of southern black voting can be sought by comparison of trends in the South with those in the nation and in the border states and by comparisons within the former Confederacy. Although all of the eleven states disfranchised Negroes at the beginning of the century, the revival of the Negro vote has been uneven. In five states, a relatively high proportion of Negroes could vote by 1958 and 1960, even before federal action became important. Arkansas, Florida, North Carolina, Tennessee, and Texas therefore will be considered "voting states," in comparison with the remaining six "nonvoting states." If the ballot provides protection, it should be evident particularly in the first group of states.

Recent voting by southern Negroes appears related to the security of life. Perhaps "the most important thing that Negroes get out of politics when they vote is legal justice—justice in the courts, police protection and protection against the persecution of the police. Even where Negroes have only a few votes in the South they have at least some opportunity to bargain for police and court protection."[61] Supporting evidence for this proposition is provided by charges of police brutality made to the U.S. Department of Justice from 1958 to 1960. A charge of brutality is not the same as a demonstrated case. However, it is likely that the complaints severely underestimate the incidence of brutality, particularly in the case of southern blacks. Nevertheless, a sharp regional disparity is evident. In the North, 117 complaints were made by blacks and 193 by whites, while 25 blacks and 33 whites in the border states felt aggrieved by local police. In the South, however, a majority of complaints, 319, came from blacks, compared to 280 from whites.[62]

Does voting account for these differences? A limited number of local community studies indicate the relationship. Even in Florida towns where the Negro vote was controlled by whites, "fair and decent treatment" by the police resulted from the whites' "calculated choice based on strategic considerations of

[61] Myrdal, Vol. I, p. 497.

[62] U.S. Commission on Civil Rights, *Report* (1961), Book 5, pp. 26, 264.

the Negro vote."[63] In Durham, North Carolina, police brutality declined, and blacks received better court treatment and began to serve on juries after winning the vote.[64] Among Black Belt counties of high Negro population, a distinct difference was found between areas in which blacks did or did not vote. "In all of the voting counties (and some of the nonvoting counties) Negroes regularly serve on, or at least appear on the panels for, juries. There were no allegations of police brutality, mob violence or illegal police practice in any of the four voting counties. Yet, although white informants often disagreed, Negroes complained of these practices in many of the others."[65] In eight Mississippi areas with varying levels of Negro political participation, there was a "strong correlation between Negro registration and equality in the administration of justice."[66]

Capital punishment is the extreme case in which the state fails to protect the right to life. Although this is a macabre instance, political factors are relevant, for they may affect ambitious attorneys, juries selected from voter lists, elected police chiefs and judges, and governors with the power to commute sentences. Discrimination at the ballot box can lead to discrimination in the execution chamber.

The existence of discrimination is tested here by comparing executions among blacks and whites convicted of felonies. (For purposes of this comparison, we make the unlikely assumption that blacks and whites receive equal treatment in the earlier phases of law enforcement.) An index has been constructed in which "equality" is indicated by 1, while discrimination in favor of or against blacks is indicated, respectively, by a lower or higher number. In Table 9.4, executions in 1940

[63] Alfred Clubok *et al.*, "The Manipulated Negro Vote: Preconditions and Consequences," *Journal of Politics*, Vol. 26 (February, 1964), pp. 121–24.

[64] Keech, "The Negro Vote as a Political Resource," pp. 106–16.

[65] U.S. Commission on Civil Rights, *Report* (1961), Book 1, p. 193.

[66] Hugh Stephen Whitaker, "'A New Day': The Effects of Negro Enfranchisement in Selected Mississippi Counties" (Ph.D. dissertation, Florida State University, 1965), p. 102 and chap. 5. Rank-order correlation yielded a coefficient of .86. The Civil Rights Commission reached a similar conclusion in *Law Enforcement* (1965), pp. 87–99.

and 1961–65 are compared for the nation as a whole, the border states, four states in which blacks were relatively free to vote in 1960, and five states in which their franchise was restricted.[67]

Table 9.4 Civil Executions, 1940 and 1961–65

		1940			*1961–65*	
Area	*Black*	*White*	*Index*	*Black*	*White*	*Index*
United States	75	49	3.9	57	74	1.4
Border States	8	6	2.7	2	6	.6
Voting South	21	8	4.1	5	7	1.0
Nonvoting South	19	3	4.1	15	10	1.5

It is obvious that the number of executions among both races has declined, that discrimination against Negroes existed in all areas of the nation in 1940, and that this discrimination has lessened universally and considerably. The regional comparisons indicate some association between voting and relative equality. Even in 1940, Negro felons received greater consideration where members of their race could vote, such as the border states. Among the Confederate states in 1940, there was no judicial difference, just as there was no difference in Negro voting. In more recent years, the border and voting states have achieved equality on death row, but there is still discrimination in the other states.[68]

[67] The index is simply calculated as: Negro Executions ÷ White Executions × Number of White Felons in Prison ÷ Number of Negro Felons in Prison. Texas is omitted from the voting states because its record indicates an unusual propensity to exact the death penalty, a possible result of unusual laws and/or a remaining frontier tradition. Among the nonvoting states, Mississippi is omitted to balance the comparison and because of its unusual harshness toward Negro felons.

[68] The sources for Table 9.4 are U.S. Bureau of the Census, *Prisoners in State and Federal Prisons and Reformatories 1940* (1943), pp. 33, 69, for 1940. The number of felons in the later period is taken to be the number in 1960, obtained in U.S. Department of Justice, Federal Bureau of Prisons, *Characteristics of State Prisoners 1960* (1965), p. 40. The number of executions is obtained by state by subtracting the total numbers to 1960 from the totals through 1965. These are available in U.S. Bureau of Prisons, *National Prisoner Statistics,* Bulletin No. 20 (March, 1961), pp. 5–6, and *National Prisoner Statistics,* Bulletin No. 39 (March, 1966), pp. 1–13.

To turn to the second inalienable right, the new black vote in the South has not yet proven its potency in removing segregation as a restriction on liberty. In some cases, extreme defenders of the separatist doctrine have been retired from politics with the aid of black voters. Campaigns are no longer waged exclusively on the segregation issue, and many white southern politicians have turned to other questions in an effort to win black support. From Texas to Virginia, and even in South Carolina and Mississippi, more stress has been placed on economic, not racial, policy. In other cases, however, the effect of new black enfranchisement has been no more than symbolic. Thus, George Wallace of Alabama retained control of his state, although he only changed from the frank espousal of racism to the subtle rhetoric of states' rights.[69]

Where eliminated, segregation usually has fallen by means of direct action, federal legislation, and court tests, rather than by Negro votes. In Durham, for example, integration was achieved by sit-ins and court orders. However, the desegregation of lunch counters was facilitated by the mayor elected with Negro support, and public officials offered no resistance to court actions on public facilities. Voting may have indirectly promoted these outcomes.[70] In the Black Belt, as in rural Florida, "segregation is just as much a fact of life where Negroes vote as it is where they do not," but a slight relationship exists in Mississippi between registration and desegregation.[71]

Desegregation has been most contentious in regard to the public schools. Other influences than the black vote have been clearly important in this case, from the original Supreme Court decision in 1954 to the recent guidelines of the federal Office of Education. On a statewide level, however, there has also been a relation between black voting and desegregation. In both the

[69] See *The New York Times*, April 14, 1966, p. 27, for the effects in Alabama, and April 8, 1967, p. 30, for Mississippi.

[70] Keech, "The Negro Vote as a Political Resource," pp. 176–206.

[71] U.S. Commission on Civil Rights, *Report* (1961), Book 1, p. 192. Cf. Whitaker, pp. 125–29, Clubok, p. 128.

border states and the voting states of the South, the first integration of schools occurred voluntarily. By contrast, in all of the states with a low proportion of black voters, court orders were required before integration began.[72]

Differences among the states are highlighted by the record through 1964, when the federal bureaucracy assumed major responsibility for the school program. In the border states, aside from Delaware, all but 19 of 631 districts acted voluntarily. In southern states with Negro voters, 325 districts acted voluntarily, in contrast to 32 court-ordered actions. In the nonvoting states, however, only 37 districts acted voluntarily, while 29 were required to accept common schools by judicial intervention.[73]

Negro voting alone certainly did not accomplish desegregation. Separate schools were ended in many places where Negroes did not vote, just as integration was thwarted in some areas where they exercised the franchise. The importance of other factors is shown by statistical analysis on a county, rather than state, basis. On this level, any relationship which exists between Negro registration and school desegregation is found to be the result of the underlying social factor of the concentration of Negro population. Desegregation is most likely where Negroes, whether voters or not, are a relatively small proportion of the total population.[74]

These findings suggest that white attitudes, rather than black ballots, are the key factor in school integration. However, a survey of white opinion in 1963 indicated that whites in both segregated and desegregated school districts were opposed to

[72] For a general account of desegregation, see Benjamin Muse, *Ten Years of Prelude* (New York: Viking, 1964).

[73] Southern Education Reporting Service, *Statistical Summary of School Segregation-Desegregation in the Southern and Border States* (1963–64), p. 38. For differences in the states' legislative responses, see *Southern School News*, Vol. 10 (May, 1964), p. 5B.

[74] Donald Matthews and James Prothro, "Stateways Versus Folkways: Critical Factors in Southern Reactions to *Brown v. Board of Education*," in Gottfried Dietze, ed., *Essays on the American Constitution* (Englewood Cliffs: Prentice-Hall, 1964), pp. 148–54.

biracial schools and that the difference in their attitudes was relatively slight. The black vote may have helped to account for the differences in actual behavior in these areas.[75]

Furthermore, it is difficult to make comparisons of counties across the entire South because of the importance of state laws on this subject. Even if local communities had been willing to act in response to Negro constituents, state action in opposition to desegregation might have prevented it. An examination of a single state, Virginia, eliminates this complication. The Old Dominion is a special example of the influence of the vote. Although regarded as moderate on racial questions, the state was one in which relatively few Negroes voted before 1960. Virginia led the campaign in the South for "massive resistance" to desegregation, and it was one of the only states in which schools were closed to avoid entrance of Negro pupils. As Negro voting climbed, Virginia also became one of the most educationally integrated states in the region.

Further evidence is available in the individual counties and cities of the state. Of 51 areas with desegregated schools in 1963, blacks voted in relatively high proportions in 37. Of 64 areas with full segregation, on the other hand, only 34 had a high proportion of blacks registered to vote. The coefficient of correlation (Yule's *Q*) is a significant .40. The relationship is not automatic or complete, in Virginia or the entire South, but there is discernible association between the freedom of the ballot and the liberty of desegregated schools.[76]

Most Negro education in the South has continued to be provided in segregated schools. If we are to judge the quality of

[75] Paul B. Sheatsley, "White Attitudes toward the Negro," *Daedalus*, Vol. 95 (Winter, 1966), p. 221.

[76] Only the 115 counties or cities in which Negroes constituted at least 2 per cent of the population in 1960 were considered. Negro voting was considered relatively high where the Negro proportion of the total registration was at least half of the Negro share of the total voting-age population. Voting and population data are from U.S. Commission on Civil Rights, *Report* (1961), Book 1, pp. 302–7. Desegregation figures are from Southern Education Reporting Service, *Statistical Summary*, p. 53.

this instruction, therefore, and the consequent protection of the right to the pursuit of happiness, we must compare separate, rather than integrated, schools. This measurement of quality is not meant to challenge the Supreme Court's 1954 finding that segregated education is inherently unequal.

The deterioration of black schools continued after disfranchisement until the 1930's. At that time, the NAACP began a broad program of litigation to equalize the condition of black and white schools. Since segregation had been justified on the fiction that the separate schools would be equal, the civil rights group attacked from a position of legal strength. State and federal courts began to order parity in teachers' salaries, the provision of high school education for both races, and the admission of blacks to previously all-white colleges. By 1950, the Supreme Court insisted on equality even in intangible qualities.[77] Judicial, rather than political, action was clearly a major method for achieving educational benefits in this period.

All districts did not respond to the new demands to the same degree. There are many indications of the use of the vote as a further means of equalizing school facilities between the races. Myrdal credited the black vote with obtaining free textbooks for black children in Louisiana under Huey Long and with various local improvements elsewhere, including provision for new schools in Atlanta and Dallas.[78] More recent evidence underlines the point. In the Black Belt in 1961, the Civil Rights Commission found, "the gap in quality between white and Negro schools is generally less in the voting than the nonvoting counties as is the gap between white and Negro median educational levels."[79] Almost all of the white high schools in the

[77] See *Sweatt* v. *Painter,* 339 U.S. 629 (1950) and *McLaurin* v. *Oklahoma,* 339 U.S. 637 (1950).

[78] Myrdal, Vol. I, pp. 499–500.

[79] U.S. Commission on Civil Rights, *Report* (1961), Book 1, p. 177. For the entire South, Matthews and Prothro find no relationship between Negro registration and differences in median educational level—*Negroes and the New Southern Politics,* pp. 126–29.

Black Belt counties studied were accredited by the state. Of the Negro high schools, less than a third of those in counties without Negro voters were accredited, while four of five in the voting counties did receive state approval.[80] In Mississippi today, schools for Negroes are not necessarily better where Negroes have voted, but they are quite likely to be more similar to white facilities in such areas.[81] In Durham as well, similar education has tended to be provided for both races. In some cases, equality resulted from explicit bids for the Negro votes necessary for the passage of bond issues. In other cases, the educational authorities seem to have anticipated the need for black support by making provision for the schools of both races.[82]

High school education in North Carolina also is related to voting differences. In 21 of the state's counties in 1962, no blacks (but some whites) were enrolled in schools approved by the regional accrediting association. In only one of these counties was there a relatively large and long-standing black electorate.[83] Of all counties with accredited schools in the state, the Negro schools were comparable to the white schools in 33 counties. The black vote was relatively high in 18 of these counties and relatively low in 15 cases. Black schools were clearly inferior to white schools in 20 counties. The colored vote was relatively high in 8 of these cases and relatively low in 12 instances. There is a real, but not strong, relationship between the quality of the schools and the level of black registration (Yule's $Q = .29$). The principal exceptions are in counties where Negro voting is very recent or where new black schools prob-

[80] *Report*, pp. 354–57.

[81] Whitaker, pp. 111–13, derives a rank-order coefficient of .94 between expenditures per Negro child as a percentage of expenditures per white child, and Negro registration. This figure is unrelated, moreover, to the relative wealth of the areas, as indicated by total school spending.

[82] Keech, "The Negro Vote as a Political Resource," pp. 121–58.

[83] *Equal Protection of the Laws in North Carolina*, p. 110. Some Negroes, but no whites, were enrolled in accredited high schools in only four counties.

ably resulted from late attempts to preserve segregation by providing superior facilities for colored children.[84]

For the South generally and the border region, Table 9.5 shows the changes in four important aspects of education. In each case, comparisons are made between the position of Negroes at some point before 1942 and their position shortly before the *Brown* decision eliminated legal segregation (and sepa-

Table 9.5 Educational Improvements in Southern States

	Nonvoting South	*Voting South*	*Border States*
Racial Disparity in Average Number of School Days Attended			
1941–42	20.4	10.0	0.6
1951–52	8.6	0.4	–3.1
Percentage Change	*57%*	*96%*	*100%*
Racial Disparity in Average Annual Teacher Salaries			
1941–42	122%	59%*	6%*
1951–52	27%	9%*	1%*
Percentage Change	*78%*	*82%*	*83%*
Racial Disparity in Pupil-Teacher Ratios			
1929–30	14.5	11.0	1.0*
1949–50	6.7	4.0	1.0*
Percentage Change	*54%*	*64%*	*0%*
Racial Disparity in High School Proportion of Student Population			
1929–30	7.75	7.78	4.55
1951–52	4.67	3.10	2.00
Percentage Change	*40%*	*60%*	*56%*

* Racial data not reported for all states in this group. The figure in the table is based on the reporting states or calculated on the basis of other data. See note 85 for sources.

[84] Areas of relatively high Negro voting are considered those in which the Negro percentage of the county registration in 1960 was at least half of the Negro share of the total voting-age population. Negro schools are considered comparable to whites' if the proportion of Negro pupils in accredited high schools is at least half of the proportion of white pupils in such schools. The voting data are from U.S. Commission on Civil Rights, *Report* (1961), Book 1, pp. 278–82. The educational data are from *Equal Protection of the Laws in North Carolina*, pp. 245–46.

rate school statistics). The data make it evident that there was improvement, at least in measurable terms, in Negro education. This improvement took place in all states, but it is evident that it took place faster in the states where the black vote was one possible consideration in the minds of politicians. In school attendance, for example, the nonvoting states showed the greatest disparity between the races in 1941. Although they thereby had the greatest opportunity for improvement, their progress was not as rapid as former Confederate states where blacks voted. In the latter group, the disparity was virtually eliminated, while the black position in the border states became actually better than the whites'. The same pattern is evident in the relative elimination of disparities in salaries, pupil-teacher ratios, and in the proportion of students attending high school. The blacks generally began in a better position in the voting states, and they also progressed faster where the franchise was available.[85]

Improvement in Negro conditions has not been complete in the voting states, nor absent in the nonvoting areas. The new enfranchisement of the Negro in the South is still continuing, and it is too soon to know the full effects of these current developments. Neither the extravagant hopes of some Negroes nor the extraordinary fears of some whites are likely to be realized. Voting alone has not brought racial betterment, for the public's attitudes, the states' wealth, and the courts' pressure were also

[85] The sources for Table 9.5 are—1929–30: U.S. Office of Education, *Biennial Survey of Education 1928–1930* (1932), Vol. I, p. 607, Vol. II, pp. 53, 85; 1941–42: *Biennial Surveys 1940–42* (1944), Vol. II, pp. 110–11; 1949–50: *Biennial Survey of Education 1948–50* (1954), p. 195; 1951–52: *Biennial Survey of Education 1950–52* (1955), pp. 44, 89, 97.

The terms are defined as follows—*Attendance:* the mean of the number of days attended by Negroes in each group of states subtracted from the average for whites in each group of states. *Salaries:* the average white teacher's salary divided by the average Negro teacher's salary, minus 100 per cent. *Pupil-teacher ratios:* the number of white pupils per white teacher, subtracted from the number of Negro pupils per Negro teacher. *High school population:* Percentage of all Negro pupils in high school, subtracted from percentage of all pupils of both races in high school.

vital. Negroes, furthermore, have had other resources in recent decades—moral stature, increased economic wealth, and able leadership. Yet, the ballot too has made a difference. Where Negroes vote, the protection of their lives, even on death row, is more assured; segregation is less blatant and widespread; and educational facilities are more equal even while they remain separate. The vote is one important means to secure the inalienable rights of men of all colors.

PROTECTION AND VOTING

As they seek to eliminate the accumulated problems of centuries of maltreatment, American Negroes have placed considerable reliance on political power. In keeping with the beliefs of political theorists and the behavior of many other groups, they have seen the vote as a crucial weapon with which to defend and promote their interests. But the record of human existence, from the time of Eden, indicates the absence of panaceas for mortal ills. In and of itself, the franchise will certainly not eliminate the discrimination, poverty, and despair of colored Americans.

The history of the Negro, particularly in the South, shows that many other factors can limit or supplement the power of the vote. At different times, the same cause can operate in opposite ways. Federal officials supported the Negro's political aims in Reconstruction, neglected his needs after 1877, and have again come to his aid in recent decades. Among blacks, other resources than the vote are necessary before full citizenship can be achieved. Without economic and social influence, political participation is only of marginal significance; with such additional influence, the margin may be crucial.

In terms of absolute improvements in the condition of their race, the evidence presented here indicates that the vote has not been necessary, in logical terms, for blacks. There have been gains even when black suffrage was eliminated in the South. Lynchings declined, desegregation was accepted, and schools were improved at times and places where blacks were without the franchise. On the other hand, both in the South and North, the vote has not been a sufficient condition for black advancement. Even when and where they voted, blacks have faced police brutality, legal segregation, and inferior schools. Whether voting or voteless, their condition has been affected greatly by broad social trends, underlying attitudes, and the actions of nonelected officials.

Protection, however, is a relative, rather than an absolute, term. Individuals and groups are conscious of protection or oppression in relation to the position of others, by comparison to their significant "reference groups," not according to some fixed standard. Life may be dangerous, freedom restricted, and opportunity closed, but these conditions will not be resented unless alternatives are evident in the status of other persons.[86] The first axiom of the Declaration of Independence is the equality of men; their unalienable rights follow from this underlying premise. The demand for protection is similarly at its root a demand for shared consideration, for common, not complete, security of the rights of life, liberty, and the pursuit of happiness.

In winning relative protection, the vote appears crucial. In the history of the southern Negro, his position has been better or has improved more rapidly in relation to whites' when and where he had the vote. A causal relationship cannot be proven, but an association does exist. Although this association has not been invariable, it has been highly consistent. "Insofar as the Negro vote has helped to secure the improvement Negroes now enjoy in those areas under discussion here, it has done so in Durham in large part because of standards of fair play and equality, not by seeking special favors for political support."[87] Similarly, throughout the South, enfranchised Negroes have

[86] See E. G. Runciman, *Relative Deprivation and Social Justice* (Berkeley: University of California Press, 1966).

[87] Keech, "The Negro Vote as a Political Resource," p. 228.

been more secure from lynching and capital punishment, more free of legal segregation, and more able to pursue their quest for education.

The future effects of Negro voting remain to be seen. Many social trends and political events have combined to increase the potential impact of black suffrage. Migration out of the rural South and into urban areas throughout the nation has reduced the perceived threat to whites and increased the likelihood of black voting. The Supreme Court has eliminated many barriers, from malapportionment to the poll tax. Congress has passed statutes to secure voting rights, and the last of these acts, in 1965, eliminated virtually all formal barriers. These actions have been followed by extensive voting drives among southern blacks and by the organization of integrated factions within the Democratic party or "black power" groups.

Negro influence will depend on many factors other than the vote alone. The actions of administrative officials, the quality of Negro leadership, the degree of party competition, and the attitudes of whites will also be vital. "A large Negro populace may not only expect to influence the commitments and behavior of a governor, but it also may expect to arouse the fears of many whites. The larger the Negro population, the greater the perceived threat (in the eyes of whites) and thus the greater the resistance to broad civil rights laws."[88]

The full development of Negro equality remains to be decided in the future. In this chapter, we have been concerned to see the history of the southern Negro as a case study in the protective functions of elections. The vote alone has not eliminated inequity or brought perfect security. Yet, Negro votes in the past have made a contribution to governmental protection of the unalienable rights of man declared upon the nation's birth. From the evidence available, we can reasonably believe that the franchise will help to fulfill the promises of the American Creed.

[88] James Q. Wilson, in John P. Davis, ed., *The American Negro Reference Book* (Englewood Cliffs: Prentice-Hall, 1966), p. 453.

The effect of elections is again seen to be indirect, but real. Politicians are not compelled to act in particular ways by the mandate of the voters. Even when enfranchised, southern blacks have hardly been in a position to demand detailed policies. Politicians do respond, however, to the perceived interests of their constituents. Officials have promoted the interests of blacks during periods of black enfranchisement and have neglected them during periods of political deprivation. Protection appears to be an empirical result as well as a theoretical benefit of the ballot. Elections are significant, and democracy is viable.

CHAPTER 10

ELECTIONS AND DEMOCRATIC POLITICS

IN THE previous chapters, we have examined various aspects of popular participation in government. We have focused on the alternative possibilities of direct voter control or indirect voter influence on American public policy. In this conclusion, we will briefly summarize our findings, and then sketch some elements of a theory of the relation of elections to democracy.

Political theorists have emphasized the dangers of direct voter control, while finding benefits in indirect influence. Our examination has revealed little evidence of the former process, but we have uncovered many indications of the latter. American institutions serve to limit the electorate's command over government actions, but they do provide many opportunities for the expression of voters' demands. The character of the electorate is consistent with these expectations. The voters are not prepared to exercise a sovereign control over policy, but they are ready and able to press their personal interests.

Empirical studies confirm these generalizations. In presidential elections, the voters' principal role has been to maintain or displace the party in power. Programs have followed from the actions of the governing coalition, retrospectively judged by the electorate, not from explicit popular directives. In gubernatorial contests as well, the voters have not consistently demanded either low state taxes or high spending, but have responded differently to the varying initiatives of politicians.

These initiatives, as expressed in national party platforms, have been relatively specific and related to the apparent interests of the citizenry. Despite the apparent lack of direct control, therefore, there appears to be a linkage between the appeals of parties and the demands of the electorate. The existence of such a linkage is confirmed by actions on platform promises. Politicians do redeem most of their promises, and the parties reveal considerable internal unity and interparty difference in their actions. Another indication of linkage between official policies and voter interests is provided by the history of southern Negroes. Despite their generally depressed state, blacks have found better protection of their natural rights when they have had the vote as a means of defense.

The policy effects of elections are not their only functions. Many other results may follow from popular selection. For example, the choice of rulers by ballot promotes the recruitment of officials with characteristics distinct from those designated through inheritance, lot, or force.[1] Suffrage may also affect the personal characteristics of the citizens. Mill believed that individuals developed more competence, awareness, and ambition when they participated in government.[2] In the contemporary struggle for civil rights as well, "The vote is a symbol of full citizenship and equal rights, which may contribute to Negro self-respect."[3]

[1] Change in the character of public officials upon the advent of universal suffrage is illustrated in Robert A. Dahl, *Who Governs?* (New Haven: Yale University Press, 1961), chaps. 2–5.

[2] John Stuart Mill, *Considerations on Representative Government* (New York: Liberal Arts Press, 1958), chap. 3.

[3] William R. Keech, "The Negro Vote as a Political Resource: The Case of Durham" (Ph.D. dissertation, University of Wisconsin, 1966), p. 231.

A major function attributed to elections is the promotion of political stability.[4] Through its votes, the populace is seen as expressing its allegiance to the existing constitution. Whether elections are only ritualistic as in the Soviet Union, or involve some real choice, their common effect is to bolster the legitimacy of the holders of power. "Elections commit the people to a sense of responsibility for their own betterment . . . . It seems clear that they are essential to us as props of the sentiment of legitimacy and the sentiment of participation."[5]

Our stress has not been on these important intangible effects of elections, but on their policy consequences. It remains now to draw our varied findings together in a general conception of the effects of popular intervention on the action of government. We will first examine the theory of elections as mandates. Subsequently, we will analyze the process of indirect electoral influence and its implications for American politics.

ELECTIONS AS MANDATES

A mandate would be the most general form of direct voter control. In this theory, political contests are seen as debates over future governmental policies, and the ballot as the means of resolving the debates. Consequently, voting is presumed to result in a relatively specific set of instructions by the electors to officials. Voters are principally concerned with issues, and candidates elected on the party ticket and platform are bound to implement the policies prescribed by the electorate. This theory has been particularly associated with the Labour party of Great Britain, although it is supported in other nations as well.

[4] The "allegiance-maintaining" function of voting and the choice of leadership through elections is stressed in the thorough survey of Richard Rose and Harve Mossawir, "Voting and Elections: A Functional Analysis," *Political Studies*, Vol. 15 (June, 1967), pp. 173–201.

[5] W. J. M. MacKenzie, "The Export of Electoral Systems," *Political Studies*, Vol. 5 (October, 1957), p. 256. Cf. R. S. Milne, "Elections in Developing Countries," *Parliamentary Affairs*, Vol. 18 (Winter, 1964–65), pp. 53–60.

Under the mandate principle, issue conflicts or broad policy innovations are decided by "going to the country" for a final decision. According to this rule, even a party's legislative majority "does not necessarily entitle it to introduce a major change of policy, of a kind likely to arouse intense public controversy, if the electors have not had the chance to express their view on the subject."[6]

For example, the British Liberal party in 1906 successfully campaigned on behalf of a low-tariff policy. Finding the results a mandate, the Commons subsequently resolved, "That this House, recognizing that in the recent general election the people of the United Kingdom have demonstrated their unqualified fidelity to the principle and practice of Free Trade, deems it right to record its determination to resist any proposal . . . to create in this country a system of Protection."[7] Similarly, in the United States in 1964, many persons interpreted the Johnson landslide as a mandate for limitations on American involvement in Vietnam.

For elections to serve as mandates, three conditions would need to be fulfilled: (1) Governmental institutions would facilitate the implementation of popular verdicts in official policy; (2) voters would be concerned primarily with future policy questions; (3) majority preferences on these questions as expressed in elections could be ascertained. However, in the United States at least, none of these three conditions is substantially satisfied.

It would be difficult to implement a mandate in America. A popular program must overcome the multiple cracks of federalism, the decentralized party system, the independent

[6] A. H. Birch, *Representative and Responsible Government* (London: Allen & Unwin, 1964), p. 117.

[7] Cecil S. Emden, *The People and the Constitution*, 2nd ed. (London: Oxford University Press, 1956), p. 225. The discussion of mandates, in both normative and empirical terms, is related to the debate over "responsible party government." This issue is ably discussed by Allan P. Sindler, *Political Parties in the United States* (New York: St. Martin's Press, 1966), chap. 5.

powers of bureaucracies, courts and public authorities, and manifold checks and balances. If public support for a given proposal is strong and definite, these barriers are not insurmountable. In most instances, the electorate's wishes are not so clear.

Moreover, voters are not primarily activated by policy considerations, at least not in the coherent and prospective fashion suggested by the mandate theory. Traditional partisanship and candidate personalities account for much of the balloting. While many voters are concerned with their particular interests, few are aware of or interested in the entire range of policies or in general ideological postures. The relevant "issues" of a campaign therefore differ from one individual or group to another, and a common interpretation of the mandate of an election would be difficult to secure. Furthermore, voters are more conscious of past than future policies. They make retrospective judgments on the record of the incumbent party, not prospective choices between alternate programs.

Even if voters were primarily motivated by future policy questions, the popular mandate would be difficult to define. Victory for a given party does not necessarily mean that a majority supports each of its programs. Voters are not always consistent in their policy or partisan preferences. In the postwar period, the electorate has generally favored the Democrats on domestic welfare issues, but has been more favorable to the Republicans on questions of foreign policy.[8] In state politics, voters may support either lower taxes or increased spending, and often the same persons will be in favor of both contradictory objectives.[9]

To the extent that voters are concerned with policy questions, their involvement extends only to a limited number of these questions. On any given issue, the party's voters include not

[8] Donald E. Stokes, "Some Dynamic Elements of Contests for the Presidency," *American Political Science Review*, Vol. 60 (March, 1966), pp. 20–21.

[9] See Robert Axelrod, "The Structure of Public Opinion on Policy Issues," *Public Opinion Quarterly*, Vol. 31 (Spring, 1967), pp. 51–60.

only advocates of its position, but also many who are indifferent to or ignorant of this position, and some who oppose the party, but still vote for it because of other considerations. In fact, by combining "passionate minorities," it is theoretically possible for a party to win a majority vote, even though each of its individual policies is supported only by a fraction of the electorate.[10]

A total popular majority is composed of many policy minorities. Rarely, if ever, is this minority united on all particular issues. The victory of a party cannot be interpreted correctly as endorsement of its total platform. As the Republicans complained of President Johnson's legislative program in 1965, "It seems that when every bill comes up now it is referred to as a mandate of last November's election—the school bill, the medicare bill, the Appalachia bill, and I assume the voting bill. I wish someone were wise enough to allocate the number of votes that belongs to each of these programs . . . . I should like to know the number of votes one might assign to the President for saying that Mr. Goldwater was 'trigger happy' and might bring on a war, and therefore, 'If you don't want war, vote for me.'"[11]

Furthermore, even a majority of voters would not include a majority of the total adult population. A third to a half of American adults do not participate in presidential balloting. If politically activated, it is possible that this group, concentrated among persons of low social and economic status, might have sharply different policy views from those of the voters.[12] Similarly, a mandate issued by voters over the age of twenty-one (particu-

[10] See Anthony Downs, *An Economic Theory of Democracy* (New York: Harper, 1957), pp. 55–60, and chapter VII, *supra*.

[11] James Utt, in *Congressional Record*, Vol. 111, 89th Cong., 1st sess. (April 8, 1965), p. 7129.

[12] On the social sources and consequences of nonvoting, see Angus Campbell *et al.*, *The American Voter* (New York: Wiley, 1960), chap. 5; Seymour Lipset, *Political Man* (Garden City: Doubleday, 1960), chap. 6; E. E. Schattschneider, *The Semi-Sovereign People* (New York: Holt, Rinehart & Winston, 1960), chap. 6; and Herbert Tingsten, *The Problem of Democracy* (Totawa: Bedminster Press, 1965), pp. 101–3.

larly on such issues as the military draft) may seem less imposing if one considers the views of those under the common age of enfranchisement.

For a mandate to be valid, it should be based on an informed choice of the electorate. If a party's voters support its policies without thought and simply because of their partisanship, this loyalty clearly does not impose any restraints on the government. Nor is a mandate discernible if no alternatives to the winning party's program are available. In order for the voters to make a decision on public policy, they must have a defined choice. On most issues, American parties do not offer clearly different policies. This similarity is often due to the fact that both parties support a program of proven popularity. In other cases, however, the absence of a choice makes it dubious that the voters clearly supported the policy in question.

Mandates are difficult to achieve, determine, and implement. The difficulties were made evident in the presidential election of 1920, which Woodrow Wilson had hoped would be a "great and solemn referendum" on American participation in the League of Nations. His hopes were disappointed. National institutions did not provide for a referendum or any other direct test. In the presidential campaign, the issue was clouded by other questions, by vagueness, and by the personalities of the candidates. Interpretation of the results was difficult. "The Republicans and Harding, however, victors by a seven million vote majority and hence free to interpret the election results as they saw fit, declared that the American people had, once and for all, rejected the notion of the League of Nations."[13] If a mandate could not be clearly obtained on this issue, policy decisions in elections must be unlikely in general.

[13] Richard L. Merritt, "Woodrow Wilson and the 'Great and Solemn Referendum', 1920," *Review of Politics,* Vol. 27 (January, 1965), pp. 78–104. The quotation is from p. 103. The Republican platform was ambiguous, the party pledging no more than "such agreements with other nations as shall meet the full duty of America to civilization and humanity"—Kirk H. Porter and Donald B. Johnson, *National Party Platforms, 1840–1964* (Urbana: University of Illinois Press, 1966), p. 231.

The Vietnam issue provides further illustration of the complexities of popular mandates. It is commonly argued that the Johnson victory in 1964 resulted from a popular desire for military restraint and that the President's later escalation of the war was a violation of that mandate. Detailed examination of voter opinion does not support this view. Among a national sample of the 1964 electorate, there was relatively little relationship between candidate and policy preference, with Johnson winning the support of both "doves" and "hawks." While 63 per cent of those favoring withdrawal from Vietnam voted for the President, so did 52 per cent of those who favored "a stronger stand even if it means invading North Vietnam," as did 82 per cent of those who preferred to "keep our soldiers in Vietnam, but try to end the fighting."[14]

A careful study of public opinion in early 1966 also fails to demonstrate the President's violation of an election mandate. By this time, American escalation of the war had proceeded for a year. While Johnson voters were somewhat less favorable to the war's expansion than Goldwater backers, all Republicans, whatever their vote, were less "hawkish" than all Democrats—but none of these differences were statistically significant. Moreover, the voters did not seem to regard the Johnson policy of bombing North Vietnam as contrary to their expectations. As seen in Table 10.1, Johnson voters of 1964 were most likely to approve the 1966 actions, while Goldwater voters were more critical.[15]

These opinions do not eliminate the evident inconsistencies between the President's 1964 campaign pledges and his 1966 actions, nor do they show that the election was a mandate for

[14] These figures are calculated by John Kessel from the Survey Research Center's 1964 election study. See *The Goldwater Coalition: Republican Strategies in 1964* (Indianapolis: Bobbs-Merrill, 1968), chap. 9.

[15] Sidney Verba *et al.*, "Public Opinion and the War in Vietnam," *American Political Science Review*, Vol. LXI (June, 1967), pp. 319, 325. Table 10.1 here is recalculated from Table 1, p. 319, in this article. As is typical of election winners, the reported vote for Johnson is inflated above the actual vote. The coefficient of association (Yule's *Q*) is .49.

escalation in Vietnam. The results do reveal that support for Johnson in both years was simply unrelated to the question of American policy in Southeast Asia, but was an expression of personal and partisan confidence in Johnson—as a candidate in 1964 and as commander-in-chief in 1966. The voting majority gave no explicit command on Vietnam, and the President, whatever the wisdom of his new policy, violated no popular mandate.

Table 10.1 Vote in 1964 and Opinion on Vietnam
(In Percentage of National Opinion)

	Vote in 1964	
	Johnson	*Goldwater*
Approve Johnson Policy on Vietnam	50 (486)	13 (123)
Disapprove Johnson Policy on Vietnam	21 (202)	16 (158)

The general absence of mandates is consistent with our specific findings on direct voter control. We have found few programmatic directives by the citizenry in presidential elections, gubernatorial contests, or southern history. In these instances, as in the debate on Vietnam, "The vocabulary of the voice of the people consists mainly of the words 'yes' and 'no'; and at times one cannot be certain which word is being uttered."[16]

POWER AND INFLUENCE

The effect of elections must be indirect. Initiatives in a democratic system lie not with the voters, but with politicians. A realistic theory of elections would define mandates, when they exist, not as programmatic, but as personal. As British Conservatives and Liberals have argued, "the party which wins an election has 'a mandate to govern,' it being understood that un-

[16] V. O. Key, Jr., *Politics, Parties and Pressure Groups*, 5th ed. (New York: Crowell, 1964), p. 544.

less the election happens to have been dominated by a single issue (which is exceptional), the government should be free to pursue whatever policies it finds appropriate."[17]

An electoral victory does not commit the politician to the voters' program, but rather serves as popular endorsement of his policies; the politician offers a proposal, and the electorate approves, condemns, or fails to respond. A proper analogy might be an auction, with the candidates and parties offering their wares, and waiting hopefully for a response from the audience. It is this sort of endorsement which Lyndon Johnson requested and received in 1964, when he declared, "I ask the American people for a mandate, not to preside over a finished program, not just to keep things going. I ask the American people for a mandate to begin."[18] The voters granted the mandate, but the President and his party largely determined its content.

Politicians in a democracy enjoy wide discretion. "The leading statesmen in a free country have great momentary power. They settle the conversation of mankind . . . . It is they who, by a great speech or two, determine what shall be said and what shall be written for long after . . . . In excited states of the public mind they have scarcely any discretion at all. The tendency of the public perturbation determines what shall and what shall not be dealt with. But, upon the other hand, in quiet times statesmen have great power; where there is no fire lighted they can settle what fire shall be lit."[19]

Elections are important as limits on these initiatives. In a theoretical sense, elections are significant not as *power in* government, but as an *influence on* government. Power "manifests itself by the behavior of a person or group when it conforms to the preferences, whether expressed or implied, of another

[17] Birch, pp. 116–17.

[18] In accepting the Democratic nomination, *The New York Times*, August 28, 1964, p. 12.

[19] Walter Bagehot, *The English Constitution* (Garden City: Doubleday Dolphin Books, n.d.), pp. 18–19.

person or group." If mandates controlled official behavior, then voters would be exercising power, but the absence of mandates also implies the absence of power. What the voters do exercise is influence, an effect rather than a control, on the conduct of officials. Influence "rests upon the capacity of human beings to imagine and thus to anticipate the reactions of those who are affected by their actions. Influence flows into the human relation whenever the influencer's *re*action might spell disadvantage and even disaster for the actor, who foresees the effect the action might have and alters it more or less in accordance with this foresight."[20] Because politicians might be affected by the voters in the next election, they regulate their conduct appropriately.

To exert their influence, voters have the most obvious and vital sanction: they control the politician's job. They can quickly and bloodlessly dismiss an offensive official and thereby end his power, prestige, and profit. No explanations need be given by the electorate, and no appeal can be taken from its decisions, however arbitrary and capricious. The voters are not informed or interested enough to decide specific policy, but their final control over the politician means that he must make great efforts to satisfy popular needs and notions, wants and whims.

The existence of the vote does not make politicians better as individuals; it simply forces them to give greater consideration to demands of enfranchised and sizable groups, who hold a weapon of potentially great force. As De Tocqueville wrote, "The men who are entrusted with the direction of public affairs in the United States are frequently inferior, in both capacity and morality. . . . but they will never systematically adopt a line of conduct hostile to the majority; and they cannot give a dangerous or exclusive tendency to the government."[21]

There are other means of influence than the pressures of elections. Money, status, and skill can be used by groups devoid of

[20] Carl J. Friedrich, *Man and His Government* (New York: McGraw-Hill, 1963), pp. 199, 201.

[21] *Democracy in America*, ed., Phillips Bradley (New York: Vintage, 1954), Vol. I, p. 248.

any significant number of votes, as demonstrated by the political strength of such diverse interests as physicians and criminals. The influence of elections is still unique because votes provide a vital sanction. The ability to punish politicians is probably the most important weapon available to citizens. It is direct, authoritative, and free from official control. Other pressures upon politicians gain in potency when supported by votes, whereas the lack of votes diminishes the impact of alternative methods. "It is because there are elections from time to time that the precise demands made on the people's behalf are always listened to. Elections are most important not only for what happens at them but for what happens because of them."[22]

The voters employ their powerful sanction retrospectively. They judge the politician after he has acted, finding personal satisfactions or discontents with the results of these actions. Such judgment is within the competence of the electors. They need not be experts, able to judge the technicalities of law or the merits of contrasting proposals for the future. They need only be able to perceive improvement or deterioration in their personal situation. An uneducated South Carolina Negro in 1877 perfectly expressed the workings of retrospective control. Explaining his rejection of the Redeemers' promises, he explained, "Den say dem *will* do dis and dat. I ain't ax no man what him *will* do—I ax him what him *hab* done."[23]

The fact of retrospective judgment affects the politician's initiatives as well. Knowing that a day of reckoning is fixed by the calendar, he must strive to make that day pleasant for the voters. Knowing the voters' past attitudes, the parties must plan their future behavior accordingly. Having made promises for which they will be called to account, they must seek to fulfill these pledges. Politicians are free from popular dictation, but not from popular responsibility. "By virtue of the combination of the electorate's retrospective judgment and the custom of party accounta-

[22] John Plamenatz, "Electoral Studies and Democratic Theory: A British View," *Political Studies,* Vol. 6 (February, 1958), p. 9.

[23] George B. Tindall, *South Carolina Negroes 1877–1900* (Columbia: University of South Carolina Press, 1952), p. 13.

bility, the electorate can exert a prospective influence if not control. Governments must worry, not about the meaning of past elections, but about their fate at future elections."[24]

The issue of Vietnam is illustrative. The war in Southeast Asia became politically important in 1966 and 1968, when the effects of the Johnson administration's actions had been brought home to the voters, not in the pre-escalation year of 1964. The electorate responded to the results of that policy, not because it violated a presumed mandate. For their part, critics of the war did not emphasize their own alternative policies, but instead concentrated on retrospective and adverse judgments. Thus in 1966, Republicans were split on Vietnam, but still reaped the political benefits of voter opposition to the administration. As House G.O.P. leader Gerald Ford recognized, "We don't have to talk about it. It isn't good politics or good national policy to try to exploit the situation for political gains. Nevertheless the war will have its impact. By election time, there will be three times the present casualties among American troops."[25]

As the 1968 presidential balloting neared, the impact of elections became more evident. Declining public support of the war brought all major candidates to promise its end. The Republican party, and particularly Richard Nixon, joined in this pledge, but provided no specific programs, instead seeking the support of all voters inclined to criticize past actions. Within the Democratic party, discontent with the administration found expression in the nominating campaigns of Senators Eugene McCarthy and the late Robert Kennedy, both astonishing efforts contrary to the established rules of American politics. Lyndon Johnson then broke most of the remaining rules. Partially as a reaction to these political threats, the President renounced political ambition, refused renomination for a second term, and revised his Vietnam policy. The party convention then pledged a peace effort.

[24] V. O. Key, Jr., with the assistance of Milton C. Cummings, Jr., *The Responsible Electorate* (Cambridge: Harvard University Press, 1966), pp. 76–77.
[25] *Newsweek*, Vol. 67 (April 18, 1966), p. 37.

Despite these developments, no specific mandate was likely to be presented in the presidential election. Public opinion polls and primary elections from New Hampshire to California demonstrated voter discontent with the war, but the truce negotiations in Paris clouded the issue. Expression of this discontent had come to be focused most effectively in the campaign of Robert Kennedy. His tragic murder severely limited the use of the electoral process for a direct repudiation of the war. Nevertheless, this opposition had great impact. As the balloting neared, no major candidate favored the war's continuance or escalation. Furthermore, the voters could still express an effective retrospective decision. Most obviously, a Republican victory would be a definite adverse judgment on the incumbent party.

Whatever the eventual outcome in Vietnam and the vote, these astounding events demonstrated the influence of elections. The ambiguous mandate of 1964 had become a major issue for the citizenry in 1968. Incumbent and prospective Presidents heard, solicited, and responded to the retrospective judgment of the electorate. The political process provided an outlet for criticism, an opportunity for choice, and a means of change. Furthermore, the voters' judgment would also have a prospective effect on the next administration. Whatever its diplomatic or military justifications, the war was clearly an electoral liability, hardly to be accepted readily by any future President. The political consequences of Lyndon Johnson's Asian initiative made another Vietnam unlikely. Even without a mandate, opponents of the war had brought a policy reversal. The governors were shown ultimately dependent on the consent of the governed.

LINKING GOVERNED AND GOVERNORS

Decisions at the ballot box are intermittent and generalized. An election for any particular office occurs only once every two or four years, and the judgment made is of a total record, not individual actions. The influence of elections extends beyond these limited occasions. Their influence is considerably magnified by politicians' anticipations of the reactions of the voters. These anticipated reactions are the vital link between the interests of the voters and the actions of government. They affect politicians continuously and on all issues. In most cases, the politician "is free to act as he thinks best because the ordinary citizen is not pounding on his door with demands for action." Nevertheless, the politician remains responsive, for "his freedom to act is limited by the fact that he believes there *will* be pounding on his door if he does not act in ways that are responsive."[26]

In looking ahead to the next election, politicians cannot take comfort in the ignorance or apathy of the majority of voters on any particular problem. We have seen, in chapter IV, that voters are aware of their particular interests, even though they are not typically concerned with the broad range of issues. Winning politicians therefore believe that their policy positions are important and act accordingly.[27] Victory may depend on marginal votes, and the politician must therefore be sensitive to any group which can provide that crucial margin. "Public spokesmen, be they congressmen or others, have a sharp ear attuned to complaints that foreshadow discontent. They react, not to actual opinion, but to their image of what opinion could become if not forestalled by action on their part. And often they are right. The very lack of concern for small grievances might well crystallize a genuinely hostile community sentiment."[28] The electoral threat feared by politicians may not actually materialize, but "because of its *possible* occurrence, the person or persons under the influence of another will anticipate the reaction of him who exercises the influence."[29]

[26] Gabriel A. Almond and Sidney Verba, *The Civic Culture* (Boston: Little, Brown, 1965), p. 352.

[27] John W. Kingdon, "Politicians' Beliefs about Voters," *American Political Science Review*, Vol. LXI (March, 1967), pp. 137–45.

[28] Raymond A. Bauer, Ithiel deSola Pool, and Louis A. Dexter, *American Business and Public Policy* (New York: Atherton, 1963), p. 315.

[29] Friedrich, p. 204.

Anticipation of voter reactions is manifested in the policies that politicians reject, adopt, and propose. One important, though elusive, manifestation is the exclusion of certain issues from political debate. "Leaders respond to many elements of public opinion that *could* affect an electoral decision, even though these opinions may not have influenced the public's choice in any actual election. In gauging popular attitudes, political leaders develop a strong sense of what the permissible bounds of policy are."[30]

Illustratively, while the issue of federal aid to education is still debated, the more fundamental question of the desirability of free public education is so fully accepted that it never becomes an election issue. The consensus of the society is maintained by the parties' foresight of the electoral consequences of denying that consensus. By contrast, the massive Goldwater defeat of 1964 followed the apparent Republican denial of the settled principle of governmental responsibility for social welfare.[31] In chapter IX, we also found protection for Negroes associated with suffrage. Oppressive actions were less likely to be taken when the oppressed might retaliate at the polls.[32]

Anticipated reactions help to account for the actions politicians take as well as those they forego. Parties and officials follow policies they believe the voters want, even though there is no demonstrable mandate. As discussed in chapter V, the advent of a national majority party usually results in new public policies to meet the presumed interests of the party's voting coalition. Judging past performance, the voters continue the existing majority party in office, in a Maintaining or Converting election, or install its opposition in a Deviating or Realigning contest. In

[30] *The American Voter,* p. 547.

[31] See Philip Converse *et al.*, "Electoral Myth and Reality: The 1964 Election," *American Political Science Review*, Vol. LIX (June, 1965), pp. 321–36.

[32] Another example is provided by the former leader of Tammany Hall. He finds that electoral tickets "balanced" among ethnic groups are required to avoid potential protest, rather than to satisfy any explicit demand—Edward N. Costikyan, *Behind Closed Doors* (New York: Harcourt, Brace & World, 1966), pp. 181–82.

state politics, governors raise and lower taxes and expenditures in anticipation of popular demands. These actions follow more from the governors' commitments than from decisions at the polls. Intervention by the voters does not dictate, but legitimizes, party control and programs.

Similar behavior is evident in Congress. The representative must rely on his own perceptions of the voters' present and future demands, rather than awaiting an electoral mandate. "A Congressman has a very wide range of choices on any given issue, as far as his constituency is concerned. There is no district viewpoint as such to be represented on the overwhelming majority of issues. A few will care one way, and a few the other, but the issue will be insignificant or unknown to the great majority."[33] In his actions, the representative must guess the uncertain reactions of the electorate. Congressmen are apt to vote as they believe their constituents desire. In fact, these perceptions are more strongly related to the congressman's roll call votes than either his personal attitudes or even the district's surveyed opinion.[34]

Such anticipated reactions also account for deviations from typical political behavior. In Congress, the normal practice is that a representative votes with his party. When he bolts, it is usually because he foresees local demands. Examples of the relationship are plentiful. In postwar debates over agricultural policy, Democrats have tended to support high parity prices, while Republicans have favored more flexible supports. Within each party, however, constituency pressures have made Democrats from farm districts most cohesive in support of high prices, while rural Republicans have often bolted their party in fear of

[33] Lewis A. Dexter, "The Representative and His District," *Human Organization*, Vol. 16 (Spring, 1957–58), p. 4.

[34] Warren E. Miller and Donald E. Stokes, "Constituency Influence in Congress," in Angus Campbell *et al.*, *Elections and the Political Order* (New York: Wiley, 1966), pp. 362–66. See also Charles F. Cnudde and Donald J. McCrane, "The Linkage between Constituency Attitudes and Congressional Voting Behavior: A Causal Model," *American Political Science Review*, Vol. LX (March, 1966), pp. 66–72.

farmer reactions. A similar pattern exists in regard to labor, urban, resources, and civil rights policy.[35]

In seeking to satisfy the voters, politicians also deal with emerging questions. Many of their initiatives are attempts to arouse a favorable response from the electorate, so as to maintain and increase their own popular support. Candidates are advanced who may catch the public fancy. Promises are made in the hope that the voters will be attracted to a new program. Governmental benefits are provided for the citizenry and then stressed in the incumbents' campaign for re-election. These actions are not necessarily demanded by the voters. They are trade goods offered by politicians in the speculative hope that constituents will purchase them with the currency of their votes.

We have seen, in chapters VII and VIII, how the parties anticipate the desires of the voters, making specific pledges of future action in their platforms, particularly on issues involving tangible and divisible benefits. Having made a large number of such pledges, the winning party honors most of its commitments, thereby mitigating opposition attacks, and then seeks reelection on its achievements. Relative party cohesion on disputatious pledges and the concentration of platforms on the incumbents' performance allow the voters to render a retrospective judgment on these initiatives.

Similar behavior has been evident in the South, as discussed in chapter IX. Negroes have rarely had control over state governments, but the existence of a black electorate has been associated with the protection of vital rights. To appeal to Negroes, white officials have protected life, limited segregation, and promoted education. Anticipated reactions have brought politicians to favor a degree of racial equality in their initiatives.

Elected governments are not completely unique. Anticipated reactions may influence all regimes, and a sensitivity to public

[35] David R. Mayhew, *Party Loyalty among Congressmen* (Cambridge: Harvard University Press, 1966), esp. chap. 2. On civil rights, see Miller and Stokes, pp. 362–70.

opinion is expedient even in primitive or authoritarian societies. When faced with electoral sanctions, however, the government not only may, but must, anticipate these reactions. Recent history indicates the efficacy of the ballot. No freely elected leader has made the disastrous decisions of a Hitler to engage in a suicidal war or of a Stalin virtually to destroy his nation's defense or of a Sukarno to impoverish a richly endowed country. Leaders in democracies have not necessarily been personally wise or moral, but they apparently have been restrained by the need to win public favor in an election. Elections can provide the protection envisioned by theorists favorable to democracy.

Without elections, some protections are still available, but they are extraordinary and uncertain. A tribal chief who is especially unfit may be killed or abandoned.[36] Assassinations, revolutions, and foreign intervention are available to remove officials who are particularly onerous. Government may have the good sense to restrain itself. Nevertheless, without the ballot, as Mill recognized, rulers "can with impunity disregard" the citizens' desires, but they "are under a necessity of considering the interests of those who have the suffrage."[37]

The ballot does not guarantee full responsiveness on the part of rulers. They may misperceive or disregard citizen needs. As the history of the Negro in both South and North has demonstrated, other resources are useful, and even necessary, for the full protection of individuals. The limitations of elections can be particularly serious for such socially deprived groups. They are unlikely to have other resources, and their reliance on the ballot must be correspondingly greater. Failure to achieve their goals may cause bitter despair and even rejection of the electoral process, as exemplified by the extreme advocates of "black power."

Elections still remain the primary way of achieving popular goals. Deprived groups with few resources other than their num-

[36] See I. Schapera, *Government and Politics in Tribal Societies* (London: C. A. Watts, 1956).

[37] Mill, p. 131.

bers must be aware particularly of the uses of politics. Their vital resource must be employed where it is most effective—at the polls. The ballot does not guarantee improvement, but it does create opportunities for the amelioration of social conditions by bringing officials to consider the interests of any significant group. Elections in democracies allow a change of rule in ordinary ways and without awaiting extraordinary occasions. In such systems, therefore, officials avoid not only the extremely unpopular action but even the uncomfortable. A greater sensitivity by politicians to the anticipated reactions of the public is necessitated. No better means of protection has been devised. Security has not been provided by depending on the good will of rulers, on the presumed identity of interests between governed or governors, or on institutional controls, such as a federal structure, or supervision by a monopolistic political party. To the ancient question "Who will guard the guardians?" there is only one answer: those who choose the guardians.

CONCLUSION: THE MEANINGFUL BALLOT

To provide guardianship, elections must be well designed. There is no protection from the ballot unless each of the links in the chain between governed and governors is tempered and strong. To forge these links, however, is difficult. The initiatives of politicians may be irrelevant or appropriate. Their anticipations of voter reactions may be erroneous or accurate. The voters may be ready or unprepared to express their interests and to exercise a retrospective judgment. Meaningful elections require more than the casting of ballots. Other important conditions must be met.

Implicit in this study has been the assumption of an appropriate election structure. Without attempting an elaborate analysis in this conclusion, we can suggest some of the elements of this structure.[38] The first necessity for meaningful elections is

[38] For a fuller discussion, see Henry B. Mayo, *An Introduction to Democratic Theory* (New York: Oxford University Press, 1960), chaps. 5–8.

an organized party system. Throughout the previous chapters, we have noted the vital role of political parties. They provide the means through which voter needs and discontents are heard and resolved. Without a choice between at least two competing parties, the electorate is powerless to exert its influence.

A related vital requirement is for free competition between the parties. The voters must be able to hear diverse opinions and be able to make an uncoerced choice. To provide this opportunity, the parties must be allowed significant opportunities to make their appeals. Nomination and campaigning must be available to the full range of candidates, and the means provided for transmitting their appeals to the electorate. A legitimate democratic election also requires that all of the adult population be enfranchised, that the ballot be intelligible to the voters, and that the winning party have some claim to explicit or tacit support by an electoral majority. It is also obviously necessary that the votes be honestly cast and counted.

Although elections are common in modern times, these conditions are not commonly fulfilled. The existence of meaningful popular decisions is consequently limited. The 1967 presidential election in South Vietnam provides one example, among many in the world, of failure to meet these standards. No meaningful electoral organizations existed, other than the army led by the incumbent candidate. There were eleven different candidates, and no provision was made for a runoff contest, thereby complicating the voters' task and foreclosing a focused choice by the electorate. Freedom in campaigning was severely restricted. Some antigovernment figures were forbidden to run. Newspaper space, funds, transportation, and other means of reaching the voters were virtually denied to opposition candidates. The incumbents, however, made effective use of the existing military and civilian government structures. Furthermore, a considerable number of persons were disfranchised, and the entire election was conducted in the midst of civil and international war. The honesty of the actual polling in 1967 was also disputed. Even if the ballots were properly cast and counted, the democratic significance of the entire election was certainly debatable.[39]

The contrast with American contests is strong. Elections in the United States do largely meet the standards of meaningful popular decisions; true voter influence exists. The two parties compete freely with one another, and the extent of their competition is spreading to virtually all states. Access to the voters is open to diverse candidates, and no party or administration attempts to control the means of communication. Suffrage is virtually universal, and voters have fairly simple choices to make for major offices. In the overwhelming number of cases, finally, voting is conducted honestly.

Proper conditions exist in America for meaningful electoral influence. Indeed, major national trends seem to be fostering an even closer linkage of politician and public. Spurred by the problems of an urbanized nation, the two parties have accepted the need for policy initiatives to meet social problems. Increasing citizen involvement in the parties has also meant a greater attention to policy issues and commitments. Politicians are better able to anticipate the reactions of voters in an age of public opinion polls, television, and mass protests. The electorate also seems more ready to attempt political activity. The reduction of the work week, the growth of the mass media, and the spread of education are likely to make voters better able to exercise a retrospective judgment on governmental action. The turmoils of the 1968 presidential election are indicative.

These trends may presage a new kind of politics in America, in which politicians increasingly rely on appeals for popular support as the means of achieving their goals. As did Johnson in 1964, other candidates may be able to seek a personal mandate for their programs. The obstacles to this kind of direct popular intervention have been sharply reduced in the last thirty years.

[39] See the analysis of R. W. Apple, Jr., in *The New York Times* (September 6, 1967), p. 2. For a favorable evaluation of the election, see the comments of Professor Richard Scammon, in *The New York Times* (September 5, 1967), p. 1.

National elections have come to focus on the Presidency and on the programs and records of national parties. The incohesion of the parties and the separations between President and Congress have been diminished. Cooperative federalism is fully established. As a foreign observer summarizes this argument, "The hidden meaning of 'consensus' is quite simply, the mandate. The 'sleeper' in a constitution which is based on popular sovereignty has been awakened: the results for democratic practice and thought everywhere can only be remarkable."[40]

Whatever the future may hold, present conditions in the United States do enable the voters to influence, but not control, the government. The evidence of this study does not confirm the most extravagant expectations of popular sovereignty. Neither are elections demonstrably dangerous or meaningless. Most basically, we have found the ballot to be an effective means for the protection of citizen interests. Elections in America ultimately provide only one, but the most vital, mandate. Echoing the words but not the despair of Linda Loman, of *Death of a Salesman,* the voters authoritatively command: "Attention must be paid."

[40] Henry Fairlie, "America—1965: The Hidden Meaning of Consensus." *New Republic,* Vol. 154 (January 1, 1966), pp. 15–20. The quotation is from p. 18.

APPENDIX TO CHAPTER 5

The following tables provide the statistical evidence for locating stable eras in presidential elections. The statistical hallmark of a stable period would be a high linear correlation of the state-by-state results between any pair of elections in the period, even when these elections are more than four years apart. Each election would constitute a variable (and each state a case of that variable), to be correlated in turn with every other election, or variable, in the period. The era of electoral stability would consist of those consecutive elections which are highly correlated with all other elections in the period.

The tables present the correlation coefficients between individually paired elections for four overlapping periods. The correlation for a particular pair will be found at the intersection of the row representing one election and the column representing the other election. Figures enclosed in solid lines constitute a stable electoral era. Figures in parentheses refer to the coefficients which result when a different percentage is used to represent the Democratic vote in a particular year.

Correlation of recent elections, for example, indicates a stable electoral era from 1932 to 1948. Each election in this period is related to every other contest at a high level, and no correlation coefficient is lower than .84. Elections before and after this stable period show a lessened relationship, and the correlations to 1964 are spectacularly low.

Table 5.2 Correlation of Democratic Vote in Presidential Elections, 1828–64

	*Election Years**									
	1832	*1836*	*1840*	*1844*	*1848*	*1852*	*1856*	*1860*		*1864*
1828	.93	.05	.38	.68	.60	.67	.82	.79	(–.37)	.39
1832		.22	.50	.77	.65	.74	.77	.77	(–.25)	.08
1836			.71	.62	.46	.48	.24	.17	(.25)	.06
1840				.84	.53	.61	.45	.36	(.14)	–.02
1844					.79	.80	.74	.70	(–.09)	.27
1848						.78	.79	.69	(.15)	.31
1852							.81	.84	(.12)	.46
1856								.89	(–.24)	.60
1860										.55

* Figures in parentheses in 1860 column refer to Douglas vote alone.

Table 5.3 Correlation of Democratic Vote in Presidential Elections, 1856–1900

	*Election Years**										
	1860	*1864*	*1868*	*1872*	*1876*	*1880*	*1884*	*1888*	*1892*	*1896*	*1900*
1856	.88	.60	.53	.70	.80	.82	.83	.73	.61	.67	.64
1860		.55	.62	.67	.77	.83	.85	.79	.54	.84	.76
		(–.06)	(–.26)	(.03)	(–.19)	(–.29)	(–.16)	(–.23)	(–.31)	(–.26)	(–.34)
1864			.84	.55	.64	.62	.59	.67	.16	.09	.23
1868				.62	.63	.67	.57	.56	.38	.32	.39
1872					.75	.57	.46	.32	.28	.21	.19
1876						.87	.80	.70	.49	.47	.53
1880							.89	.86	.67	.63	.77
1884								.93	.61	.60	.79
1888									.70	.63	.85
1892	(.80)	(.31)	(.40)	(.30)	(.58)	(.74)	(.73)	(.80)		.54	.73
1896											.82

* Row figures in parentheses refer to the Douglas vote alone in 1860 and the combined Democratic and Populist vote in 1892.

Table 5.4 Correlation of Democratic Vote in Presidential Elections, 1896–1928

	Election Years[*]								
	1900	*1904*	*1908*	*1912*	*1916*	*1920*	*1924*		*1928*
1896	.82	.52	.66	.53	.73	.58	.47	(.70)	.46
1900		.87	.92	.87	.93	.88	.83	(.87)	.77
1904			.94	.95	.88	.94	.95	(.81)	.81
1908				.91	.93	.92	.90	(.87)	.79
1912					.91	.93	.92	(.87)	.79
1916						.90	.85	(.90)	.80
1920							.96	(.82)	.75
1924									.77

[*] Figures in parentheses in 1924 column refer to the combined Democratic and Progressive vote.

Table 5.5 Correlation of Democratic Vote in Presidential Elections, 1924–64

	Election Years[*]									
	1928	*1932*	*1936*	*1940*	*1944*	*1948*	*1952*	*1956*	*1960*	*1964*
1924	.77	.79	.78	.88	.86	.88	.72	.54	.18	−.59
	(.79)	(.95)	(.93)	(.87)	(.84)	(.88)	(.57)	(.59)	(.07)	−.73
1928		.78	.76	.80	.82	.85	.58	.43	.22	−.56
1932			.93	.86	.84	.90	.58	.64	.09	−.73
1936				.93	.91	.90	.66	.66	.15	−.74
1940					.98	.94	.78	.64	.27	−.67
1944						.94	.80	.67	.30	−.68
1948							.77	.71	.21	−.68
	(−.43)	(−.29)	(−.32)	(−.36)	(−.41)	(−.33)	(−.16)	(−.08)	(.16)	(.65)
1952								.84	.56	−.39
1956									.38	−.47
1960										.32

[*] Row figures in parentheses refer to the combined Democratic and Progressive vote in 1924 and the vote of Truman alone in 1948.

APPENDIX TO CHAPTER 6

Below are explanations of the techniques used in this chapter.

VOTE CHANGE

In each year, the vote for a given candidate is considered the number of percentage points (calculated to one decimal place) by which he exceeded or trailed the median percentage received by all of his party's gubernatorial candidates in the given election year. (To avoid complications from negative figures in the computer program, a constant of 50.0 percentage points was added to all figures.) The vote change between elections is then defined as the change in this deviation from the party average. As an illustration, suppose a candidate received 55 per cent of the vote in successive elections, while his party's national average fell from 55 to 50 per cent. His vote change would be: (55 – 50) – (55 – 55), or +5. Symbolically, where c represents the candidate, p his party, and subscripts 1 and 2 successive elections, then:

$$\text{Vote Change} = (c_2 - p_2) - (c_1 - p_1)$$

GOODMAN-KRUSKAL GAMMA

This statistic measures the association between two sets of data arranged to constitute ordinal variables. An ordinal variable is one in which the data are grouped into classes with higher and lower values, but the intervals between the classes are not specified. "Ordinal scales permit discussion of 'moreness' or 'lessness,' but they make no assumptions as to how much more or less."[27]

The procedure is illustrated, using the data in Table 6.4, by calculating the association between changes in the vote and percentage increases in taxes for 28 gubernatorial elections in 1950. Six steps are involved:

1. Arrange the deviations from the national party trend in order, from the highest deviation above to the highest deviation below the trend, as in the horizontal rows of Table 6.4.

2. Divide this array into three groups, with an approximately equal number of states in each group. When victory is defined as the measure of political success, only the two categories of victory and defeat are employed.

3. Arrange the percentage increases in taxes in order, from the lowest to the highest, as in the vertical columns of Table 6.4. It is important that the orderings be in the direction predicted by the hypothesis.

4. Divide this array into three groups.

5. Construct a 3 × 3 table, counting the number of states which fall into each of the resulting nine cells.

6. Calculate *gamma*, by the formula:

$$G = \frac{f_a - f_i}{f_a + f_i},$$

*Table 6.4 Vote Change and Per Cent Increase in Taxes, 1950**

	Per Cent Increase in Taxes Since Last Election		
Vote Change	*−18.1 to 6.6*	*6.8 to 24.7*	*27.6 to 273.6*
9.8 to .5	5	2	2
.2 to −5.2	1	6	3
−5.5 to −17.6	3	2	4

* The number in each cell is the number of states with the designated vote change and percentage tax increases.

[27] Linton C. Freeman, *Elementary Applied Statistics* (New York: Wiley, 1965), p. 7.

in which, "to compute f_a we multiply the frequency in each cell by the frequencies in all the cells that lie both below and to the right of it. By adding these products together, we obtain f_a. . . . To compute f_i we multiply the frequency in each cell by the sum of the frequencies in the cells which lie below and to the left of it and add these products."[28]

In this case, f_a is equal to:

$$5\,(6 + 3 + 2 + 4) + 1(2 + 4) + 2(3 + 4) + 6(4) = 119,$$

and f_i is equal to:

$$2(6 + 1 + 2 + 3) + 3(2 + 3) + 2(1 + 3) + 6(3) = 65.$$

By the formula above,

$$G = \frac{119 - 65}{119 + 65} = \frac{54}{184} = .29$$

There is a moderate relationship in 1950 between tax increases and political results. Governors who were relatively stringent in their tax programs were likely to improve their electoral performance compared to other candidates of their party.[29]

The same procedure is used for the analysis of spending. In the analysis of both first-year taxes and last-year spending, the financial data are ranked from high to low. Concentrating taxes in the first year, or spending in the last year, will therefore result in a positive coefficient if these actions are truly related to political success. In the calculation of the spending-taxes ratio, the absolute and percentage increases in spending in a term are divided, respectively, by the absolute and percentage increase in taxes. After they are ranked from low to high, they are correlated with the political variables.

[28] Freeman, chap. 8 and p. 85. The original source of this statistic is Leo Goodman and William Kruskal, "Measures of Association for Cross Classifications," *Journal of the American Statistical Association,* Vol. 49 (1954), pp. 733–64.

[29] This result is not very impressive. A test of significance indicates that a similar coefficient might occur by chance as often as one of five times. See Freeman, chap. 13.

YULE'S Q

This measure, mathematically a special case of *gamma,* is used in the second set of correlations. The small number of cases in each group permits use of only 2 × 2 tables. Each coefficient represents the correlation of vote change and per cent annual tax increase for the designated group in the designated year. For all election years combined, a gross measure of association can be obtained by combining the figures from individual elections to achieve a grand 2 × 2 table. This total coefficient is listed in the last column of Table 6.3.

The procedure for calculation is similar to that for *gamma,* except that each array is divided into two, rather than three, groups. The coefficient of association is derived through the formula:[30]

$$Q = \frac{ad - bc}{ad + bc},$$

in which a, b, c, d correspond to the four cells of the table, and ad and bc are the diagonal products. An illustration of this statistic is provided by Table 6.5, which shows the relationship, for Democratic gubernatorial seats in 1950, between vote change and per cent annual tax increases. In this case,

$$Q = \frac{5(5) - 1(2)}{5(5) + 1(2)} = \frac{23}{27} = .85$$

The relationship is strong, although the small number of cases limits its significance.

*Table 6.5 Vote Change and Tax Increase, Democratic States in 1950**

	Per Cent Annual Increase in Taxes	
Vote Change	*−9.0 to 6.6*	*6.7 to 68.4*
2.9 to 4.4	5	1
−4.6 to −17.6	2	5

* The number in each cell is the number of states with the designated vote change and annual percentage tax increase.

[30] See M. J. Moroney, *Facts from Figures,* 3rd ed. (Baltimore: Penguin Books, 1956), pp. 264–66.

APPENDIX TO CHAPTER 7

The following standards were used in classifying platform sentences among the content categories.

1. *Rhetoric and Fact*

Approval of commonly accepted values; appeals to "valence" issues without any specific context; support of diffuse symbols; citation of truisms and clichés. All purely factual statements, if not in a particular context, are also included.

2. *Evaluations of the Parties' Records and Past Performances*

All statements referring to past actions, policies, leaders, and conduct of the parties, including references to historical events which are attributed to the parties. There are four minor categories included here:

(*a*) *General Approval*

Favorable citation of the party or its leaders; nonspecific citation of achievements and personnel; reference to national achievements (not government policies) in the context of praise for the given party.

(*b*) *General Criticism*

Unfavorable citation of the opposite party or its leaders in statements analogous to (*a*).

(c) Policy Approval

Reference to designated policy actions of the party or its leaders of alleged social benefit. A definite policy must be cited to justify inclusion in this category, but no proof of the benefits of the policy is necessary.

(d) Policy Criticism

Unfavorable reference to designated policy actions of the opposite party or its leaders, in statements analogous to (*c*).

3. *Statements of Future Policies*

The six minor categories are in order of increasing commitment and specificity. The degree of party commitment is judged by the verbs employed, and the degree of specificity by the character of the sentence object. Pledges to oppose or refrain from an action are considered as relevant as positive promises. Since the categories are constructed on more than one criterion, these categories are nominal classifications and do not constitute a continuous, unidimensional scale.

(a) Rhetorical Pledges

Future support of commonly accepted values, "valence" issues, truisms, and clichés. A simple test of a sentence in this category is to state the opposite. If the resulting sentence is absurd and could not be a logical policy, the pledge of future support is only rhetorical. A pledge that is not logically required, even though politically necessary, such as support of social security, is not rhetorical and is not included here.

(b) General Pledges

Statements with a policy content which is unspecified or unclear, but is not logically necessary. Typically, these statements could be made by either major party, and a reader would find it difficult to attribute the pledge to one party or the other. Unlike the rhetorical pledges, there is some relation to governmental action but, like the former, it is difficult to measure performance on pledges in this group.

(*c*) *Pledges of Continuity*

A pledge to maintain present governmental policy, but without specification of its character, or with reference only to the general nature of a program. Verbs such as "continue," "support," "renew," "press," and "strengthen" are used, followed by indefinite objects. Although the details of future policy are unclear, a pledge in this category would provide the voter with a notion of future actions, if he were informed of present policies.

(*d*) *Expressions of Goals and Concerns*

Stated intentions to meet a specific problem or to achieve a particular goal, but without specification of the means to be employed, or without complete commitment to the goal; recognition of a need or statements of concern, without the promise or possibility of government action. Verbs used in this category include "aid," "foster," "develop," "promote," "seek," "encourage," "endeavor," and their opposites. Object nouns may be qualified by adjectives such as "feasible," "reasonable," "sound," and "constitutional."

(*e*) *Pledges of Action*

Definite promises of the direction of policy, as well as of the problems to be considered, although detailed provisions are not included. Pledges in this category dealing with government finances or other quantitatively measurable policies indicate the direction, but not the amount, of intended changes. These provisions include verbs such as "insist," "offer," "favor," "oppose," "resist," "extend," "increase," "restrict," and "decrease." Object nouns tend to be unqualified or modified by adjectives of quantity, such as "additional," "greater," "decreased," and "reduced."

(f) Detailed Pledges

The character of the action pledged, as well as its direction, is stated. A specific bill or executive action may be mentioned, or its context explicated. Pledges to continue specific past policies or to exact quantitatively defined policies are included as well. Even in this category, however, specificity must be understood as considerably less than the details of an actual law. Verbs such as "endorse," "recommend," "pledge," and "commit" are followed by a definite object, often modified by strengthening adjectives such as "immediate," "prompt," "complete," and "full."

The following topics were included in the nine policy areas. These areas roughly correspond to the functions grouped in cabinet departments before 1964 and to the groupings used in legislative analysis by *Congressional Quarterly:*

(1) *Foreign policy*

Diplomacy; the United Nations; foreign aid; collective security agreements unless exclusively military in character; policy toward Israel or other specific nations; East-West Center.

(2) *Defense*

Conduct of war and military strategy; the draft; living conditions of military personnel; weapons systems; military research; civil defense; United Nations armed forces; disarmament and testing of nuclear weapons.

(3) *Economic Policy*

Control of business cycles; federal fiscal policy and taxation; regulation of business; distribution of military procurement contracts; science and nonmilitary research; transportation, including mass transit and rivers and harbors; depressed areas.

(4) *Labor*

Regulation of labor unions; employment conditions and minimum wages; retraining programs; employment services; equal pay for women; farm workers; standards in government contracts other than nondiscrimination.

(5) *Agriculture*

Farm commodity, storage, loan, and income policies; food reserves; foreign distribution of agricultural surpluses; agricultural research; production and marketing controls; food stamp programs; school lunches; fisheries; rural electrification.

(6) *Resources*

Policies relating to minerals, fuels, and other raw materials; depletion allowances; water, forest, and game policy; air and water pollution; conservation and recreation; atomic energy for domestic purposes; regional development; electrical and hydroelectric power policy, excluding rural electrification.

(7) *Social Welfare*

All programs related to health, hospitals, education, and social welfare; social security, including unemployment insurance; programs for the aged and handicapped; consumer protection; housing, urban planning and renewal other than transportation; Department of Urban Affairs; veterans.

(8) *Government*

Administration; loyalty programs and civil liberties; management of the civil service; federalism in general terms, including programs of federal-state tax adjustment; federal budgeting and spending levels apart from particular programs; the national debt; statehood, government of territories and the District of Columbia; regulation of elections; legislative apportionment; congressional procedures other than Senate cloture.

(9) *Civil Rights and Ethnic Policy*

All provisions related to discrimination against Negroes, including segregation in the armed forces, schools, etc.; social welfare programs specifically designed to deal with racial discrimination; Senate cloture; immigration policy; American Indians; discrimination against women.

APPENDIX TO CHAPTER 8

The methods employed in this chapter are explained in detail below.

FULFILLMENT OF PLEDGES

The 1,399 platform pledges were listed separately by topic and election year. Each platform pledge was then compared to the actions of the national government in the following four years. A full examination was made of all enacted laws and of bills debated in Congress, and a general, but less detailed, examination was made of presidential and administrative actions. A judgment was then made of the proper category of fulfillment for each platform provision. The illustration in the text relates to PL89–601 (89th Cong., 2nd sess., 1966), which fully met the 1964 Democratic commitment to raise the minimum wage, but only partially satisfied the party's pledge to extend coverage to all workers in interstate commerce.

This method is greatly dependent on individual judgment and persistence. Mechanical or electronic methods cannot be easily employed. One vital aid is available—the compilations and explanations of national government by Congressional Quarterly News Services. Their publications were relied on heavily to provide information on the actions of the national government during this period. Without these sources, this research is all but impossible.[21]

Judgments on fulfillment are inherently subjective and are subject to two opposite kinds of error. First, the standards used are admittedly imprecise and perhaps too liberal. However, given the assumption that platforms are disregarded in Congress, and the considerable obstacles to performance in American government, one would expect little platform fulfillment. To be able to make any useful analysis, some flexibility in the standards may be permissible. Secondly, errors of the opposite kind are also possible. Some actions related to platforms may have been taken, but may not have been discovered in this search. Omissions are particularly likely in regard to administrative actions or to minor provisions included in omnibus legislation. Hopefully, these two types of error partially offset one another.

SIMILARITY AND CONFLICT IN PLEDGES

The Democratic pledges were listed for each topic in each platform. Repetitious pledges were grouped together, although counted separately. The Republican pledges on a given topic in a given year were then compared to the corresponding Democratic commitments. Each pledge was then classified as a one-party pledge when only Democrats or Republicans dealt with the specific subject, a bipartisan pledge when the parties were essentially in agreement, or a conflicting pledge when the parties were basically opposed. After enumerating the pledges in each topic of each year, totals and percentages were calculated for the entire

[21] My major source has been *Congress and the Nation: 1945–1964* (Washington: Congressional Quarterly Service, 1965). This is an astoundingly detailed, comprehensive, and highly accurate source on the twenty-year period. I have also used the *Congressional Quarterly Almanac*, Vols. IV–XX (1948–64), and the official *Congressional Record* where necessary for supplemental information for these years. For the 1965–66 period, I have used the latter two sources as well as *Congressional Quarterly Weekly Report*, Vols. 23–24 (1965–66). A small attempt similar to the research here was attempted in "Platforms vs Performance in Congress," *Congressional Quarterly Almanac*, Vol. V (1949), pp. 72–78, but the effort was never repeated.

topic and election year. (This procedure parallels that employed to measure fulfillment. In reality, the analysis of similarity and conflict in pledges was performed first.)

Illustratively, only the Democrats in 1964 promised an increase in the minimum wage, and only the Republicans pledged reorganization of the National Labor Relations Board. The parties were agreed on expansion of government programs for retraining workers displaced by automation. They were in conflict on the coverage of minimum wage laws. The Democrats pledged expansion "to all workers employed in industries affecting interstate commerce," while the Republicans proposed "incentives for employers to hire teenagers, including broadening of temporary exemptions under the minimum wage law."[22]

PARTY COHESION AND LIKENESS ON CONFLICTING PLEDGES

Indexes of party cohesion and likeness were calculated for congressional roll calls on conflicting platform pledges. The 136 conflicting pledges involved 45 different issues. For each of these 45 issues, I selected one roll call in the House and one roll call in the Senate which was closely related to the issue. The significant roll call was not usually the final vote on passage of a bill. A roll call on an amendment, or a motion to "recommit," and thereby kill, a bill might be far more crucial. Often more than one roll call was relevant. The invariable rule was to select the first congressional vote after the election year which significantly dealt with the issue at hand. In fewer cases, there was no relevant roll call in one or both chambers. In all, for the total of 45 issues, 70 "conflict roll calls" were examined.

Party unity is measured by Stuart Rice's "index of cohesion."[23] This simple index is obtained by calculating the percentage of

[22] Porter and Johnson, pp. 646, 683.

[23] See Stuart Rice, *Quantitative Methods in Politics* (New York: Knopf, 1928) and "The Behavior of Legislative Groups," *Political Science Quarterly*, Vol. XL (1925), pp. 60–72. A good introduction to these techniques is Lee F. Anderson *et al.*, *Legislative Roll-Call Analysis* (Evanston: Northwestern University Press, 1966).

the party favoring a measure, and then subtracting the percentage opposed. When the party is completely united, the index will be 100 (100 per cent favoring −0 per cent opposed). When the party is evenly divided, the index will be 0 (50 per cent favoring −50 per cent opposed). (If the percentage opposed is larger, it is calculated first.)

Similarities and differences between the parties is measured by another technique developed by Rice, the "index of likeness." This index also varies from 100, when the parties take similar positions, to 0, when the parties are completely different. To obtain the index, we calculate the percentage of Republicans favoring a particular position and then subtract the percentage of Democrats taking the same position. The resulting difference is then subtracted from 100. Arithmetically,

$$\text{Index of Likeness} = 100 - (\text{per cent Republicans} - \text{per cent Democrats})$$

(If the Democratic percentage is larger, it is calculated first.) Where the index of cohesion shows unity within each party, the index of likeness shows how much the two parties agree on the same position.

The 1966 bill to extend coverage of the minimum wage (HR13712) is illustrative. A proposed amendment to increase exceptions was directly relevant to the conflicting party platform pledges. On this amendment, House Democrats divided 84 in favor and 186 against. The division among House Republicans was 111–14, Senate Democrats 21–34, and Senate Republicans 20–7. Party cohesion scores on this roll call are therefore:

$$\text{House Democrats:} \quad \frac{186 - 84}{186 + 84} = 38$$

$$\text{House Republicans:} \quad \frac{111 - 14}{111 + 14} = 78$$

Senate Democrats: $$\frac{34 - 21}{34 + 21} = 24$$

Senate Republicans: $$\frac{20 - 7}{20 + 7} = 48$$

The indexes of likeness would be:

House: $$100 - \frac{111}{111 + 14} - \frac{84}{186 + 84} = 42$$

Senate: $$100 - \frac{20}{20 + 7} - \frac{21}{34 + 21} = 64$$

Party cohesion and likeness on all conflict roll calls in a period is simply the average of the figures for individual votes. These average indexes are reported in Table 8.4.

GENERAL CONGRESSIONAL VOTING

For purposes of comparison, measurements of party cohesion and likeness are also presented for all roll calls in Congress. These general measures are further divided into party-unity votes, in which a majority of Democrats oppose a majority of Republicans, and bipartisan votes, in which a majority of each party takes the same position.

The basic data for these measures is derived from the performance records published by *Congressional Quarterly Almanac.* The average "party unity score" presented there is equal to the average percentage of the party on the majority side on party-unity votes, and the average "party opposition score" is equal to the average percentage opposing the party stand. The index of cohesion is therefore the average "party unity score" minus the average "party opposition score." Similarly, on bipartisan votes, the index of cohesion is the average "bipartisan support score" minus the average "bipartisan opposition score." For all roll calls, the various scores must be weighted by the proportion of all roll calls which are party-unity or bipartisan votes.[24]

The general index of likeness can be calculated in a similar manner. On all party-unity votes, Democrats and Republicans will be taking conflicting positions. Therefore the average "party-opposition score" for one party, e.g., the Republicans, is subtracted from the average "party-unity score" for the other party, e.g., the Democrats. In accord with the previous formula, the resulting difference is then subtracted from 100. On bipartisan votes, the parties are taking the same position. Therefore the average "bipartisan support score" for one party is

[24] A correction for absences must first be made. Under its current practice, *Congressional Quarterly* does not take account of absences. Thus a "party-unity score" is the percentage of roll calls on which the congressman supported his party, even if he were absent on some. The Rice index, however, is based on the percentage of those voting. Moreover, the *Congressional Quarterly* measure has changed in important details over the years. Some recalculation is therefore necessary for comparability. To derive the percentage of the party supporting the majority on party-unity votes, the following measures from the annual volumes should be used: 1949–51—Party Unity Score; 1953–54—Party Unity Score divided by Attendance Score; 1955–date—Party Unity Score divided by the sum of the Party-Unity and Party-Opposition Scores. The analogous percentage for bipartisan votes is: 1949–54—Bipartisan Support Scores: 1955–date —Bipartisan Support Score divided by the sum of Bipartisan Support and Bipartisan Opposition Scores. For party-unity votes, the index of cohesion is then:

$$\text{Corrected party-unity score} - \text{Corrected party-opposition score.}$$

For bipartisan votes, the same process is used with bipartisan scores. For all votes, the combined index of party cohesion is:

$$\begin{aligned}
&\Big[\text{Corrected Party Unity Score} \times \frac{\text{No. of Party-Unity Roll Calls}}{\text{No. of All Roll Calls}} \\
&+ \text{Corrected Bipartisan Score} \times \frac{\text{No. of Bipartisan Roll Calls}}{\text{No. of All Roll Calls}}\Big] \\
&- \Big[\text{Corrected Party Opposition Score} \times \frac{\text{No. of Party-Unity Roll Calls}}{\text{No. of All Roll Calls}} \\
&+ \text{Corrected Bipartisan Opposition Score} \times \frac{\text{No. of Bipartisan Roll Calls}}{\text{No. of All Roll Calls}}\Big]
\end{aligned}$$

simply subtracted from the average support score of the other party, and the difference then subtracted from 100.[25]

[25] To take account of absences, the corrected figures, described in the previous footnote, are again used. For all roll calls, a combined, weighted figure must be calculated, through a formula frightening in appearance, but simple in operation. The combined index of likeness is:

$$100 - \left[\left(\text{Democratic Party Unity} \times \frac{\text{No. of Party-Unity Roll Calls}}{\text{No. of All Roll Calls}} + \text{Democratic Bipartisan Support} \times \frac{\text{No. of Bipartisan Roll Calls}}{\text{No. of All Roll Calls}}\right) - \left(\text{Republican Party Opposition} \times \frac{\text{No. of Party-Unity Roll Calls}}{\text{No. of All Roll Calls}} + \text{Republican Bipartisan Support} \times \frac{\text{No. of Bipartisan Roll Calls}}{\text{No. of All Roll Calls}}\right)\right]$$

FOR FURTHER READING

Readers will find complete references to many of the works cited here in individual footnotes. This list is designed to provide a small number of books for those interested in pursuing a particular subject.

On the theory of democracy, the study of normative theory could begin with T. H. Green's *Lectures on the Theory of Political Obligation*, John Locke's *Of Civil Government*, and John Stuart Mill's *Considerations on Representative Government*. Useful modern interpretations include E. F. M. Durbin, *The Politics of Democratic Socialism*, Henry B. Mayo, *Introduction to Democratic Theory*, and Giovanni Sartori, *Democratic Theory*. More empirical theories of democracy are presented in Robert Dahl, *A Preface to Democratic Theory*, Anthony Downs, *An Economic Theory of Democracy*, and Joseph Schumpeter, *Capitalism, Socialism, and Democracy*.

The place of parties in American government has been dealt with by many analysts. Among the most important general works are W. N. Chambers and Walter D. Burnham, eds., *The American Party Systems*, V. O. Key, *Politics, Parties and Pressure Groups*, Samuel Lubell, *The Future of American Politics*, E. E. Schattschneider, *Party Government*, and Frank Sorauf, *Political Parties in America*. More comparative studies of parties include Maurice Duverger, *Political Parties*, Seymour Lipset and Stein Rokkan, *Party Systems and Voter Alignments*, and two classics, Robert Michels, *Political Parties*, and M. Ostrogorskii, *Democracy and the Organization of Political Parties*.

Particular aspects of party organization, nominations, and campaigns are dealt with in such works as Samuel Eldersveld, *Political Parties: A Behavioral Analysis,* Paul David, *et al., The Politics of National Party Conventions,* and Nelson Polsby and Aaron Wildavsky, *Presidential Elections.* There is a large body of literature on particular American election campaigns. Among the best works of this genre are Murat Halstead, *Three Against Lincoln,* John Kessel, *The Goldwater Coalition: Republican Strategies in 1964,* Florence Weston, *The Presidential Election of 1828,* and Theodore H. White, *The Making of the President 1960.*

Studies of state politics are particularly relevant to the discussion of Chapter 6. Among the important works on this subject are Thomas Dye, *Politics, Economics and the Public,* Herbert Jacob and Kenneth Vines, eds., *Politics in the American States,* V. O. Key, *American State Politics,* Duane Lockard, *New England State Politics,* and John Wahlke, *The Legislative System.*

Studies of voting are obviously critical in regard to the impact of elections. The basic works are those of Angus Campbell, Philip Converse, Warren Miller, and Donald Stokes, *The American Voter* and *Elections and the Political Order.* More distant elections are analyzed by Bernard Berelson, *Voting,* and Paul Lazarsfeld, *The People's Choice.* On recent elections, the work of V. O. Key and Milton Cummings, *The Responsible Electorate,* Seymour Lipset, *Political Man,* and William Flanigan, *Political Behavior of the American Electorate,* is vitally important.

The pressing political problems of black Americans could easily provide sufficient material for a separate bibliography. I will cite here only a few relevant books: William Brink and Louis Harris, *Black and White,* Stokely Carmichael and Charles Hamilton, *Black Power: The Politics of Liberation in America,* W. J. Cash, *The Mind of the South,* V. O. Key, *Southern Politics,* Carl Lewinson, *Race, Class and Party,* Donald Matthews and James Prothro, *Negroes and the New Southern Politics,* Charles

Silberman, *Crisis in Black and White,* and C. Vann Woodward, *The Strange Career of Jim Crow.*

Finally, there is the basic question of the linkage of governed and governors, the central theme of this book. This issue has been dealt with normatively at least since Plato, and is now receiving great empirical investigation. Important works encompass Gabriel Almond and Sidney Verba, *The Civic Culture,* Lloyd A. Free and Hadley Cantril, *The Political Beliefs of Americans,* V. O. Key, *Public Opinion and American Democracy,* Warren Miller and Donald Stokes' forthcoming volume, *Representation in Congress,* and the excellent readings included by Norman Luttbeg in *Public Opinion and Public Policy.*

INDEX